D1598582

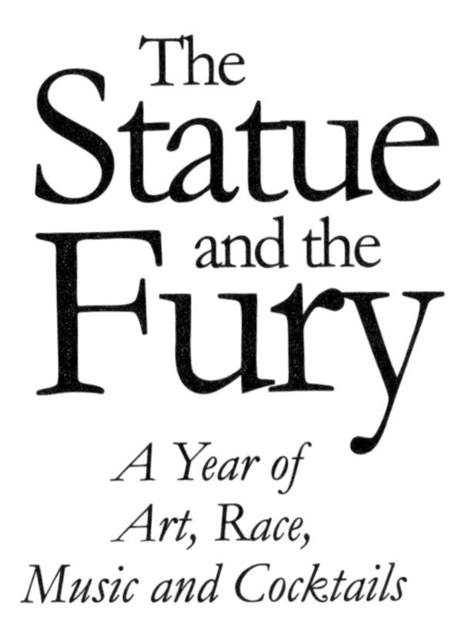

The Statue and the Fury

A Year of Art, Race, Music and Cocktails

Jim Dees

Nautilus Publishing

For information contact
Nautilus Publishing, 426 South Lamar Blvd., Suite 16, Oxford, MS 38655.

ISBN: 978-1-936946-80-8

The Nautilus Publishing Company
426 South Lamar Blvd., Suite 16
Oxford, Mississippi 38655
Tel: 662-513-0159
www.nautiluspublishing.com

First Edition

Front cover design by Le'Herman Peyton.

Library of Congress Cataloging-in-Publication Data has been applied for.

Printed in Canada

10 9 8 7 6 5 4 3 2 1

For

MICAH

In Memory

Charlie and Duff; Larry and Barry

"A book is the writer's secret life, the dark twin of a man:
you can't reconcile them."

William Faulkner, *Mosquitoes* (1927)

Foreword

Is there a dicier, more humiliating stance, than trying to get backstage after a big-name concert? On some level you feel like a schmuck. You try not to look like a Trekkie. While you await clearance, you might check your watch, or even yawn. You channel casual.

On this night I had papers, had written the PR department and actually been granted an interview with the one and only, the great Willie Nelson. Our interview was to be conducted on board his bus, the Honeysuckle Rose II, one of the most mythical vehicles in show business. It felt like securing an audience with the Pope. The Pontiff of Puff. Breathing his seat cushions might give me a contact high.

Of course, when I presented myself and my letter of transit, Dave, the tour manager, took in my recorder and pad and said, "You're here to do an interview? OK. Not sure I heard about this… uh, Hold on."

He popped into the bus and left me standing in the after-show clatter. I looked around and saw stage hands and roadies dismantling the stage, stragglers still hanging out, crew rolling road trunks out the door, the lighting rig being lowered. In my mind, I could see Dave stepping back out and telling me there must be some mistake, and sorry, but he didn't have Willie scheduled for an interview tonight, and he's tired and unavailable, but thanks for coming out.

After what seemed an hour but was probably five minutes, the bus door opened. It sounded hydraulic, just like it does at the Greyhound station, and there was Dave saying, "All right. Welcome aboard." The stairs were steep, and before I could mentally geek out that this was really happening, I had to focus on those steps. Stumbling and biting my tongue and bleeding on the carpet was not how I intended my encounter with Willie Nelson to start off. My journalistic mission aside, I was a fan. In my fey youth, a buddy and I drove to Austin from Mississippi to buy Willie's *Red Headed Stranger* album on Willie's native soil.

I watched my step carefully as I slowly ascended, up… up, up, nod to the driver, and…I was on the bus. Deep breath. Here goes…

The very first thing I noticed was that it smelled like Christmas… or at least Christmas trees. Dave showed me to the booth like you might see in a small diner, and I took a seat across from a bulletin board filled with photos and Willie ephemera. The board was dominated by a large color picture of Willie and Keith Richards. Lord have mercy… I hadn't been nervous, but somehow seeing this picture of Willie and Keith put a little rattle on me. Good Lord, Keith and Willie. Buries the needle on the Cool Meter.

Almost by magic, Willie appeared, hair in tight braids, a quick whiff of musk, sliding into his seat across from me. His eyes were so large and piercing I thought maybe he could see through me and see my heart beating and my organs twitching.

"How ya doing?" he asked, holding out his hand.

1

Early Days

The vile newsroom coffee was just beginning to pry open our hangovers when the staff received word a body had been found on the town square. For house fires, car wrecks, flash floods, construction accidents and mysterious deaths, small-town reporters and photographers jump up into full-scurry mode, like firemen hitting the pole.

I learned on the way. I was hired at age forty as a cub reporter at our local paper, the *Oxford Eagle* in Oxford, Mississippi. They were doing me a favor. I had been downsized from a federal literacy program at the local university, Ole Miss. I was writing scripts for educational television for which I had no experience. Education I mean. I had *watched* a lot of television.

A newspaper gig had other ramifications, at least for my psyche. It meant I could still call myself a writer. I was still on the "art" side of the ledger. Someone else would have to flip the burgers and wear the hairnet. At age forty the *Eagle* gig became the first job I ever had where I was older than my boss. While my contemporaries were saving towards retirement, I was starting a career in journalism.

My two bosses, Steve Mullen and Jonny Miles, weren't the sorts to bust the newbie's chops but rather seemed happy to have some help. And not with actual news but more with the droning, soul-sucking minutiae of the small-town paper: the daily duty of obituaries, Rotary Club check pass-offs, new business ribbon-cuttings, birth announcements, garden club lectures, late soccer scores, Knights of Columbus meetings, police reports and the occasional big scoop: "Hey, just wanted y'all to know there's a raccoon roaming the Square. If y'all wanted to get a pitcher or anything."

My second day on the job, I found myself telling a high public official that we were running a story on the front page describing in detail how he was well behind in his child support payments, and there was a warrant for his arrest. The man was on the state college board. I could hear him gasping and hacking before saying, "You'll have to speak to my attorney."

I felt a Woodward and Bernstein chill down my back. Two days before, I had been lounging on my couch in boxer shorts watching Jerry Springer and licking Cheetos powder off my fingers. Now I was wreaking fire and pestilence down upon the High and Mighty.

On this bright December morning the unbelievable call came: a jogger, early on Sunday morning, glanced up to see a body up on one of the town square's New Orleans-style balconies. It was sitting upright with a single bullet wound to the chest. Discovered later was his pipe and scotch nearby. The victim was a leading figure in town — a prominent merchant and arts patron. As a boy, he had spent time at the home of William Faulkner. He was classmates with Faulkner's daughter Jill. This would be front-page news. Jonny was assigned the story, which would run with a photo. I was assigned to call the deceased man's friends for a comment.

That's when I realized my tongue was stuck to the roof of my mouth, and my throat felt like I had gargled gravel. My head was pounding like Godzilla jogging. My eyes bled water. I questioned life itself. A hangover proves a word to the wise isn't sufficient. I was the last person to be calling innocent people in their time of bereavement. I rose from my tiny desk and grabbed another unspeakable cup of over-cooked Folger's, picked up the phone, and hoped my breath didn't carry over the line.

Speaking to the grief-stricken had a sobering effect. I quickly learned the deceased was a fine-clothing store owner, small press publisher and amateur historian of Oxford and Lafayette County. He was deeply invested in his community, which he loved like family. His death, coming in December 1996, spared him the changes that were about to occur in the coming year. The upcoming controversies over how to celebrate the centennial of his beloved William Faulkner would have made him laugh — and cry. He, especially, would recognize 1997 as a turning point in the life of Oxford.

He wouldn't have to witness many of his favorite homes and haunts being razed to make way for condos, townhouses and parking lots. Jonny Miles, in quickly checking the facts, discovered the deceased had Air Force service and went to graduate school in history before opening his clothing store with his dad in 1958. As a young store owner, he had immersed himself in the culture of his homeland, which Jonny wrote as being: "Ole Miss football, literature, duck hunting and Southern history — in short, the tweedy passions of a gentleman."

He became a publisher in 1975 and brought out works by Faulkner and Faulkner's brother John, the artist Theora Hamblett and others. He was the kind of man who could walk through the local cemetery and recite the histories of the deceased but so full of the living he met a coffee klatsch of friends every morning at a diner called Smitty's.

"You could really warm your hands with him," his friend Ed Morgan told me.

As we worked the phones, the clock ticking until our eleven a.m. deadline, Jonny discovered that one of the deceased's stated wishes was to have his hearse circle the Square twice: "Once to say goodbye to the store, once to say goodbye to Oxford."

Once Jonny had all the quotes he thought he needed, it was time to actually craft the obituary. Jonny was tallish with a crown of curly hair, an eye for detail and a nose for trouble. He wasn't exactly handsome — who was? — but somehow exuded enough bad-boy airs to pique the local ladies. Many mornings, he came in with the rumpled dishevel of one who hadn't been home.

Before writing, he took a moment to compose himself. Seconds roar by at times like these. He paced the newsroom floor — all six feet of it — popping his fist into his palm like a prizefighter. There is an undeniable adrenaline rush in knowing your thoughts, your gut reaction, your first-blush feelings will be in print in two hours, irretrievable and permanent. Or worse, crumbled in the trash.

Our motto was, *This morning's inspiration is that afternoon's finger smudge.*

Jonny paced up and down the hallways. It would probably be the most-read story he had ever written. He had to psyche himself. We all did. The entire town was going to read words that were being wrangled together under duress, deadline and, on this day, alcohol poisoning. Jonny, typing furiously, lashed his text together in about an hour, interspersing the quotes Steve and I fed him over the cubicle. One quote we found was from the Memphis, Tennessee, *Commercial Appeal* in which the deceased had said, "Oxford used to be so quiet at night that the only thing you could hear was the single piston pumping away at the ice house. Hear it a mile away."

Jonny, Steve and I couldn't help thinking that no one heard the pistol go off so many years later on that cold December night at the end of the century. Maybe the gentleman took one last listen before firing.

Perhaps it was actually an opening volley…

2

The paper came out that day and sold out, and our aging publisher, Mr. Jesse, shuffled through the newsroom and acknowledged all of us. "Good job today, boys. We got out a heartfelt piece in a timely manner." After such a wrenching day, the hair of the dog wagged its tail. The three of us clocked out in unison and made the 310-step walk to City Grocery. The Grocery, as it is known, has world-class high-dollar dining downstairs, complete with white linens and bow-tied waiters, and a more modest, homey neighborhood tavern upstairs. I've heard it described as a dive. We called it the "Upstairs Bureau," and it truly became an extension of the office. We'd generally be early arrivals and could read our work in civilian surroundings. Funny how the paper seemed like it was written by someone else when we read it up there.

If a story had played well, people would tell us. If they thought we were full of it, they weren't shy. At all. As it developed, the Upstairs Bureau, along with being an excellent place to quench more than a thirst for knowledge, was a handy barometer of public opinion. So steadfast was our devotion to the Bureau, when the time came for the bartenders to add more customer names, along with their favored drink, to the brass plaques lining the fabled bar, i.e., "Joe Blow — Budweiser," all three of us made it. It was a proud day when we saw our names engraved into the boozy pantheon of our fellow regulars. Hard-drinking newsmen is an age-old tradition, and lucky for us, we were newsmen.

The Grocery was also known for its cozy outdoor balcony that looked out over the Oxford town square, neat and picture perfect, Disney World meets Harper Lee. The too-good-to-be-true amusement-park vibe aside, on certain nights that balcony felt like the best place on earth to hoist a drink. Perhaps it was strange to be in celebratory mode after a day putting together a successful obituary, but strange was part of the job.

The range of stories that year ran an amazing gamut, and we even had a rare murder in Oxford in November 1997. Pizza Bob, the town's endearing pizza proprietor, came up rather viciously killed. His truck had stalled on Highway 30 east of town and was off the road. His body was found the next day by a resident out for a morning walk. (Luckily, we have exercise enthusiasts in this community.) Bob had suffered fatal blunt-force injuries. Two men were rumored to have pulled over to offer "assistance." The sheriff did his usual, "No comment," when I called for details. While talking with the chief of police, friendly rivals with the sherriff's department, the chief told me that there were sworn affidavits from witnesses, the arresting officer and the suspects themselves on file at the County Justice Building. It was standard procedure. Of course, the sheriff felt no need to volunteer this information.

"Just heigh-ho your happy ass down there and check it out, Jimmy Olsen," the chief cracked.

I walked over to the courthouse. Like everything else, it was basically across the street. The ladies behind the glass at the records office were sweet with a rural cordiality, but they wouldn't let me photocopy the documents. However, in a move I found both baffling and charming, they allowed me to stand there and copy them longhand. So there I stood, off to the side, copying the important parts in long hand on a legal pad. It took me about a half hour. But the details were compelling enough: He had been beaten with a pick axe, which was found 375 feet from the body. (One came to love the exactitude of police-speak.) A statement from one of the suspects admitted they had been smoking marijuana. I thanked the ladies, and as I left, I got the distinct impression they thought I was nuts.

On the front page that day, we ran the murder story with the sheriff's no comments but also the grisly quotes from the affidavits that I had handwritten. The paper wasn't out an hour before the sheriff called my desk.

"Hey, man, we need to talk. Can you come over?" His office was… right across the street. I went to the bathroom to look at myself before walking into the lion's den. I had never been in a law enforcement facility sober and of my own free will, but I still expected an ass-chewing. I ambled over, determined not to let him see me sweat.

"You can leave the door open if you want," he said when I arrived.

"Oh, that's good," I said sitting down. "In case you want to shoot me."

I wasn't really joking. We were joined by one of his deputies; I'll call him No-Neck. He had one of those Resting Bitch faces that frowned even when he was smiling.

"I didn't lie to you guys," I started in, rather brashly. "Everything you told me off the record, I kept off the record."

The sheriff pursed his lips. He looked like a bear with a crew cut who had decided not to eat what he'd just caught. "Well, my problem is I told the family I wouldn't release any other information, and then they have to read all about their daddy being pick-axed on the front page of the *Oxford Eagle*. They think I lied to 'em."

I could see his point. "I'm sorry, Sheriff, the documents are open to the public, and I was just assigned this story. Everybody knew Pizza Bob."

"I understand that," he replied. "Everybody's just doing their job." I looked at No-Neck. His features looked fiercely pissed, at all times. I got the feeling he could snap at any moment.

I was so intent on getting a good story — and this was a big one — I'd not thought about the effect on Pizza Bob's family. The details, "the juice," were what made the story so good, so distinct from others. Reporters were looking to ride that juice wave of murder and mayhem with just the right twist. A pizza man, a pick axe and a roll of money fit the bill. The sheriff had made his point, and I felt some sort of bond with him. At least we were dealing with each other straight up.

"I appreciate you working with me, Sheriff," I said, standing up. I shook the sheriff's hand and No-Neck's hand and headed back to the office, checking my fingers for any signs of tobacco spittle. I was learning the lesson of real human cost in all this. These weren't just stories I was writing, although when you're there at the desk with the clock ticking and a certain set of facts, it's in your DNA to make it crackle.

In the case of Pizza Bob, he was cherished by generations of customers. His place, the Pizza Den, was dark and funky with crappy faux-Italian murals and old newspapers, sort of stacked, on mismatched tables. But people weren't coming for the décor. One regular customer, Jeff Callaway, upon hearing of Pizza Bob's death, wrote as only a fan could:

"I know folks that loved his pizza and his pasta, but for most of us, the real treasures were those sandwiches; big, giant, sloppy sandwiches baked in that ancient, time-blackened oven where they gathered little, black, burned cheese crinklies that clung to the bottom of the fresh New Orleans Reising bread as it cooked to just the slightest crunch, then were slathered by the trusty paint brush that lived perpetually in a weathered saucepan of melted butter. It was our little corner of heaven, with Reverend Bob doling out his sermons on Styrofoam plates full of the majesty of the muffaletta or the glory of the stromboli, the sandwich of the gods.

"It was our haven in the storm. It was church. It was peace."

Ironically, Whiteaker himself was a witness in a rare Oxford murder trial ten years before. In that case, Doug Hodgkin, a twenty-one-year-old business major brutally murdered his girlfriend, Jeanie Gillies, twenty-four, a nursing student, after a night out. One of the last stops the two made on that May night in 1986 was at Pizza Den to pick up sandwiches to go. Besides her murderer, Pizza Bob was thought to be the last person to see her alive.

At the trial, Whiteaker was called to testify as to whether the couple seemed to be fighting at the time of their visit to his restaurant. After raising his hand and being sworn in, defense attorney Jack Dunbar asked the witness his name.

"Bob Whiteaker."

"Now, Mr. Whiteaker, is there a nickname by which you are commonly known around town?"

Whiteaker looked around the courtroom rather sheepishly before answering, "Yes… uh, Pizza Bob."

I was in the courtroom that day; it was the first murder trial I had ever seen in person. As the packed room tittered and smiled, I still remember Bob acknowledging his nickname as a pure moment of quaint, small-town theater. On that day, who would have ever dreamed that, some ten years later, Bob himself would be the victim of murder?

After my visit with the sheriff, I walked back to the office, again marveling at the life-and-death issues in which I now found myself entangled. Of course, I had no way of knowing that the biggest story of the year was waiting for me when I got back to the office…

OXFORD

MAYOR
JOHN O. LESLIE

BOARD OF ALDERMEN

MAYOR PRO-TEM
DEVON JONES
WARD I

H.C. FRANKLIN
WARD II

JOHN W. BOUNDS
WARD III

(COACH) ULYSSES HOWELL
WARD IV

DR. WILLIAM (BILL) BAKER
WARD V

JOE HUDSPETH
WARD VI

TOM SHARPE
ALDERMAN-AT-LARGE

CITY ATTORNEY
F. EDWIN PERRY

DEPARTMENT HEADS

CITY CLERK & TAX COLLECTOR
VIRGINIA H. CHRESTMAN

CITY TAX ASSESSOR
DEBBIE T. McLARTY

ELECTRIC DEPARTMENT SUPT.
JOHNNY EARNEST

SOLID WASTE SUPERINTENDENT
SHIRLEY MICHAEL

CHIEF OF POLICE
STEPHEN D. BRAMLETT

FIRE CHIEF
WILLIAM TERRY McDONALD

PARK & RECREATION DIRECTOR
ALLEN A. JONES

DIRECTOR OF PLANNING
AND DEVELOPMENT
BEN A. SMITH

CITY SHOP FOREMAN
TOMMY COBB

PUBLIC WORKS DIRECTOR
DAVID BENNETT

THE CITY OF OXFORD
COURTHOUSE SQUARE
OXFORD, MISSISSIPPI 38655
(601) 236-1310

NEWS RELEASE

FOR IMMEDIATE RELEASE

CONTACT: Mayor John Leslie
601/236-1310; FAX 601/232-2375

OXFORD, MISSISSIPPI, TO HONOR NATIVE SON WILLIAM FAULKNER ON HIS CENTENNIAL WITH STATUE

OXFORD, Miss. -- December 6, 1995 -- William Faulkner's hometown will celebrate his centennial in a very special way.

Oxford, Miss., will erect a life-size bronze statue of the Nobel Prize laureate in front of the City Hall on the historic courthouse square, Oxford Mayor John O. Leslie announced today.

"William Faulkner is the most important literary figure of this century," said Leslie. "We wanted to honor him and his contributions to world literature."

The city will dedicate the statue amid appropriate pomp and ceremony on September 25, 1997, the hundredth anniversary of Faulkner's birth. Local sculptor William Beckwith will design the statue.

In the 30-odd years since the author's death, Oxonians have witnessed a steadily-increasing interest in the writer and his ties to the local scene.

Private and corporate donations will fund the project, estimated to be $50,000.

###

NOTE TO MEDIA: Keep up with the latest on the Faulkner statue project and other happenings in Oxford by checking the Oxford home page on the Internet, debuting today, at http://www.ci.oxford.ms.us

A NICE PLACE TO LIVE

Press release from the City of Oxford

3

It began like most life-changing moments…with a press release. On December 6, 1995, the mayor of Oxford, John Leslie, issued a press release announcing the city was going to commission a statue of author and Nobel Prize winner William Faulkner. Faulkner lived in Oxford most of his life and had a roster of kinfolk still calling Lafayette County home. His former residence, Rowan Oak, a five-block walk from the town square, attracts thousands yearly. Our immediate reaction as the announcement peeled off the fax machine was that it would make a nice story to the people of Oxford and would be very easy to report. Regurgitate press releases, phone up the mayor (a garrulous six-termer, the dean of Mississippi mayors), lard it up with a couple of literary nuggets from the author and head to the bar. No problemo. But this story, one that began mundanely enough, would prove to be very different and strange.

If we were ill-equipped to handle child-support malfeasance and plain ole murder, we certainly were not prepared for the year-long roller coaster that erupted over a public work of art to honor our small-town giant. Faulkner will forever be this town's most widely-known native son. Not many towns of 10,000 can claim a Nobel Prize winner in literature.

The ruckus over the statue evolved in a serpentine fashion, a real-life mirror of the great man's fiction. In some quarters of town, on the corner, at the grocery store, bumping into friends on the street, we discovered that a statue honoring Faulkner was considered a sell-out, a gross stab at tourist dollars. "Oxford is a good town to sell," I recall one particularly oleaginous speaker telling our Board of Aldermen. "Our execs in Baltimore are very excited about Oxford."

The statue proposal came three years after a row of five one hundred-year-old oak trees, presiding across the street from Faulkner's mother's (Miss Maud's) house on South Lamar, were chopped down with no notice or hearing. The massive trees offered morning shade to an entire block, including the Nobel Laureate's family, but were felled to make way for a turn lane and a bank. The occupants of Miss Maud's house, Dean Faulkner Wells (the author's niece) and her husband, author Larry Wells, shed tears of rage. The city seemed tone deaf from chainsaws and perpetrated other overzealous tree cuttings on Lamar Blvd. (the town's stately thoroughfare into the Square), causing the couch potato populace to rise up. Enraged citizens, usually polite and apathetic, began the process to establish a Tree Board and the drafting of strict guidelines.

As the city beat reporter, I attended the twice-monthly board of alderman meetings, and in the past they were strictly snoozers. But more and more, as developments and shopping malls came up for approval, crowds filled the chambers with rowdy booing and hissing. Despite the hostility, a retirement/golf villa was approved for south of town, and a shopping center development to the west. The edges of town seemed on the verge of being slowly pecked away by rabid ducks.

The project that stirred the most ire was a major five-lane highway plan that was working its way through the city's legislative process. It would require the cutting of hundreds of trees to add two lanes to Oxford's western entrance. City engineers said the project would provide a "safe artery" to the mall and the ever-expanding group of businesses springing up west of town. A safe artery for the life blood… the mall. It's ironic that such medical terminology involving the aorta was actually cutting out the heart of Oxford — at least in the minds of many we interviewed and from those who wrote angry letters to the editor.

A "trees vs. improved access to the mall" debate was readily understandable. Economically, it was a good problem for a small Southern town to have at that time. Many small towns in 1997 Mississippi were drying up, beginning the long, inexorable slide into plywood windows and graffiti-covered nonexistence. A statue of a novelist was the last thing on their minds.

In January 1997, the mayor announced the site for the statue would be in front of Oxford's City Hall and a magnolia tree there, the official tree of the state of Mississippi, would have to be "removed."

Oh, boy…

"Your cause is doomed. The Old Cumberland Church was the only building on or near the Square still standing in 1865. It was tougher than war, tougher than the Yankee Brigadier Chalmers and his artillery and all his sappers with dynamite and crowbars and cans of kersosene. But it wasn't stronger than the ringing of a cash register bell."

William Faulkner
letter to the *Oxford Eagle*, March 13, 1947

4

January
Chainsaw Leadership

Faulkner wouldn't recognize much of his hometown these days, but he would recognize the awkward civic wrangling during his centennial year. He would recognize the petty squabbling, court injunctions, arrests, raucous board meetings, scathing letters to the editor, and all the sound and fury. What he might not understand is why his hometown was going to such lengths to honor him on his 100th birthday. After all, most of the town had pretty much disdained him while he was alive except for his last two decades when he won the Pulitzer and Nobel prizes, and even then, their admiration was tempered with bemusement. (He was known derisively as "Count No Count," an eccentric who often dressed flamboyantly and "put on airs" but had trouble paying his bills.)

If Faulkner could stroll around Oxford now, he would indeed be flabbergasted by the condos and apartments, the interstate bypass, the traffic. He would be disgusted by the pulsating taverns on his beloved Square with loud, live music. He would be shotgun-grabbing mad at the twenty-four-hour convenience store *next door* to his Miss Maud's house. The over-sized space-age roofing, the fluorescent lighting, the drunken coeds whooping and buying cigarettes at two in the morning and squealing over chicken-on-a-stick.

Indeed, what would the old existentialist make of chicken-on-a-stick?

In 1997, Oxford was a small southern town — in Faulkner-speak, "a hamlet." In that year, the population was 11,000 souls and another 11,000 students at the University of Mississippi, a mile away. The town was tiny and woody but became "discovered" through news stories about mega-novelist John Grisham, a recent resident. Oxford's attributes as a retirement community further upped its national profile.

In the days and weeks following the mayor's announcement about the statue and plans to "remove" a tree to make way for it, he also announced that the second magnolia tree at the site was diseased, and it too would have to go. With the current pro-tree outcry going on, these plans amounted to a raised middle finger to the citizens. Jonny and I decided to call a local tree surgeon and get health appraisals on both trees. It was a total juice move with hopes to stir up the mayor and maybe our readers as well.

Willie Phillips, owner of Oxford's J&J Tree Service, agreed to meet us at City Hall and inspect the trees for us. He had the relaxed air of an outdoorsman and the worn hands of patience. What he found was a long cylindrical hole in the trunk of the north tree. Diseased, he told us, but certainly not doomed. "With a tree like this, we normally dig all this out of there, spray the fungus and fill it up with concrete. Once you fix the hole, nothing can get in there to eat it up. The tree will eventually heal over the concrete."

He then pointed to the south tree, the healthy one slated for the axe. Phillips explained that both trees were so healthy they would grow and expand and eventually have to be cut away from the wall of City

Hall, a task easily accomplished.

"You could stand on the ground with a trim pole and cut that back." He stood back and regarded both trees with a smile.

"Man, when they bloom, they sure are pretty."

Under the headline, "City Hall Trees May Get the Axe," Jonny and I paired quotes from Faulkner with Willie Phillips, surely a first. We ran this excerpt from a letter Faulkner wrote to the *Oxford Eagle* on March 13, 1947: "We have gotten rid of the shade trees which once circled the courthouse yard and bordered the Square itself, along with the second-floor galleries which once formed awnings for the sidewalk; all we have left now to distinguish an old southern town from any of ten thousand towns built yesterday from Kansas to California are the Confederate monument, the courthouse and the jail. Let us tear them down too and put up something covered with neon and radio amplyfyers.[sic]"

The following Monday, a cold January morning brooding with slate skies, all Faulkner broke loose. Our sharp-eyed photographer, Bruce Newman, was walking to work, looked over at City Hall and noticed the magnolia tree was gone, nothing remaining but a stump. He quickly picked up his pace and stormed into the office.

"They cut the tree down," he said to no one in particular as he lunged to his desk and loaded up his gear, grabbing cameras, bags, lens. Jonny and I looked at each other like kids hearing the recess bell. It probably wouldn't take both of us to write it, but we both grabbed up our notepads and scurried over to City Hall, which was, again, right across the street (a large portion of our lives took place in a three-block radius).

Walking over, we could see the south windows on City Hall, thanks to the tree no longer there to block the view. The other tree looked lonely. They had cut down the healthy tree and left the diseased one standing. All that remained was a small stump with sawdust all around it, a bell that couldn't be un-rung, death by chainsaw. The tree-cutting, we found out later, occurred at dawn on the Saturday after New Year's when half the town felt like I did on so many days. On that Monday, January 6, only one week into the Year of the Genius, the mayor and his allies handed us solid gold. Upon seeing the stump we ran back to the office and began working the phones, trying not to sound giddy. In those days we rarely used a recording device when conducting phone interviews, relying instead on the true art of jotting down people's comments using our own weird version of shorthand.

The man who actually did the tree-cutting was very matter-of-fact and I'm sure had no idea how much he was helping me grease this story just by simply stating the facts.

Johnny Earnest, superintendent of the Oxford Electric Department, told me, "We cut the tree down early Saturday morning after the Christmas decorations came down on Friday but before traffic hit the square on Saturday."

Seems perfectly reasonable, but reasonable don't sell papers. To get the yin to Earnest's yang, my next call that morning was my ace-in-the-hole for all things Faulkner: Dr. Evans Harrington. Evans was a retired Ole Miss English professor and one of two preeminent Faulkner scholars in town (Dr. Donald Kartiganer, the other). I asked him for a comment on what Faulkner would have thought of a tree being cut to make way for a statue of himself.

"When I conduct tours of Rowan Oak," he began, as if lecturing, "I take people to the northeast side of the house and point out a pear tree stump. In the 1950s, the wind blew down the pear tree and left nothing but a small root sticking up. Faulkner propped that root up and took care of it. He planted a pecan tree next to it in case the pear tree died. The pear tree survived and continued to bear fruit long after he died."

Evans was a poet, playwright and novelist, not to mention a professor of literature, and he talked like all three without sounding showy.

In our digging around perusing the alderman agenda, we noticed the Saturday cutting of the City Hall magnolia occurred before a new tree ordinance was to take effect on Monday. The new ordinance banned the cutting of non-hazardous trees on city property.

Steve noticed it on the agenda and stepped over to Jonny and me.

"I guess what we have here is an ah-ha moment," he chuckled as he waved the agenda around. Not only had the city cut down a healthy tree, it appeared it was done to get under the wire of a new law. We didn't have total proof of that, but then again, you don't often see city work crews out at dawn on a Saturday.

Jonny wrote the story that day: "This spot on the Square, along with the woods behind his home, or the Delta cane breaks where he hunted in the autumn, was where Faulkner gleaned much of what some would term his inspiration: families driving in from the country for their mail and ice cream, the old men in overalls sitting still and cool beneath the shade of the trees circling the courthouse and lining the square. Most of the trees are gone now, of course."

I phoned one of the statue supporters, the octogenarian Dr. Chester McLarty, who, as a younger physician, had actually treated Faulkner.

"You either cut the tree down, or there's no statue. I'd vote for Mr. Faulkner over a tree any day," he told me, seeming to enjoy the grievances. "I think even a tree-hugger would have a hard time arguing with that."

The story ran on page one with a Bruce Newman photo of the stump. Indignation poured in over the phone and in letters to the editor. "It challenges common sense, killing a magnolia tree for a statue that few people want," wrote one. "If I had snuck downtown with my chainsaw early some Saturday morning and cut the tree, I would probably have been arrested. If I were dealing out justice, the mayor would have to replace the tree he killed with one of equal size and vitality and personally have to care for." The letter was signed, "Larry Watts, Tree-hugger." The Associated Press picked up our story, and we saw the tree-cutting make international newspapers. The watering hole wags spoke of recalling the mayor. Or at least rolling his yard.

One columnist, the inestimable Rheta Grimsley Johnson of the *Atlanta Journal Constitution,* wrote: "A town lousy with magnolias can spare one for Faulkner."

True enough, perhaps, but that sentiment can't see the forest for the ducks. The statue project seemed to have been hatched in secret and seemed like just one more ineluctable bulldozer being shoved down the town's throat. The secretive project seemed to be all too indicative of the way local government had been operating recently.

Mayor John Leslie had grown a little brusque in his role after six terms. He was amiable and cordial, but there was an edge. As a reporter, I never had a problem getting information from him or getting him to return phone calls, but he could be gruff and clam up when it suited him. The public perception in some quarters was that things went "his way or the highway." When I called him that Tuesday morning to ask his comment on citizens taking exception to the tree-cutting, he shifted into defiant mode.

"I learned a long time ago that you're not going to get one hundred

Oxford Mayor John Leslie, 1997

per cent unanimous approval on anything. We're putting the statue in front of City Hall because the folks who gave us $45,000 wanted it there."

"Who are the donors, Mr. Mayor?"

"It's no big secret. We'll reveal them at the proper time."

"When will that be?"

"Don't worry, we'll alert the press at the proper time. I'm sure the donors will appreciate the positive publicity."

Here we go again. Time to "Heigh-Ho My Happy Ass" to the truth. Such mild stone-walling might suffice in some cases, but not with this story. It was so easy to pick up the phone and call around and find the identity of the statue donors, and if that pissed off the mayor, well, that was a good day at the office.

The deadline clock was ticking.

"OK, thanks, Mr. Mayor."

Will Lewis is one of Oxford's leading merchants as the owner of Neilson's, a fine-clothing store and one of the South's oldest, in business 135 years. In 1997, he served on the board of Union Planters Bank. Lewis is an avid reader and an erudite gentleman who fully appreciates public debate

"The mayor's right; the identity of the donors is no big secret," Lewis told me when I called him after hanging up with mayor. "The donors are First National Bank, Union Planters Bank and Chester McLarty. We each gave $10,000, but no one asked us about location. In fact, I'm personally against the City Hall location. I think a better place would be south of City Hall in front of the tourism building. And of course, I prefer a more statue *verite* rather than Faulkner just standing erect holding his pipe."

The president of First National Bank, Bill Gottshall, confirmed his bank's $10,000 donation.

"I don't recall any suggestion of location," he added.

While we were assembling our stories for that day's paper, we received word there was to be a "spontaneous demonstration" to mourn the magnolia tree. Jonny and I chuckled as we headed over.

We arrived at City Hall in time to find the "ceremony" under way. A black wreath had been placed at the site and a statement read: "The chain-saw-style of leadership has really thwarted the democratic process." The speaker was photographer and art professor Tom Rankin, a friend of ours. His son, Julian, adjusted the black wreath. Rankin smirked and looked over at Jonny and me before plunging on.

"This happened at a time when people of good faith are trying to compromise on a tree ordinance. This cowardly act was wielded at an invisible hour on a Saturday morning in a college town."

Right on cue, young Julian piped up.

"Daddy, if William Faulkner loved trees so much, why'd they cut it down?"

Good stuff, no doubt. We hurried back to the office, where Jonny had another story going. He received a phone tip about classic small-town shenanigans at the city automotive repair garage. Seems some of the good ole boys were selling surplus police cars to their girlfriends for $10. Man, oh man, we found ourselves living in a world of above-the-fold gold.

Jonny phoned the mayor for a comment and got the standard political recant: "This is the first I've heard of it, but I know one thing: when you find out about a problem and don't immediately correct it, you're part of the problem."

If you didn't know better, you'd say we were earning our paychecks. Good stories were falling into our laps and into the paper. We

Julian Rankin at the tree mourning

even brought home the brass; we won writing awards, and Bruce won best photographer accolades from the state press association. For those two or three hours in the morning where we labored to write and edit, we cared about the stories. We would pace the floors or run to the dictionary for the exact word. We would make that extra call in search of the killer quote. We certainly wanted to be accurate but get in as much back-door subversion as possible.

After all the writing was done, we'd crowd around Steve's computer and toss out headline ideas, most too dirty to actually use. We even developed a deep affection for sub-heads. As editor-in-chief, Steve could have done this on his own. He didn't owe it to us, but he enjoyed it. It was comic relief and gave us the opportunity to cackle and indulge our inner idiot, (sometimes not so inner). Jonny would have spit bubbles foaming in his mouth before spitting on the floor. This was the level of our humor. And we were the yahoos entrusted with bringing the daily news to one of the hottest towns in the South.

We ran a front-page photo of the stump, the black wreath, young Julian with his great quote and other comments. Once again we covered a story secretly hoping the controversy would continue. Objective journalism is tooth fairy stuff. Journalism is as objective as the human beings who write it.

That night, after our splashy coverage in the afternoon, the board of aldermen was meeting to take up the tree ordinance. There wasn't even time to bask over beers at the Grocery. When I arrived, the meeting room was overflowing, and no one was smiling. I took my usual seat on the second row, directly behind the chief of police. The tension, even anger, in the room was palpable, and in spite of myself, I felt a momentary twinge of remorse at any part I may have played in stirring it up. But then, seeing the mayor and board squirm up at the dais goosed me. This was different. These people were mad. They actually gave off heat. The mayor, no doubt literally feeling the heat and facing the fire, quickly addressed the question of the night.

"We were only doing what we thought was best for the city. There is no doubt that the statue will be a real tourist attraction. Look, I'm a tree lover. I personally planted that tree, and I have a right to do that, so I took it down. I don't see why everyone is so upset about this one tree."

He then opened the floor for comments, and Susan Hannah approached the lectern. She was an administrator of the Hume art museum on campus and wife of the outlaw novelist Barry Hannah. You couldn't be married to Barry and be a lightweight. Susan leaned into the microphone.

"It's not just the tree, Mr. Mayor." She was shaking, and her words slithered out of clenched teeth. "It's the overall attitude that you seem to display towards the citizens of this community. It really has nothing to do with the tree. It's the fact that you seem to have lost sight of the fact that this city belongs to the people. If this continues..." she trembled, biting her lip, then pointing at the board, "we…will…vote…you…out of office!" She pounded the lectern and walked back to her seat to roaring applause.

Jimmy Faulkner approached the podium, setting off a buzz of anticipation, the tension in overdrive. Jimmy, Faulkner's nephew, was the last of the living male Faulkners who had actually known William. He was the author's hunting and drinking buddy and, in the author's later years, caretaker. It was Jimmy, the nephew (more like the son he never had) who took Faulkner on his last trip to the sanitarium in nearby Byhalia, Mississippi, where the author passed away on July 2, 1962.

Jimmy looked like a rounder, more garrulous, version of his famous uncle. He had the white hair, the mustache and the sad eyes. "I want to go on the record," he said, shaking his finger. "I'm speaking for the entire Faulkner family now. I want to let the people know we do not, nor would we ever, condone cutting a healthy, living, beautiful tree to erect a cold, inanimate object in its place. I don't ever remember Uncle Will gazing across the Square from City Hall, as has been suggested." Then he added an explosive addendum that, in this war of words, amounted to the nuclear option, at least in these parts:

"The way this tree was done is how the Snopeses would do it."

To call someone a Snopes is to invoke the notorious, conniving backwoods clan of Faulkner's fiction. Cousins, uncles and brothers with names like Montgomery Ward Snopes and Wall Street Panic Snopes, and the slimiest one of all, Flem Snopes. Based on a long-ago family in Oxford, they are the epitome of poor white trash who rode into town on stolen horses and swindled their way into nouveau wealth. The designation "Snopes" relegates one to a social strata lower than trailer trash. Indeed, in Faulkner country, it is the equivalent to using the "N" word.

The board passed an emergency motion that no more city trees would be cut until further notice. The next day, Steve wrote the story and called us into his office. We gathered around his screen, and his headline read, "No More City Trees Will Be Sucked."

"Whaddaya think?"

Jonny spit on the floor.

We amended it to "No More City Trees Will Be Cut," in fourteen-point type, just a couple of notches below a declaration of war. The sub-head read, "Aldermen take action following fierce criticism." The tree vote and Jimmy's remarks, including the Snopes line, went out on the Associated Press wire, and quickly, the *Eagle* received calls from

National Public Radio and the *Chicago Tribune*. A week later, I was asked to call and get a comment from Jill Faulkner Summers, Faulkner's daughter and only child. As I waited for her to come to the phone that day, I could hear happy grandchildren in the background, and you could almost taste the fresh air. Summers lived in the horse country outside of Charlottesville, Virginia. She was very pleasant and had indeed just come in from riding horses.

"I'm against this statue," she said in a warm, soft, southern voice that seemed to stretch back to the long-ago days of her Nobel Prize-winning dad. "My father was a very private man. He wouldn't like this. I'm against it particularly since they cut down the magnolia tree." She mentioned she had written a letter to city officials in care of Jimmy.

"It's up to him if he wants to read it to the board. I gave him permission."

"Would you consider legal action to stop the statue?"

"You know, I used to be a reporter," she said, giving me the smooth Faulkner brush off. "I worked at the *Oxford Eagle* briefly and at the *Charlotte Observer*. I've been in the position of asking the questions. So you'll understand this is not something I'm going to tell you right now."

"Who else could make them fight? Could have struck them so aghast with fear and dread? Who else could have declared a war… except men who would believe that all necessary to conduct a successful war was not acumen nor shrewdness nor politics nor diplomacy nor money nor even integrity and simple arithmetic but just love of land and courage."

William Faulkner, *Go Down, Moses* (1942)

5

Dr. Chester McLarty inherited the Faulkner family as patients back in 1946 when their family doctor, Dr. John Culley, moved into surgery. As a patron of the arts ("an interested consumer," he said), a major donor to the statue project, as well as a good talker, I knew his thoughts had to be part of the story. Dr. McLarty had a Clark Gable mustache and could be seen around town nattily dressed, often wearing a racing hat at a rakish tilt.

"My people have been in this county since the 1840s," he told me in one of several interviews. "Nobody read Faulkner until *Sanctuary*. They debated whether there was a little porno in there. Everybody in town was whispering about it. Bridge parties were big in Oxford in those days, and there was much talk among citizens. People read it under their mattress or in the john."

McLarty was at Tulane in New Orleans in 1936 and enjoyed seeing the apartment Faulkner rented in Pirate's Alley some ten years before. "It's for sale for a million dollars now."

In 1946, when he began his practice, scores of Ole Miss students were back from the service and marrying their high school sweethearts and starting families.

"I started OBY. Ended up delivering about 1,000 babies," he laughed.

"It was an easy arrangement with the Faulkners, Bill, Estelle (Faulkner's wife) and Jill. Bill didn't need much doctoring. He wasn't sick all that much. His drinking bouts were the main part of it. He'd periodically have injuries, mainly from trying to jump horses. He was pushing sixty when he went to Virginia and started jumping horses. Well, you know, that's a little late in life to start going over fences on horses, and he had one fall after another is what killed him."

McLarty then recounted one particularly gruesome fall. Faulkner was practice jumping one day, and the horse started over an obstacle and almost stumbled, and when the author lunged to hang on, he tore his adductor muscle on his upper thigh.

"Tore his 'ductor muscle right in two," McLarty recounted casually. "It's not serious, but it hurts like hell. Bleeds, then swells up."

"He came up to my house," McLarty continued. "Came and knocked on the door. 'Janey,' he asked my wife, 'does Chester have his surgery here?' When you do operations in your home you have what is called a 'surgery box.' I fixed him up and assured him it wasn't serious, but I told him we could get a second opinion. We called one of my doctor friends in Memphis, Dr. Calatrusio. I said, 'I'm sitting here with Bill Faulkner, and he has a torn 'ductor…' Well, he didn't want to talk about Bill's injury; he began lecturing me how Faulkner was our last great hope for the novel. 'Oh, he's our last great hope for the novel.'"

I asked Dr. McLarty to elaborate on Faulkner's much-discussed drinking. "You mentioned his drinking bouts. What do you think precipitated them?"

"Well, that's a very complicated subject. There really wasn't that much social drinking going on. Women didn't drink, maybe young flappers just getting the hang of it, but middle-aged people just didn't drink that much, Prohibition and everything. So the men that did drink couldn't drink at home; their wives would give them hell, so it just wasn't worth the trouble."

McLarty said Oxford menfolk of this era would get a driver to drive them up to Memphis to the Peabody Hotel for two-day benders. In the summer, there were fishing expeditions to the nearby Tallahatchie River.

"If you messed around and fell out drunk," McLarty pointed out, "the mosquitoes would eat you up." In the fall, trips to the Delta were booked for deer hunting with libations.

"There wasn't a deer in Lafayette County until the mid-1930s, when they turned about half a dozen loose, and when we came back from World War II, you couldn't move for 'em." McLarty said that prior to that, in Faulkner's day, the 1920s and '30s, the deer camps in the Delta offered game and camaraderie. Much of the area was bayous, low country that flooded every year and wouldn't grow cotton or anything else. Instead, there were hardwoods and deer, not to mention bear, bobcat, even panthers.

McLarty said Faulkner would go over to deer camp and "stay drunk as long as he could." Upon returning to Rowan Oak from deer camp, many times the diminutive author would have to go over to the hospital in Byhalia for three or four days to dry out.

"I remember Faulkner once coming back from Memphis after a bender, and he was blue, cyanotic," McLarty recalled. "Somebody called ahead and said, 'Get the oxygen ready.' He was thirty-eight or forty years old at this time. You have to be quite a drinker to get noticed in Hollywood. I remember [director] Howard Hawks shaking his head and saying, 'I never saw a man drink like he's trying to kill himself.'"

We then returned to the subject at hand. "Tell me about this centennial year," I said.

"The thought came to me in the spring of 1995 that we ought to build a statue of Faulkner. I believed [Bill] Beckwith was the person to do it, and the timing was absolutely right; we had two years until September of 1997: a year to raise the money and a year to build it."

McLarty said he had seen Faulkner standing at the old post office (now City Hall), gazing off into the distance, an image that had stuck with him, despite Jimmy Faulkner's dismissal of the notion. He could already see the statue in his mind. When he ran into Beckwith at the annual Faulkner picnic (across the street from Rowan Oak), he asked him for a figure. Beckwith said $50,000, and when McLarty went to City Hall and relayed the number to Mayor Leslie, the mayor said to run with it.

"We looked out the window and at first thought of the north side of City Hall," McLarty said, shaking his head. "It's such a jungle over there, so we settled on the south side. We looked and saw that the tree would have to be cut, and we laughed and thought that might give somebody a couple of bad days, but it's not of any consequence, and we laughed about it, and in any rational society, that would be true.

"But it all started out innocently."

McLarty said he visited with Bill Gottshall, the president of the First National Bank, and also wrote him a letter. He reminded him that his bank had been on the outs with the Faulkners since 1912, and here was a chance to make amends. (McLarty was referring to a spat the original founder, the "Young Colonel" John Faulkner, had with the bank's board, causing him to remove all his money, reportedly in a wheelbarrow.) Gottshall was the first one to write a check. The Faulkner Centennial Fund received $5,000 from First National Bank and the same from Union Planters.

"The city money is $25,000," McLarty said. "That's in the bank, in the Faulkner Centennial Fund. It's tourism money approved by the board of aldermen, but as you know, we don't lack for conflict around here."

"Maybe that's why so many writers come from Oxford."

"Well writers, whatever they write about, it boils down to the fact that they're writing about interpersonal relationships. If you look at Oxford over the last few months, you see some pretty intense relationships."

"What do you think Faulkner would have made of all the fuss?"

"Everybody I see knows how Faulkner thought about everything," McLarty exclaimed, a fire in his eye. "Oh, he was a nature-lover, but that has nothing to do with the tree. He would have been in favor of cutting the tree down, not because he is or isn't a nature lover, but because he's not a damn fool."

Jimmy Faulkner's declaration that the entire statue episode was handled the way "a Snopes would have done it" wounded McLarty. Despite both men being elderly, the war of words had a schoolyard feel to it.

"He called me a Snopes," McLarty would later say. "We've entertained Jimmy two or three times in the past year. I'm not going to be rude to him, but you won't see him back in my house."

Silly season was in full swing.

Editor Steve Mullen did his part by penning what he thought was a satirical editorial. Under the headline, "Faulkner statue not enough;

how about Faulknerland?" Steve wrote: "City officials see the statue as a tourist draw… If it's tourists we want, why stop with one statue? We need to offer them something more than just concrete and bronze. That something? Faulknerland. A theme park based on the writings of William Faulkner… All theme parks need roller coasters, and ours will have *Absalom, Absalom!* Since that book was written in circles, the coaster will have several loops in it.

"'Addy Bundren's Wild River Ride' will take screaming tourists, seated in coffin-shaped canoes, through a swollen creek featured in *As I Lay Dying*. Fast-paced thrills will be plentiful at the 'Barn Burning' attraction, similar to the *Backdraft* ride at Universal Studios. We can pay for the whole thing through the two-percent food and beverage tax and through corporate sponsorships. Jack Daniels Distillery might join in, as well as Birdseye, which could sponsor the informational, 'Popeye's Wonderful World of Corn.'"

Steve ended the editorial with, "I respectfully submit this plan to our city leaders… We want visitors and more gawking visitors, clogging our streets, shops and restaurants, spending their money."

Steve deserved points for the Faulkner references, but one reader in particular, sculptor Bill Beckwith, who was commissioned to create the statue, failed to appreciate the humor. He wrote a fairly blistering reply: "I find this editorial to be neither funny, nor cute, nor clever. The best description would be stupid. This editorial can only incite trouble and ill will. Please, Mr. Editor, do your job and edit; save Steve Mullen from embarrassing himself and your newspaper any further. Trash cans are very useful things."

The problem was, of course, Steve *was* the editor.

6

The following week, the next board meeting was like a fight rematch, with Jimmy the challenger, further emboldened, not only by a sense that he was righteous in his fight, but armed with Jill Faulkner's letter and the favorable national publicity that was starting to percolate. In his blue blazer, full head of white hair and ample girth he looked like the old squirrel hunter and former Marine fighter pilot he in fact was. After reading aloud Jill's letter — "I'm against it particularly since they cut down that magnolia tree. Tell them I do not want a statue of my father on the Square or anywhere else…" Jimmy looked dramatically over his glasses and struck a pose probably not unlike that of his ancestors when dueling.

"We have respectfully asked that you cancel your project. Sir, when will we have an answer to our request?" John Leslie looked over his glasses like the town druggist filling a prescription, which he did for forty years.

"Well, we've got contracts signed. We've got dignitaries booked, like Willie Morris. Shelby Foote is coming and Judge Neal Biggers."

"Are you going to build this statue, yes or no?"

Leslie looked away from Jimmy and addressed the audience, which was packed and frothing.

"You know, in Mississippi, we don't have a law like they do in Tennessee that guards a person's likeness or image. I guessed they passed that because of Elvis. But we don't have that law like they do up there. In Mississippi, there is no such law. When a person dies here, that's the end of it."

"Are you going to build this statue, yes or no?" Faulkner thundered again.

John Leslie could mount a poker face when he needed too. His countenance would go blank and you could read no actual emotion he may have had. He let his words do the job: "Well, it's not necessary to have the family's permission. The board has approved the money and the site. Yes, we're going to build the statue."

Ward VI Alderman David Magee interrupted. Magee was a new-breed Republican who grew up in Oxford and loved the town. He could always be counted on as pro-tree vote despite his political affiliation.

"I think we're walking into some uneasy territory here. We don't want to be stuck forever with 'the statue the family didn't want.'"

"We'd certainly like to have the family's blessing," agreed Devon Jones, a good ole boy, long-time, very conservative resident with a handsome shock of slicked-back white hair. Alderman-at-Large Tom Sharpe weighed in. Sharpe was aptly named. He was a brilliant guy with a professorial gray beard. He worked tirelessly for economic development but had a tree-hugger's soul. He turned to face Jimmy Faulkner. As always, he spoke deliberately, the words coming out in a measured, thoughtful flow.

"Can we form a committee to sit down and see if there is an accommodation that we can come to that is in the best interest of the Faulkner family and the community and honors Faulkner as we were originally trying to do?"

Jimmy replied that the family was willing to talk, and Sharpe immediately put his words into a motion that passed unanimously. Sharpe asked Jimmy how many Faulkners should be on the committee: "Two or three?"

"All of us!" Jimmy roared.

The Faulkners had indeed "fought" City Hall and won — at least this round. The tension from the meeting would surely be ramped up now, and Jonny and I did all we could to throw gas on the fire. Once again, our eagerness for a story clouded our vision that there were very real-life consequences involved for real human beings. It wasn't just a story. This statue represented the biggest, most prestigious commission for the chosen artist, Bill Beckwith. All the black wreaths and political hissing were luxuries to him. While we giggled through deadlines and racked our mushy brains for just the right pun in a headline, this was life-and-blood seriousness to Beckwith. Our "juice" was his sustenance.

Beckwith and I were both raised in the Mississippi River town of Greenville in the heart of the Delta. I remember him a grade or two ahead of me in high school. We both made our way to Ole Miss and stayed. Beckwith set up shop in Taylor, seven miles south of Oxford, out in the sticks. At any given time, Taylor (pop. 323) had half a dozen working artists. Rent was cheaper. The quiet, slow vibe was a notch or two down from the increasing hum of Oxford.

There was certainly a psychic transformation one felt when transitioning from the Delta to the hills. It gets colder for one thing. There's less unbridled looniness. I've concluded Deltans suffer from

Sculptor Bill Beckwith

"too much sky" syndrome. When you can see too far across endless, flat land, it skews the brain. Thank God.

For me, Oxford in the late 1970s into the '80s had a nice buzz to it: music, vibrant bars, culture and literature, quality fishing nearby, of course SEC sports and, let's not deny it, world-class beauties. Unlike Beckwith, I had no marketable skills, but there were still manual labor jobs to be had. It seemed a safe move for a clueless nineteen-year-old. Of course I never dreamed in 1978, when I moved here, that it would be my last move — at least for all intents and purposelessness.

Oxford and Lafayette County are located in the north central part of the state, eighty miles southeast of Memphis. The Chickasaws lived here before the white man came along with a series of treaties, the terms of which kept changing. The original European settlers were beguiled by the land, which they considered valuable. Such was their drive to obtain this acreage from the Indians, government officials began monitoring Chickasaw behavior for insights in how to deal with (cheat) them.

One of their reports read, "When the more pressing work had been accomplished, many members of the tribe repaired to an open area in the center of town for dancing and athletic activity. As hunting and warfare became less of a viable vocation, the warriors found considerable time on their hands, and proceeded to occupy most of it in entertainment, usually involving drunkenness."

And so it is to this day.

My professors at Ole Miss and I mutually decided I could benefit from a "gap year" (if not decade), so I left school. Wanting to remain in Oxford for all the above reasons, I hired on with the state highway department, Oxford office. At the time, two crews out of Oxford were helping with the massive four-lane project to nearby Batesville.

Early on, I was handed a hard hat and a kaiser blade (a long-handled scythe) and instructed to start hacking my way through the jungle to Batesville — twenty miles away. I hacked and I hacked. I hacked for weeks. I drove stakes with sledge hammers in dirt like a stone floor. I hacked some more. I lost thirty pounds.

The summertime, balls-to-the-wall attitude of highway building, shall we say, relaxed a bit in the winter, especially on rainy days. During the winter, the crew would leave the office and go hide. This was literally pulling the truck up into the woods, turning off the engine and frittering away the morning until lunch, then doing the same that afternoon. Your tax dollars at work.

Guys would nap; some would play spades. I read. There were days when sitting and hiding was dragging agony. There were days when it was pretty swell. Mostly it made me realize I wanted to take my hacking to a typewriter, preferably in an air-conditioned room.

I'm no Faulkner scholar but certainly a reader, a fan and an admirer. Reading Faulkner for the first time felt like entering a country where you don't speak the language, and all the other citizens can fly. My introduction was in high school, at age sixteen, with the opening section of *The Sound and the Fury*. Faulkner readers know this as the famously hard-to-understand, "Benjy section," written from the babbling, incoherent point of view of what was then called an "idiot" child (based on an actual Oxford resident and his family). For me, it was stream-of-unconsciousness: a tale of sound and fury told by an idiot, signifying who-the-hell-knows.

The book was assigned in our senior high school English class by Nell Thomas, a revered teacher in the (then) literary town of Greenville. She fanned the flames of free thought by teaching *The Catcher in the Rye* and *The Sound and the Fury* in the same semester.

Thomas earned her master's at Ole Miss around 1940, and her thesis on William Faulkner was, at the time, the school's first on the author. She was a heavyweight. Teachers in other more redneck Delta towns might have been questioned, if not censured, for exposing tender young minds to Salinger and Faulkner and their down-and-dirty tales of suicide, incest and alcoholism. I reveled in her class until we started in on *The Sound and the Fury*. That first, bewildering read of Faulkner was like trying to make sentences out of algebra. I was lost and not only lost, but terrified that I would never be found.

Next came John Pilkington, a medicine ball of a professor at Ole Miss. The marquee Faulkner teacher at the time was the dashing and handsome Evans Harrington. I wound up with Pilkington in summer school of 1974, and back then, summer school in Oxford really was summer. The town was sleepy with plenty of parking, and no hustle and very little bustle. Our small class had an insane reading list: a novel a week, and not breezy beach tomes. We were reading *The Sound and Fury; Absalom, Absalom; Sanctuary; Light in August; Sartoris* and the pay-off pitch: the Snopes trilogy — *The Hamlet*, *The Mansion*, *The Town*. This reading frenzy put the crash in crash course. But it worked. I've been a committed Faulkner fan ever since.

In retrospect, I believe a forced feeding of too much Faulkner might be the way to go for the novice Faulkner student. Full Immersion. It would also help if you could live in Oxford while you're reading, preferably over the summer. An intense reading of Faulkner while living in his town is a seminar of ghosts: you read that the idiot Benjy, ran down the sidewalk with a stick clacking against the bars of a wrought iron fence, and that afternoon, you can walk past the very house. When Faulkner describes how the afternoon heat slants off the northwest side of the Square, you can walk to that spot and sweat.

You'll pass under Gavin Stevens' law office on your way back and then, "the cloud" itself, the courthouse. You can get chill bumps reading about the corpse propped up in bed in "A Rose for Emily" and then go visit her neighbors. You can walk out to Rowan Oak and see the east gallery, hidden behind hedges, where the great man would enjoy a late-afternoon gin and tonic. You can flip through the Oxford phone book and still see "Varner," "Bundren," "Littlejohn," "Ratliff," "Carothers," "Boatwright," even "Faulkner." The Snopeses are well represented too; they just go by different names now.

If you're unable to come to Oxford for a Faulkner sabbatical, I suppose you can read Faulkner in the comfort of your own home, in your own town, but your housemates and neighbors might notice certain changes in you. For one thing, they won't see you as much. Faulkner takes time to read, digest and absorb.

Again, I'm not any kind of Faulkner know-it-all, but if asked where to start, I would direct first-time readers to the novellas in *Go Down, Moses* or the Snopes trilogy, or, to dip your toe gently in the Faulkner sea, page-turners like *Intruder in the Dust* or *As I Lay Dying*. Then, once you have your stroke, swim out into the deep current of the above-mentioned *Fury, Absalom, Light in August*. Pilkington required us to keep notes on each character as they were introduced — just a word or phrase to remind us who they are. Although this practice slowed reading, the notes proved invaluable and greatly enhanced my understanding and eventual love of Faulkner's fiction. Thank you, Dr. Pilkington.

Living in Oxford Faulkner seems very much alive. He certainly presents a living, breathing cosmos in the pages of his books and especially in the streets (and phone book) of his town.

7

February
Petting Zoo for Poets

The next battle in the war of the statue was a February 4 "work session," with the city council and all the principals invited. The meeting was a beauty of Deep South, small-town life. Held in the middle of the afternoon in city council's chambers, it was open to the public and press. The chambers double as city court during the week. The bench and seating are fine. The usual mahogany brown, well-polished woodwork. Then the walls are shit green. Luckily for Justice, she's blind.

This meeting was pivotal. Filing in one by one and in groups were the mayor, the aldermen, all the living adult Faulkners (save Dean Faulkner Wells): Chooky, Jimmy Faulkner, Buddy, Meg Faulkner and a smattering of press. Besides me, the *Dallas Morning News* had a reporter there, the student paper and video crew, and two local filmmakers, Kent Moorhead and Elizabeth Dollarhide. They filmed the meeting as part of a proposed Faulkner documentary. Elizabeth and I were living together at the time.

Hal Freeland, the erudite and colorful lead attorney for Beckwith was there, along with his lawyer son, Tom. The two Freelands, both

Faulkner readers, were working pro bono. Their law office was the building formerly owned by Phil Stone, an early champion of Faulkner's work in the 1920s. Mr. Stone was instrumental in getting Faulkner's career under way, though he scoffed at the notion in interviews by saying, "All I did was bring water to the elephant."

The room began filling at the appointed hour, everyone dressed casually except the lawyers and politicians. Beckwith walked in lightheartedly chatting with Jane Rule Burdine, a fun-loving Delta native and photographer, now Beckwith's Taylor neighbor who was on the committee at Beckwith's request. The moment he saw the camera his entire face dropped into a dark furrow that would remain throughout the entire meeting. He sat up front with his lawyers. Mayor Leslie opened the meeting with standard welcoming remarks before turning it over to Tom Freeland. Freeland recited the work he and his father had done, which he said consisted of interviewing all the parties to get a sense of each one's desire in the matter. "The one unanimous sentiment we heard was that Bill Beckwith was the absolute right man for this job. This commission is very important to him for reasons that are perfectly understandable."

Working as arbiters who listened to both the Faulkner family, the city and then the artist's needs, Freeland rather eloquently spoke to the heart of the matter: "For the family, William Faulkner was a member of their immediate family; their father, uncle, brother. If he is to be the subject of a monument, they want it to depict him in a way that is true and is consistent with their memory of him and consistent with his wishes. Beckwith believes he can come up with a Faulkner that the community most remembers, and the family best remembers." Beckwith and Freeland passed out photos of a Mark Twain statue in which the author is seated, cross-legged on a bench. Beckwith said he liked this pose and thought it was the best option to offer the bronze Faulkner some "privacy" and to be "public but also be to himself."

The Faulkner family passed the photo among themselves. It was obvious from their body language they weren't impressed.

Jimmy was then recognized, and he unhooked his hearing aid and rose. "I want to clear up on one thing. Yes, I went out to Beckwith's, and we had a nice visit. We talked about the weather, collecting guns, he collects guns, I collect guns. We never talked about the statue." He patted his hand on the railing for emphasis.

The aldermen, spread across the front row, all turned to face Jimmy. Mayor Leslie stared straight ahead. He might have been thinking about what he wanted for dinner.

Jimmy continued. "My idea was — I thought — we'd sit around a table and see what we could come up with to get Jill's approval. This is what we'll accept: number one, Jill Faulkner Summers and the Faulkner family will have control over the pose of the statue. Jill Faulkner Summers and the Faulkner family will have control over the clothes on the statue. Jill Faulkner Summers and the Faulkner family will have control over the location of the statue. That is what we'll go with. We're against the statue, but we'll try to work something out."

Jimmy's brother, "Chooky" Falkner, rose and gave a rambling statement, the upshot of which was to have Faulkner in clothes he wore on the flight to Stockholm when he was awarded the Nobel Prize in 1948. He made this point: "Brother Will, as we called him, was a very private person (pronounced *puurson*). He'd much rather see the $50,000 go to a scholarship fund for education, for children (*chulren*) so they can better (*bettah*) themselves." He turned to Beckwith. "But there's gon be a statue, and it's gon be a wonderful statue, I know it is. But I hope it will be a standing statue and located in the cemetery by Brother Will's grave (*gr-yave*). If it's got to be, let's go to the cemetery. *Thonk ya*." Chooky shook hands with Beckwith before returning to his seat.

I was struck by the incredibly deep, rich, thick Southern accents, 19th century Southern accents at that, of all concerned, particularly the older participants. So pure and unspoiled by the homogenized television culture as to possibly require sub-titles. Mayor Leslie took to the podium to re-state that if the board decided to erect the statue anywhere besides the front of City Hall, that was fine, but "I'll return the money to all the donors, and the board can pay the full price for the statue if that is your wish."

He sounded like a man who was, by God, gonna have that statue at City Hall. Tom Sharpe, the alderman-at-large, asked Beckwith what he thought about granting the Faulkner family "control" over the pose and clothes on the statue.

Beckwith approached the podium with the weight of the world on his shoulders. He had thick, long hair; a full beard and the air of a man who works with his hands every day.

"That word 'control' is a little bit frightening," he said looking at the Faulkners. "At some point I may have to hand over my modeling tools and my clay and my armature and just step out of it. Input yes; absolute control, no. If I'm gonna do the piece, I've got to do the piece. I don't think Mr. Faulkner would give up absolute control over one of his books, and I don't think Buddy Faulkner would give up control over one of his drawings for a building. And I can't either."

Chooky jumped up. Town scuttlebutt held that Chooky was agreeable to an afternoon sip of whiskey, and it's my respectful opinion that he could have very well had a thimbleful before the meeting.

Murry C. "Chooky" Falkner was a hero in Oxford. He had been a captain with the Oxford National Guard on Oct. 1, 1962, when they were federalized by President John F. Kennedy in order to facilitate James Meredith's admission into Ole Miss. He led his troops into battle the night of the deadly riots in Oxford, on the wrong side, in the eyes of many of his countrymen.

Chooky and his men upheld their oath as federal soldiers. Rolling onto campus in their jeeps, they were set upon by the protestors, who showered them with bricks, concrete, lumber, whatever was available. Chooky suffered three broken bones as he heard a sniper's bullet lodge in his radiator. The next day, he discovered an unexploded Molotov cocktail in the back seat of his jeep.

"That was the only time I was scared," he later told interviewers. "The day after the riots."

Now, he rose to his feet in a very different kind of battle and directly contradicted what Jimmy had just demanded on behalf of the family.

"We don't want control, just input. Control? Lord no." Bang. Meeting over.

The Faulkner family gathered in Mayor Leslie's office. They were inside with Alderman Bill Baker, who was running for mayor and looked it, loving Moorehead's camera at every turn. Beckwith headed back inside to see if the family needed him, and Chester McLarty came strolling outside where two reporters — one of them me — were standing, waiting for some sort of announcement. Moorehead aimed his camera at Dr. McLarty.

"Well, Chester, what do you think?" McLarty revealed a half smile; a full seven seconds went by before he answered: "Well, it looks like these things always end up in the lap of the politicians, so I'm ready to let it repose there."

He walked over to the site and stood over it, the tree stump barely visible above the ground. He began to describe the mini-park where the statue would reside, and it was obvious he had thought about it.

"A symbolic tree — a crape myrtle will be nice — single trunk, will be planted in the back left-hand side toward the south. Keep it trimmed, it blooms all summer. You'll have a nice trunk in the winter time. The front part of the space, you'll want a hard surface on the ground. Slate maybe. A border in the back of monkey grass. Open it up on both ends for freedom. We have a gate in the front and back. I visualize" — warming to his subject now, he seemed to lose years from his face — "busloads of school kids coming through here, crawling all over him. He would have his own little plot. It would be a private space for a poet."

McLarty was genuinely charming.

"The kids will love it. It will be like a petting zoo for poets."

The doors of City Hall burst open. "Nothing happened at this meeting," Jimmy Faulkner told the student TV reporters as he walked down the steps of City Hall. "Nothing happened that I could see."

"We ain't too old to raise hell," Chester laughed to Jimmy, putting a jovial face on their cool relationship.

Beckwith walked out and stood next to me. I said something lame to the effect that it was fitting of Faulkner that this statue process had turned so twisty, but he was in no mood for literary allusions.

"I know how O.J. feels," he replied, with the slightest smile in his deadpan delivery. After we filed our stories for the day, I called Beckwith and set up a time for me to ride out and meet him at his shop.

"We are but warriors for the working day… We would not seek a battle, as we are; Nor, as we are, we say we will not shun it."

William Shakespeare, *Henry V* (1599)

8

Bill Beckwith has the kind of face you see on statues. His deep-set eyes and thick beard give him the countenance of another era, like Herman Melville or Jefferson Davis, both subjects of his work. The evocation of years gone by resonates inside his shop in Taylor. The large doors offer a welcoming entrance to the organized clutter of his tools. There are tables and stacks of cement and, of course, his "people" — sculpted figures looking back at you from all angles and directions, all possessing their own quiet dignity, inscrutability and, thanks to the artist, immortality. And what a group: there's Temple Drake, Faulkner's doomed heroine from his notorious novel *Sanctuary*, who "got off the train at Taylor" and stepped into a world of hurt, including, most infamously, being raped with a corncob by an impotent gangster named "Popeye." Across the room is a large bust of Jamie Whitten, legendary U.S. Congressman from Charleston, Mississippi, who became the longest-serving member of Congress and chairman of the House Appropriations Committee. Peering at Congressman Whitten from a table is a two-foot mockette of Faulkner. Over in the corner, there's a young boy, frozen forever in childhood as he jumps a creek.

Beckwith is never alone here in his cluttered world of muted spirits. Here he can think, mold, smoke, and those gathered never interrupt him or tell him boring stories. Looking out his two large doors as traffic lazes by on a golden afternoon I imagine it could be the waiting room to heaven. The sense of sacrificial toil from decades of creating busts, heads and sculpture are evident looking at the walls of the studio. Tools are lined up, ten rows of ten, on pegboard, and virtually every other available space was covered with hammers, bins, and stacks for storage. There were planers, drills, wrenches and compressors. All a testament to toil for creation.

And then there were Beckwith's dirty hands, dirty for thirty years. Aside from his talent and thirty years of experience — which includes bronze likenesses of the aforementioned Jeff Davis and Herman Melville along with Mississippians B.B. King and Jim Henson with Kermit the Frog, it is fitting Bill Beckwith was assigned the task of creating an eternal memorial to William Faulkner on the author's 100th birthday.

"I feel like I've worked toward this all my life," he said, shaking his head. A school bus clamored down Old Taylor Road, taking its noisy charges toward the Yocona River bottoms. Beckwith looked far away as the quiet refilled the room, then chuckled to himself.

"My daddy always had ink under his fingernails." Beckwith stood looking at his hands almost in wonder. Each fingertip was black (on this day, he explained, from rebuilding lawn mower engines). He remembered his father's career as a typesetter for the old *Delta Democrat Times* newspaper in Greenville. The paper was started in the 1930s by Hodding Carter, or "Big," as he was known. Big Hodding was renowned for his crusading editorials against racial injustice, a dangerous position to hold at that time in Mississippi but one that earned him a Pulitzer Prize. Greenville was one of the state's exceptions to racial violence back then. From 1920 through the '60s, Greenville was a cultural center known for its racial tolerance and diverse population of Chinese, Lebanese, Syrian, Jewish and Italian immigrants.

Thanks in part to the influence of poet William Alexander Percy, who wrote the influential Delta flood memoir, *Lanterns on the Levee*, the bustling river port town also became known for producing an inordinate number of writers. A partial list of Greenville writers from this era besides Carter and Percy would include Walker Percy, Shelby Foote, Ellen Douglas, Bern Keating, David Cohn, Charles G. Bell and Ben Wasson. Will Percy's home became an artistic salon that attracted visiting writers and artists from all over the world. When Beckwith's father, the Greenville typesetter, showed an interest in reading, Hodding Carter and Will Percy helped by recommending books to the young pressman.

Bill Beckwith is a product of a robust mentor/protégé tradition. It was through Will Percy's salon that Beckwith's mentor, the late Greenville sculptor, Leon Koury, began his career.

"Leon had wanted to be a writer, but Will Percy read his poetry and looked at his illustrations and suggested he pursue drawing," Beckwith says, his blue eyes twinkling. "Will's nephew, Walker Percy, who lived with him, had a mound of modeling clay in the house, and one day, Leon fiddled with it and quickly produced a torso figure." Percy introduced Koury to Malvina Hoffman, a sculptor visiting from New York who had studied under Auguste Rodin in Paris. Percy and Wasson soon sold some of Koury's pieces to friends in New York and Hollywood, and Koury was off and running, beginning a sculpting career that lasted until his death in 1983. By 1966, like his mentor

Percy, Koury's studio in Greenville had become a salon-like destination for local artists, including the then-fourteen-year-old Bill Beckwith.

"Leon did for all of us what Will Percy had done for him," Beckwith said. "After I met Leon, I knew what I wanted to do with the rest of my life. He gave us something to do with our minds, which were hungry." In 1974 as a senior at Ole Miss, Beckwith had one of his first shows, a collection of his pieces exhibited at the William Alexander Percy Library in Greenville. A review in the *Delta Democrat Times* seemed to validate Beckwith's career choice: "If you are looking for paintings or sculptures that are merely pretty or nervously namby pamby, don't go for the Beckwith display. In everything I saw, there is strength and power." The reviewer was Ben Wasson.

"I told Leon on his death bed," — Koury was dying of cancer in 1983 — "'Man, I wish you could see some of my pieces right now,'" Beckwith recalled. "'I think you'd really like 'em. I think it's just what you would have wanted.'"

"'Aw, I'll see 'em,' Koury said. 'Remember to work with the light, work in the gray areas.'"

The connection between Mississippi artists from Percy's Delta to Faulkner's hills would seem to have a made a meaningful circle with the selection of Bill Beckwith to build Faulkner. He didn't reckon on a civic fuss that slowed his work and threatened to cancel it.

"At first it scared me," he said, speaking of the controversy regarding the cutting of the magnolia tree in front of City Hall. "Then I was losing days, meeting with lawyers over slanderous bullshit. People calling the statue a 'tourist trap.' Well, I guess the Museum of Modern Art is a tourist trap. The Statue of Liberty. Rome in general. Everyone is a tourist. As soon as you leave your house, you're a tourist.

"John Leslie has balls of steel. He won't back down. He's done a good job," Beckwith said. He paused. "Leslie's also done some stuff that's had people bouncing off the walls, but he's brought us to where we are: a good town that people are moving to and want to live in."

"Tom Rankin (the photographer/protestor at the tree-cutting site) wouldn't stand in the way of a Larry Brown book or a Willie Morris book, why is he trying to stop my work? He's fucking with my livelihood. I got a family. I'm just trying to keep the roof from leaking on my baby's borrowed shoes."

We both smiled. Then he got serious.

"There's a danger here; the Faulkner family could have a negative impact now that it's national news: 'Oh we won't hire that Beckwith, he botched that Faulkner job.'"

He rubbed his forehead. "My wife bought me some more Mylanta."

The city of Oxford agreed to investigate alternative sites, as well as poses, for the statue. Within two weeks, Beckwith would be notified what kind of piece — standing or seated — and the location.

"In two weeks, I'll have Jeff (Davis) out of here. I'll have Jamie (Whitten) out of here, and everything will be clear for Mr. Faulkner," he said as he glanced expectantly around his shop.

"It will take me four months to do the model, and the foundry in Memphis will take four months to cast it, and that's really pushing it. We really need six months each, but we'll buckle down; we'll get it," he said of the looming September centennial unveiling.

"Jimmy called Jill before he came out to see me. The question of exploitation came up. "Exploitation? I don't know who puts Faulkner on a t-shirt, I don't. I got a lot to figure out. I'm going to do this piece and go fishing. We're not building a man here," he points out. "We're building a statue. You're working with texture, shadow and proportion. It's not a photograph. There are different rules and criteria that have to take over, that take precedent for aesthetic reasons."

His thoughts were interrupted by the rumble of an eighteen-wheeler headed south toward the Yocona River, what the old Chickasaws called the "Yockney-Patafa," which means "water running slowly through the flatlands."

"The piece is the most important thing," he said as his young son wandered in. "It becomes more important than reality in one sense because it exists on its own." The boy stood still and listened. "It's its own thing, and I'm really looking forward to it."

White light filled the room, an ancient edifice built in the early 1900s. A large skylight brought in the sun. The shop was a doctor's office one hundred years ago, where operations were performed, I presumed, only on sunny days.

The boy stood quietly, nervous perhaps, in front of his father's guest. I took in Beckwith's world, surrounded by family, work, commitment (he was also a captain with the Taylor Volunteer Fire Department — the red truck was housed across the street from his shop). The sculptor was a strong member of a century-long line on this landscape. He was a stalwart steward, keeping the old verities alive. Beckwith picked up his little boy, much like Beckwith's father probably did long ago in a dirty press shop in Greenville.

"What's your son's name?" I asked.

"Clay," the sculptor replied, without the slightest hint of irony.

9

Richard Howorth, owner of Square Books, one of this country's leading independent bookstores which anchors the Oxford Square and a true Faulkner scholar, watched all the name-calling and rowdy recriminations with more than a little bemusement. Finally, he could stay silent no longer. He wrote an op-ed piece in the *Oxford Eagle* in January:

"It seems somehow appropriate that we kick off the Faulkner Centennial with a fussy small-town controversy featuring an enormously heavy statue of the great little man, a magnolia removed by midnight execution and a tyrannical mayor. It is so tempting to watch this one from the sidelines rather than get involved in anything so marvelously ridiculous. It is especially easy for those of us predisposed to support the arts to let this thing go ahead, but that is primarily because we like the artist commissioned to do the sculpture and his work, Bill Beckwith.

"We believe Beckwith's Faulkner would be a thing of interest and integrity, and wouldn't mind seeing it someplace where the public could do the same. That someplace is not in front of City Hall. It's too public, reason number one. It's hard to pay your proper respect to Faulkner or Beckwith when people are walking around you, not necessarily doing the same thing you are, and cars are whizzing around behind you. One reason memorials such as the Vietnam Memorial in Washington are so effective is that they're situated in a place of sanctuary. City Hall is also a place many of us walk past as a matter of routine, and having to traffic by the statue in a completely pedestrian manner would be sort of creepy."

Stephen Hawkings from the Associated Press picked up on the dust-up. The newspaper in Elvis' hometown, Tupelo (forty-five miles east of Oxford), the *Northeast Daily Journal,* carried Hawkings' excellent, concise piece. The story ran on February 18 and was accompanied by photo of a scowling Bill Beckwith. The headline read, "Statue dispute keeps Oxford hot under the collar," and the sub-head, "The mayor had a magnolia tree cut to make way for a Faulkner statue. His decision sparked a huge debate."

As you might expect, a catchy lede: "There's a sound and fury in William Faulkner's hometown these days, all because the mayor cut down a magnolia tree to make room for another symbol of the Deep South — a statue of the author.

"'Outside looking in, it beats worrying about drive-by shootings and things,' said retired physician Chester McLarty, Faulkner's personal doctor. 'People do take things serious around here.'" Hawkings got an astute quote from Bill Ferris, the then-director of the Center for the Study of Southern Culture. "I think Faulkner would scoff at it and say it was much ado about nothing, but I'm appalled a magnolia was sacrificed in the name of Faulkner, who wrote so eloquently about nature and about the beauty of the woods and life within the woods. It was as if the one place it shouldn't be, the mayor insisted on trying to put it there."

Hawkings scooped me when he revealed the pose for the statue had been agreed upon: a seated pose. He then wrapped up his story with a justifiably cranky Beckwith: "While the tree is gone, the statue doesn't yet exist. It's supposed to be installed September 25, which would have been Faulkner's one hundredth birthday, but sculptor William Beckwith said last week that that the design has only just recently been decided: Faulkner in a sitting pose.

"'I need more time than I have. It is going to really be pushing it. All of this should have been done a long time ago.'"

10

After the Great Ice Storm of 1994, when most of North Mississippi suffered shattered trees, county-wide power outages, blocked roads and general freezing chaos, my girlfriend, Elizabeth, and I awoke to the unmistakable sound of a puppy in distress underneath our small farmhouse in Taylor. Somehow, we managed to coax the little bugger out to find a cute little female German shepherd. We had discussed getting a dog — you can't really live in the country and not possess some sort of animal(s). This was like a gift dropped from the wintry clouds. We cautioned ourselves about getting too attached. Though we lived in Taylor, a former railroad town seven miles south of Oxford (more like one hundred miles in psychic distance) we were surrounded by neighbors. Taylor was home to some 300 people, and this dog — maybe six months old — looked fed and cared for. There was every chance it had simply wandered off from somebody's place.

We posted a large notice down at the local post office, a major gathering place, much like it was in many small towns in the old days. Most everyone in town would swing by the post office at least once a week. I often passed a gaggle of good ole boys out front, hunched over a truck, trading lies, snorting laughter and drinking in the honeysuckle-laden air — and a few other things too. The postmistress, a Miss Joyce, was the queen bee of the hive of activity that the P.O. at times became. She performed tax services for many families around Taylor and pretty much seemed to always be in the know and on the phone. In fact, very often you felt you were bothering her to ask for a stamp or envelope, as this required her having to tell her caller, "Hold on." Then to you, brow furrowed, "Can I help you?" taking care of the transaction briskly in order to return to the phone. She could generally be counted on for gold-plated gossip, a clearinghouse for social buzz. She could multi-task even after a series of operations left her left hand unusable and housed in a Dr. Strangelove-like glove. We told Joyce that we had found a puppy, got her permission to post our sign inside the P.O., and, in the process, felt like we'd gotten the word out in loud capital letters.

As it turned out, no one stepped forward to claim the dog, and after a month or so, we allowed ourselves to declare ownership. Elizabeth promptly named the puppy Belle. This dog seemed to be on the smarter side of the ledger. She picked up commands pretty quickly and had the big feet of a puppy with growth promise. She was a baller, able to defend herself at our backyard soccer facsimiles. As she grew into a sleek three-year-old, I squared off against her almost daily at our backyard basketball goal with the dirt floor. Elizabeth's daughter, Corrine, an art student in New York, had painted a Hawaiian sunset on the backboard. Set among the privets in our bucolic back yard, it was like going to work out in the Garden of Eden. Many days I would drive home for lunch, play a couple rounds of hoops with her and return to the paper refreshed and ready to focus on obituaries or a special section piece on gardening rakes. She became not only a pet, but an effective stress valve.

Soon after her third birthday, Belle developed a limp and kept herself pitifully on her bed, even refusing the come on of the basketball waved in her face. On the last Friday the 13th of 1996, I stood in a vet's office as he "took me through" the $200 worth of x-rays he had taken of Belle's shoulder and described the $400 surgery she needed.

"Of course, there's a chance that once we open her up and get in there and clean the cartilage out, there's a possibility we may find small tumors behind the blister, the beginnings of possible bone cancer that could possibly spread and, of course, kill her." To the small-town scribe, these fees were formidable. I believe my salary was around $24,000, before drinks. Elizabeth was making good movie money, but jobs were scattered, feast-or-famine style. We had also added a second dog, the snow white Bingo. (Former designer Elizabeth thought the black/blonde Belle needed an all-white dog for contrast and complement).

I also kept an apartment in town at a curious housing area of small round houses set among pine trees, dubbed "Ewok Village" by the locals for its otherworldly Star Wars look. The places were cheap but functional and provided a getaway when pseudo-married life became crowded. We were nearly destitute, though you'd never know it looking at our two residences, nice house and the Volvo in the dirt driveway. We took Belle in for her surgery not knowing the clock was ticking on her abbreviated life.

"This land which man has deswamped, denuetered, and derivered in two generations… no wonder the ruined woods I used to know don't cry for retribution! The people who have destroyed it will accomplish its revenge."

William Faulkner, *Delta Autumn* (May 1942)

11

February was the Month of the Trees. The Oxford citizenry — or at least a group some 500 strong — was mad as hell and wasn't going to take it anymore. They not only wrote fiery — even weird, letters to the editor, spoke (at length) from the podium at board of aldermen meetings and even organized an actual march, complete with placards and a police escort. They formed themselves into a Concerned Citizens group with a manifesto, a list of principles, dues, meetings, press releases — the whole bit. One of the most vocal leaders was Dave Dutton, whose day job was with the U.S. Corps of Engineers. He was a tree-hugger with an actual degree in forestry. From Oregon, he was posted in north Mississippi with his family. Oxford was blessed to have outsiders leading the charge. It almost seemed at times that locals, even native Oxonians, were too polite to protest.

On February 12, he penned this beauty of a screed to the *Oxford Eagle*: "Once again, [tiny orange construction] flags are springing up all along West Jackson Avenue. The question is why? Why widen the road and, in the process, destroy hundreds of trees, some of which may have been standing since the Civil War? Talk about heritage. What

I find irritating is that the issue of widening West Jackson appeared to be dead, until Alderman Baker quietly and effortlessly resuscitated it at a meeting which was sparsely attended by the public. Now, it seems the wheels and cogs of city bureaucracy are churning again, steam rolling ahead, without any public input whatsoever. This is becoming a sickeningly familiar pattern of city governing — and it stinks! 'Panic Junction' certainly requires re-engineering, but how much safer is a five-lane road anyway? Why do you suppose they refer to the center lane as a suicide lane?"

Dutton was just warming up: "Some argue that driving in Oxford is a must, and that traffic congestion can mean the difference between life and death, saving a burning home, fixing an electrical panel shooting sparks before it becomes a fire or stopping a broken pipe flooding your house. These situations are much more important than trees. How ridiculous. I can just imagine that every time I drive down West Jackson and see those splendid oaks, that they are somehow responsible for my toilet overflowing."

No idea what he was talking about, but he later encouraged the public to get active, and many did.

Mayor John Leslie had heard and seen enough. On February 7 he announced he would not seek re-election for what would have been his seventh term. "Twenty-four years is a long run," he told Steve in a front-page story. "I decided last week not to run. I checked on my pension, and my take-home pay will be about what it is now.

"I never lost a box. The citizens have been awfully good to me." The mayor said criticism had become more mean-spirited than in the past — his own front yard was recently vandalized with toilet paper and shaving cream.

"Over the past few months, people have gotten mean and negative. All of a sudden, it's just not fun anymore."

Although I was a professional journalist and, therefore, supposedly "objective," I had to admit I felt pride in my fellow citizens at the February 17 board of alderman meeting. Led by Dave Dutton, a ragtag group of PhDs, a handful of little old ladies, intellectuals and various malcontents shouted down the bidding process for the five-lane highway west of town, the so-called, "artery to the mall." Three bids had been taken, and a motion was being made to approve the lowest one when the peanut gallery erupted and made such a commotion the board agreed to postpone any action for two weeks. It seemed to be civil disobedience in action, even if it was more disobedient than civil.

On February 18, a couple of letters to the editor were penned by bright citizens, some of whom, like Ole Miss English instructor Peter Wirth, had the added benefit of being poets. He wrote, "'The tree which moves some to tears of joy,' said William Blake, 'is in the eyes of others only a green thing that stands in the way.' In the way of what? Progress, we are told. We still have the right to say no. Better late than never. Once the trees and grass are gone, we can't get them back."

Mary Dutton, wife of Dave Dutton, wrote, "Recently a group of concerned citizens decided to time our trips along West Jackson. We started at the post office and ended at Shoney's. We traveled the speed limit (thirty mph) going both directions, in light traffic and heavy. The average time to get across town was seven minutes and twenty seconds. In heavy traffic the average was nine minutes. The two-minute time difference did not really distress us… Recently, I traveled this road at 4:40 a.m. in zero traffic and arrived at the end of town in seven minutes. I did see two deer browsing on the grass in front of Wal-Mart. I don't envy their position when this turns five lanes through the woods."

"To understand the world, William Faulkner once said, you first have to understand a place like Mississippi. One loved a place, he wrote, not so much because of its virtues, but despite its faults. Faulkner understood Mississippi in his soul, and so did Medgar Evers. It is America's Ireland. Richard Ford observes that it, as with the larger South, has produced such a wealth of writers because it is so complicated it takes that many writers to interpret it."

Willie Morris, *The Ghosts of Medgar Evers* (1994)

12

Faulkner's 100th year just happened to fall on the same year the often bedeviled University of Mississippi hired a consulting firm to assess the school's image, particularly its use of Confederate battle flags, the song "Dixie" and even its nickname, "Ole Miss," which was the affectionate moniker for the planter's wife, the lady of the big house, on old Southern plantations.

Faulkner's family, like many in the area, worked for the university, Faulkner famously as a bored, if not surly, postmaster. It was also at Ole Miss, on the graveyard shift at the school's power plant, where he wrote his classic *As I Lay Dying* using a flipped-over wheelbarrow as a desk. The school produced its first black graduate, James Meredith, in 1966 and, in 1986, Mississippi's first black Rhodes Scholar, Damon Moore.

Race, such a persistent factor on the American psyche, was, of course, an inherent part of Faulkner's real and fictional worlds. Despite his frequent use of the word "nigger" in his work, the author's biographers have shown that Faulkner was considered moderate to liberal on the question of race. During the year of 1997, the Faulkner

Centennial, Oxford and environs were visited by some of the most important civil rights figures of the 20th century including James Meredith, Johnnie Cochran, Myrlie Evers, James Brown, Will D. Campbell and… uh, 2 Live Crew.

The towering example of strength and class of the year had to be the February 26 visit by Myrlie Evers, widow of activist Medgar Evers (*Ghosts of Mississippi*), who, in 1963, was shot down in the family's driveway in Jackson, Mississippi, as his children watched. During her visit, incredibly, she was asked, "Why did you leave Mississippi?"

"I had to move," she said quietly at a press conference preceding her speech. "I couldn't get the blood out of the carpet and the bullet out of the refrigerator." She received a hero's welcome. "There could be some anger, or bitter sweetness," the Vicksburg native said later during her address, as Ole Miss Chancellor Robert Khayat looked on. "But I choose to look at it not with anger. I think of it as a sweet homecoming."

Such an attitude is truly amazing when considering the facts: she and her three children witnessed the assassination of Evers on June 12, 1963, in front of their Jackson home. He had been targeted because of his unrelenting work as field secretary for the NAACP, working to register black citizens to vote. After appearing on local television, his profile had gotten too high and became unforgivable for the arch segregationists. He had been shot in the back as he pulled into his driveway after working late and exited his vehicle. The bullet came from the overgrown vacant lot directly across the street, a shooter's nest later discovered amid the honeysuckle. When Myrlie and the children reached Medgar, even in their terrified hysteria, they saw he still had his car keys in his hand.

Author Maryanne Vollers wrote, "Everywhere Myrlie Evers turned

Myrlie Evers at her Mississippi "Homecoming"

in her house on Guynes Street, there was something to remind her of the night of the killing. There was the blood that would never quite wash off the carport; the dent in the refrigerator where a fingertip would fit; the stack of crisp white shirts still carefully folded in the closet that she didn't have the heart to give away.

"The children were shattered. Van, the three-year-old, talked endlessly about the blood on the steps and about his father. He would answer the phone and the door with the same words: 'Have you seen my daddy?' He must have said it a hundred times a day.

"Reena kept her grief hidden, and Darrell retreated into deep silences. Sometimes he would just sit under the plum tree and stare out at nothing. He had trouble at school. He slept with a toy gun by his bed. And when his mother went away, as she often did, he was terrified that she would never come back."

A white supremacist with an old-school Southern name, Byron De La Beckwith, was arrested and actually stood trial, something that was rare in white-on-black killings in that vicious era. The family endured two hung jury trials and watched the killer stroll free. As the *New York Times* noted, "The jurors could not help but notice [then-Mississippi] Gov. Ross Barnett shaking hands with Mr. Beckwith in the courtroom before they deliberated."

Finally, a third trial was held in 1994. This time, Beckwith was convicted and sentenced to life in prison. He died in 2001 at age eighty at a medical center.

Often forgotten is that Myrlie is twice a widow. She remarried in 1976 to Walter Williams, a towering (6'5") former Los Angeles longshoreman who had fought for workers' rights in the 1940s. He was a fan of Medgar's heroics in Mississippi and remembers feeling concern when he saw the young widow Myrlie on TV with her children. When they married, she kept the Evers name, and he told reporters that was fine with him. "I fell in love with Medgar before I fell in love with Myrlie." Williams passed away in 1995.

Two years later, a crowd of more than 500 jammed into Ole Miss's aged theater, Fulton Chapel, to hear this heroic figure from the Civil Rights movement. Fulton Chapel, like many buildings at Ole Miss, had its own footnote in history. In 1970, ninety black students were arrested after a demonstration that interrupted an Up with People concert. Up with People was an integrated singing group that promoted harmony and positive vibes, albeit in a "white bread" fashion. A Rebel flag was burned as part of the upheaval, and the arrestees numbered so many they overflowed the Oxford jail, and many were carted off to the dreaded state penitentiary at Parchman. (All were released the next day.) Fulton Chapel later became the university's premier concert venue.

Over the years, I saw the Neville Brothers, J.J. Cale, John Prine and many others there. B.B. King once recorded a double live album on the stage, "Now Appearing at Ole Miss."

Myrlie stepped to the podium, dignified and resplendent at sixty-three, in a blue suit, her hair swept back. She faced the crowd with the assurance of a woman who is accomplished in her own right as an activist, author, head of the NAACP and former commissioner of the Los Angeles Board of Public Works. The crowd seemed to be willing her love and, of course, hoping for some semblance of forgiveness, or a small token to let us know we weren't the devil. Speaking without notes, she challenged students in the audience to not rest on the struggles and ultimate sacrifices of the ones who had come before.

"I come from a time not so long ago when a black person who

wanted to vote had to first answer questions like, 'How many bubbles in a bar of soap?' A time when our parents paid taxes but were not allowed to go to the pool and swim. A time when we knew the Dewey Decimal System but weren't allowed to go to the library.

"I was born colored," she said. "But I have always been called the 'n' word. Negro, black, African-American have become popular. Ten years from now, I don't know what I'll be called, but I know what I'm going to be."

While acknowledging progress, she also pointed out the deep chasm of race in America.

"Connect with the Internet, and see the hate messages posted there. Pick up the paper, and see that church burnings are still going on."

Welfare and affirmative action are two questionable subjects to bring up in front of a conservative Deep South crowd, but Evers-Williams had a pedigree forged with courage.

"All welfare recipients are not my color and weighing 200 to 300 pounds that have six and ten children. We should make sure welfare reform does not leave out people who are helpless and cannot help themselves." (Semi-polite applause.)

"Corporations and universities have benefited from affirmative action. Affirmative action is in danger of being dismantled. It's one thing to re-examine. It's something else to say we can cut something that has been so important to economic development." (Crickets.)

"The criminal justice system needs to be looked at in terms of fairness and race. I support 'three strikes and you're out' laws. It should make you work hard not to strike out the second and third time, but let there be justice in giving those strike outs. We need to eradicate drugs in this society. I say there is still work to be done."

Such sentiments might seem trite when uttered by a Johnny Cochran, but Evers-Williams could read the phone book and give it gravitas. She then reminded the crowd of the importance of voting and the large significance of each and every vote.

"I would not be standing before you as chairman of the NAACP had it not been for one vote," she said, referring to the 1995 election she won — by one vote — to lead the organization.

"Take advantage of every opportunity to learn and grow. And remember your responsibility to give back to your country and your people. African-American history and discussion of the Civil Rights movement should not be saved for special months of the year. It really disappoints me when I ask children what they know of Medgar Evers, and they say, 'Medgar who?'"

She pointed out that the freedom movement needs a song other than "We Shall Overcome."

"We need a new song that moves us into the future. If we don't, we may find ourselves reliving the '50s and '60s." Then, she turned downright prescient.

"If race relations deteriorate to what they were then, many of today's youth may not turn the other cheek when hit or fall to their knees in prayer when faced with other injustices." She then described why she accepted the invitation to speak at Ole Miss, a place that might be considered enemy territory for a civil rights advocate.

"I wanted to see what Ole Miss was all about," she told the crowd.

"I wanted to see the magnolia trees, the buildings, the students walking from one building to another. I wanted to get a sense of what this most-discussed place is about." Myrlie, who had grappled with hard truth all her life, spoke for every Mississippian who loves their state even when it is hard to do so.

"Regardless of what happened in my life, regardless of what happened in Medgar's life, this is and was his state. There is a degree of anger, but also a lot of love. Mississippi is home. It will always be." The crowd rose into a thunderous ovation that was undoubtedly a reflection of love, but also a tinge of relief. After all, she could have used the occasion to tear us a new one.

13

The next day, February 27, *The Daily Mississippian* ran two front-page stories, one recounting the events of Evers-Williams' visit, and then a story on the university retaining the services of a New York-based public relations firm to advise the school on its use of old South symbols such as Dixie, the Colonel Rebel mascot, the Rebel flag, the name Rebels.

In other words, our whole way of life.

This second story, written by Jenny Dobson, the paper's news editor, showed the old juice jones starts early in the journalistic heart: "Almost fourteen years since the Confederate flag was officially disassociated with the university, other university images may face the same fate.

"Colonel Rebel, the nickname Rebels and the fight song 'Dixie' are all up for review by two independent marketing firms commissioned by Chancellor Robert Khayat to improve the image of the university."

The "symbols review" as it came to be called was first reported (accurately, Khayat said) by the student paper, *The Daily Mississippian*.

But the statewide paper the *Clarion Ledger* picked it up, as did the AP, and soon, the *New York Times* sent their Atlanta bureau chief, Kevin Sack, to Oxford, where he stayed for days filing numerous stories. In Sack's first dispatch, "Symbols of the Old South Stir a College Campus," he wrote, "Khayat announced that the university, using a private grant from an anonymous donor, had hired Burson-Marsteller, the world's largest public relations firm, to study its image and to recommend a strategy for burnishing it. The firm's chair, Harold Burson, made it clear that a review of the symbols would be a critical part of the process.

"He's asking himself, 'What are the impediments to establishing credibility and status?' and our preliminary assessment shows that the race card always comes up," said Burson, who is a 1940 graduate of Ole Miss. "If it's playing an important part, I think we should get rid of some of the symbols, the most offensive ones."

Almost immediately the "Ole Miss symbols review" became the ongoing narrative of the year, parallel with the town's growth pains by tree removal and the Faulkner Centennial and the statue. It was a perfect Mississippi story in that it embodied race and literature — the yin and yang of Mississippi's psyche; we have arguably produced the best writers in the world and the worst racists. You can throw in the ecology angle for gravy.

To the non-Southerner, these issues of symbols and mascots must have seemed trivial and even childish. *The Civil War was one hundred years ago. Surely these matters have been put to rest.*

But that just simply wasn't the case, and the answer is complicated. In 1962, two people died, and 350 were injured trying to enroll a single black man into Ole Miss. In 1983, the university officially disassociated itself from the Confederate flag. As late as 1988, a house on campus about to be inhabited by a black fraternity was burned by arson. In 1997, Sack quoted the president of the Black Student Union, Monique Brown, saying the symbols conveyed a "plantation mentality" on campus that made black students feel unwelcome. "This is a university. It's not a shrine for the preservation of the relics of the Civil War." Most Mississippi readers of the *Times* would assume a reporter was sent down here to do the usual hatchet job on the racist rubes. Khayat said he thought Sack came to the story with no pre-conceived stereotype of Ole Miss.

Sack concluded with a sharp-eyed quote from Ms. Brown. "I'm not going to deceive myself for one minute that this [dropping the Rebel flag] is about making black students happy. It's about dollars."

Letters to the editor appeared every day; talk radio reverberated; people started flying Stars and Bars flags on their vehicle — all from a smallish item in a student newspaper.

Khayat received death threats, and the FBI was called in to investigate. Khayat later wrote, "When FBI agents arrived at the Lyceum in 1997 in response to the death threats, everything about our routine was scrutinized — from how we opened the mail to how we greeted visitors. They warned us that anthrax attacks were a possibility, as were explosive devices shipped in boxes. The administrative assistants in our offices were, understandably, terrified. I was concerned for the safety of our students, faculty and staff."

This was in 1997, thirty-five years after the James Meredith riots and the assassination of Medgar Evers, a full generation later. And yet, a flag and a song could still raise such murderous passions.

Some of the reaction to the image review was more practical. One MBA student wrote *The Mississippian* sounding every inch the business major: "In the future, this campus will be facing unprecedented competition for new students because of a rapidly expanded industrial base, the emergence of junior colleges and a trend toward smaller families. Chancellor Khayat has a responsibility as CEO to investigate strategies to develop new business...the flag has been adopted as an icon by radical elements including the KKK and Skinheads who maintain a much higher media profile than this university. This creates a problem in the mind of the undecided consumer..."

Others were reliably smart-alecky: R. David Sanders, a Jackson resident, suggested in a letter to the *Clarion Ledger* that the football team be renamed "The Guilt" and the team colors be changed to blush red. Another letter to the student paper suggested why stop with nicknames; why not cut down all the magnolias trees on campus. And then, of course, there are always several variants on the old "love it or leave" refrain: "If someone is offended by this flag, our song and mascot, perhaps they should attend school elsewhere."

14

March

These people can be decent.

Moses Arthur Meredith
to his son, James (August 1963)

To have James Meredith and O.J. Simpson defense attorney, Johnnie Cochran, in Oxford within two days of each other offered a chance to compare two civil rights figures from disparate generations and verve. I couldn't imagine the natty, supremely confident Cochran being cut down with a shotgun, just as I couldn't imagine Meredith arguing and winning a high-profile double murder trial. The two visits also offered two different looks at Mississippi: present and past, a past, in Faulkner's wise words, that was "not really past."

I was given the task of interviewing Meredith over the phone in advance of his coming to Oxford to donate his papers. He peddled cheaply produced pamphlets and tracts filled with his "wisdom." To hear him speak reminded me of a doddering but charming eccentric. Also on the ledger is Meredith's confounding political support and work for such confirmed racists as David Duke in Louisiana and Jesse Helms in North Carolina.

On the day of the interview, the front page of the *Clarion Ledger* had photos of Byron De La Beckwith (Medgar Evers' assassin) and Rob Evans, black head basketball coach of Ole Miss. De La was on his way to court, sporting the latest in orange jumpsuitery, to argue that he hadn't been given a speedy trial; Evans was headed to Baton Rouge to play Louisiana State University as part of his half-million-dollar-a-year job. (A few weeks later, he would be named SEC Coach of the Year). Perhaps Beckwith had a point about a speedy trial; after all, it had been thirty years, long enough for Whoopi Goldberg to play Myrlie in the movie version of her husband's killing. (The movie, *Ghosts of Mississippi*, also featured James Woods as Beckwith).

I called Meredith and he immediately let me know that he wasn't African-American and therefore wasn't the "first black student" at the University of Mississippi. He said he was, in fact, a Choctaw Indian.

"My great-grandfather, Sam Cobb, was head of the Choctaw nation," he told me as I jotted away. "I will be donating my papers to Ole Miss on behalf of the Choctaw nation." Meredith then recited a litany of atrocities inflicted on the Choctaws, including land ripped away and forced removal of families.

"We had a smaller version of the Trail of Tears," he said. "Andrew Jackson was, of course, one of the biggest Indian fighters there was, you understand?" Meredith punctuated most of his sentences with this rhetorical query. "You understand?"

"Right."

"You understand..." Our conversation even developed a rhythm, and I imagined Meredith as some kind of gonzo African village elder handing down the old tales. "I have a new mission. I'm looking for the same thing Hernando de Soto was looking for when he discovered the Mississippi River. What they called it in his time was the Good

Life. When I took history at Ole Miss, they taught me that de Soto was there, but they didn't teach me why he was there, but, of course, he was looking for the Good Life." Meredith then veered off into a rant about his right to reparations under provisions of the Treaty of Dancing Rabbit Creek.

Trying to jolt him out of his tirade, I asked, "Has the white man done anything good for mankind?"

"One thing my daddy taught me was the reason we [Choctaws] were so humiliated was because of our foolishness and arrogance; our own [Choctaw] leaders. They did not have enough respect for the knowledge of the white man. Big mistake. Granddad said one of the principles of government that leads to the Good Life is you respect the best — be it crops or public policy." Then he went into another aside.

"Frankly, except in government — the superiority of whites in industry and even religion, we [Choctaws] must acknowledge the scientific superiority of whites and learn these things and apply them."

Even over the phone, Meredith seemed unstable. A recent bout with prostate cancer had taken a physical toll. He had visited Oxford the year before as part of his tour of state libraries and complained then about his years of bad health. If ever there was a candidate for posttraumatic stress syndrome, it was James Meredith.

And yet, he was still capable of poetry.

"I didn't feel the importance of the Lyceum (the iconic campus administrative building where the 1962 deadly riots took place) until that day last year when I visited the campus. Once that happened, my whole psychology changed. I knew the importance of Ole Miss to me. They never acted like I existed before. When I was there last year and seeing what it meant to the young students for me to be there, I realized something that had been missing that I had never realized had been missing…until I got a sense of what they had been missing, you understand?"

"Right."

"So, I'm going to do my best for all, forever, except for history. It's taken care of."

• • •

I was part of a press contingent that followed Meredith around campus when he arrived to donate his papers to the school on March 21. Especially moving was his visit to his old dorm, Baxter Hall.

"It's been thirty-four years since I walked up that hill," Meredith said as he gazed down at his old dorm like a prisoner brought back to San Quentin or a Holocaust victim returning to his internment camp. He had emerged from a university van packed with Ole Miss suits, plus Chancellor Khayat and Meredith's family. Meredith was wearing an Ole Miss cap with Colonel Rebel, the old plantation figure currently under review, displayed prominently. A black coed in the crowd said, "Somebody take that off him."

Meredith took questions right there on the curb, and the media hoarded in.

"This is a feeling of relief," Meredith said, a statement that felt like something of an understatement. Meredith is a wisp of a man, seemingly too small to have made history. The last time he had stood on this spot, people were being shot and killed just down the hill in a battle brought by him. On this day, there were tears without tear gas. Today, he arrived in air-conditioned comfort, surrounded by his loved ones, receiving a hero's welcome. "I long ago made my peace," he said.

"My father, Moses Arthur Meredith, the whole Ole Miss thing was his idea. He and my mother told me my obligation was to restore peace and dignity to our bloodline. Eighty or ninety percent of blacks in Mississippi are Native American and don't know it." He walked up the sidewalk to the front door, a small figure in a new suit wearing a silly cap but walking peacefully. The only menace now was TV lights and banal questions. University workers in nearby buildings stepped out to glimpse a little history.

Meredith reached the front door, put his hand on the handle and opened it.

"First time I ever went in the front door."

He went inside and read the plaque on the wall, which alludes to the pain and suffering but also stresses that it should never happen again. Then he was swept away by the handlers, led by university PR Director Ed Meek. Meredith was then taken to the Ole Miss Library for the ceremony of donating his papers. He entered to a standing ovation. While Meredith seemed genuinely touched, Ole Miss officials looked on with apprehension. Meredith had a reputation (well-earned) for being a loose cannon. When they brought him to campus a few years ago for the twentieth anniversary of his admittance to the university, he had minced no words: "Things aren't much better now than they were in the '60s. Don't pat yourselves on the back. It's not much better, and it might get worse."

Meredith hadn't been invited back until now.

On this day, I saw in the eyes of James Meredith steely compassion. He had his game face on. He was comfortable with the media, the public, the officials shepherding him about. Meredith still exuded power. The power to fill a room, to raise a ruckus, to write history.

James Meredith visiting the Ole Miss campus

He was slight in physical stature. With his bald head and a white beard, he seemed almost gnomish, but his place in history endures. It's all written down — in black and white.

He spoke with generosity and humility, no bombshells or untoward rants. "Thank you for being here," he told the crowd. "I hope that future generations of Mississippians and Americans can read what happened back in 1962 and be resolved we will never go back." Then, it seemed, he couldn't help himself. "I want to report to my father today in Mississippi: these people are decent. America is still a free society; people can do what they want. Ole Miss is still number one. It is the Harvard of the South."

He was then asked about the Old South symbols of Ole Miss. He replied, "It's nonsense. As hard as I fought for Colonel Rebel, and they're gonna take him away? Ain't nothing to do with black and white. He's no more dangerous than Colonel Sanders."

Irascible, irrepressible and endlessly intriguing, James Meredith is the perfect civil rights hero for Mississippi. He's as whacky as the rest of us. When he's in town, it's always a good day at the office.

15

That night, the Hale-Bopp comet was visible over the trees out in Taylor. The comet, dubbed "The Great Comet of 1997," was in the news as perhaps the most widely seen comet of the 20th Century and also the brightest. It was visible for eighteen months making it the most visible comet in almost 200 years. It was so bright it could even be seen in big cities with overpowering light pollution. News reports tracked its status and whereabouts regularly, and the comet took on folk hero status. It probably helped that it was discovered by two amateur astronomers, Alan Hale and Thomas Bopp, one of whom (Bopp) didn't even own a telescope. It was the farthest distance from earth that any comet had ever been discovered by amateurs.

After coming home from my newspaper job, which could be janky, often surreal, or moving, like the day spent covering James Meredith, it was magical indeed to step out on my back porch in Taylor with a gin and tonic and my two dogs and see the bright light fish-tailing across the night sky, visible to my naked, bloodshot eye.

Sometimes, I went to bed thinking the world was on fire in a good way.

Johnnie Cochran was an earthly comet: bright, flashy and visible for all the world to see. Of course, in more racist quarters of American society, he was reviled as an "uppity nigger." Such revulsion seemed to spring from age-old white fears about a successful black man. He was feared by the white man because of his cunning, intellect, poise, charm and presumed sexual power. In 1997, at the time of his Oxford appearance, Johnnie Cochran was his own caricature.

Cochran came to Ole Miss on March 23 to address the University of Mississippi's Black Law Student's Association. The timing was interesting. It came the day after Meredith donated his papers to the school and a month after Myrlie Evers. The events suggested careful PR coordination by the school in the middle of its controversial image survey. The Cochran event also honored Louis Westerfield, the school's first black dean of the law school, who had died in office the year before.

And yet, one of the red-hot-button issues of this year was whether to get rid of the Rebel flag. Three years away from the millennium and Mississippi was still fighting the Civil War. In another time, Johnnie Cochran would have needed James Meredith's police escort. As it was, he was chauffeured in and paid $14,000.

Cochran strode confidently into Tad Smith Coliseum, the school's funky, prehistoric basketball arena, filled with perhaps 400 people seated on the covered gym floor, and absolutely swooned 'em. Many in the crowd, I couldn't help noticing, were quite stunningly beautiful young black women. It wasn't the first time I felt underdressed.

Cochran spoke deep and velvety into the mike like an FM dee-jay: "How y'all doing? Great…to be in…Oxford, Mississippi." He had a Lou Rawls supper club persona. Jack, that cat was clean.

"Lemme hear you say: 'Yeah!'"

Cochran's remarks proceeded into an embarrassing litany of platitudes, what you might expect to read on sugar packets: "Remember it is the obstacles in the water, the rocks, that make the sound of the creek." The women squirmed, while men in the audience began to nod off. "It is the obstacles that make a babbling brook. A dam is built in front of water so the water can be harnessed into power.

"We must look at obstacles…as…opportunities…" He breathed the last words like an obscene phone call, and indeed, half the audience climaxed, erupting into applause.

"Be good, study, go to class, be the best you can be and give something back to the community." I'm not sure, but I think there were tears. "Be an eagle, don't be a chicken.

"The eagle can't possibly be a chicken because he doesn't possess chicken DNA." Just when I was thinking he would never be acquitted of being lame, he made an allusion to the OJ trials: "Some say a trial opens divides in people, but they were already there, the trials just exposed them."

During the Q and A, Cochran was asked about the university's quest to enlist an "image survey" related to Old South symbols.

"There are things that African-Americans feel strongly about, and to the credit of your chancellor, he is taking steps to evaluate the situation."

On to the next question, and soon enough, it was over. All the hot goddesses got in the receiving line to meet Cochran but I had had enough. It was all very diplomatic, very smooth, very Johnnie. We were surrounded by a multitude of beautiful black women, like I'd never see in my normal coming and going around Oxford. I obviously was hanging out in the wrong places with the wrong crowd.

Just then *Eagle* photographer Bruce Newman joined me at my

table. Bruce had a nose for news and a wall full of photography awards but also a streak of whack. He announced, "All the cars are covered in pollen. Every car has yellow fuzz on it. I bet that Hale-Bopp comet is the reason."

It was this type of comment that typified why we all loved Bruce. Off the cuff, random, original. At Happy Hour, I used to torment Jonny by goading Bruce into dancing, which resembled a car wreck with elbows.

Just then, one of the beautiful black chicks showed up near our table with a TV camera. She appeared to be shooting the event for the Ole Miss student TV station, Channel 12 UMTV. This girl was drop-dead, fuck-you gorgeous. She had to be the best-dressed camera person in the history of media.

Bruce whispered to me: "That's the new Miss Ole Miss. She won the crown on a technicality."

Technicality, my ass. If she was first runner up, I'd like to see the chick that originally won. I thought to ask later for access to the footage at some point. (Hopefully from her.) Little did I know how important the exact wording of Cochran's remarks would become…

That night, after Cochran's speech, a racial altercation involving shotguns and Rebel flags erupted in town at our local drive-through beer store, the Rebel Barn, located at the end of Fraternity Row. At the paper, we learned about it that Monday and called around to gather as many facts as possible before deadline. Jonny and our comely intern, Caroline Blackwell, banged out the following: "Criminal charges are expected to be filed today following a Saturday clash between a group of black University of Mississippi students and employees at the Rebel Barn, a confrontation that saw Rebel flags torn off the wall and destroyed and threats to do the same at other Oxford businesses.

"Police say three Ole Miss students, after an initial clash with employees at the drive-through beer and barbecue store on West Jackson Avenue adjacent to campus, returned just after eleven p.m. with a group of at least fifteen companions. The latter group, said store manager David Sage, surrounded two Rebel Barn employees, shoving one and refusing to let either use the telephone.

"They were grabbing flags and breaking sticks," Sage said. "They went on a rampage. These employees were scared to death," Sage said, adding that one employee went to the back of the store to fetch a shotgun."

The story concluded: "The incident came just hours after celebrated attorney Johnnie Cochran, addressing a crowd at the Black Law Student Association's annual award dinner, exhorted students to rid the university of the controversial flag."

I looked up from the paper. "Exhorted?" When I read that word, I knew Jonny had just thrown it in for juice. If Cochran "exhorted" anything, it was to take a nap. That afternoon when the paper came out, I found Jonny, and I told him we might want to run some kind of correction the next day. He shrugged. Running corrections was our band-aid for any cut. Print it, and if it's wrong, tell 'em we'll run a correction tomorrow.

Jonny was brilliant, one of the best pure writers I knew personally. He was working his way out of the *Eagle*. He already had an agent and was already the book reviewer for *Salon*, a brand-new, up-and-coming online journal. He had produced brilliantly written pieces published in national magazines like *Sports Afield*, *Men's Journal* and the *New York Times*. He certainly wasn't a lazy journalist. Maybe he just liked the word "exhort."

That afternoon after work, I was still mulling the word "exhort" as I was getting gas at the Stop and Go. As I stood there pumping, a local radio station was booming from the overhead speakers. Then their local news came on: "A race riot occurred over the weekend in Oxford, Mississippi, after O.J. Simpson attorney Johnnie Cochran exhorted a crowd of black students to rid the school of its racist symbols…"

I almost tripped over the gas hose. "Exhorted?" I felt certain the staff at Q97 AM "Soft Rock for Hard Times" wouldn't know the word "exhort" from cohort. Quite often, national wire services would pick up *Eagle* stories. We found it amusing, but this was different. This was misreporting on a sensitive subject that had real consequences. Once at home, I affixed my rabbit ears to the Tupelo TV channel and the little greaser news reader reported the story on their ten o'clock news and used the same phrase. "Race riot." "Exhorted."

I sat there in my uneasy chair, shaking my head in wonder.

A month later, the story showed up as the top story in the Sunday edition of the *Clarion Ledger*. Under the headline, "Old South symbols loom in background of Oxford incident," the reporter, Eric Stringfellow, elicited some truly marvelous quotes from the same people the *Eagle* interviewed, including this gem from Rebel Barn manager David Sage: "I'd like them to apologize to me for tearing my store up. I'd like to apologize to them if something in my store offended them. Work this out, and send that message to the world. It's not like we live in trailer parks and sleep with goats." Boom!

Stringfellow wrote: "At the Rebel Barn, situated just west of campus, the flags are noticeable before the beer. They are hoisted between bottles of Beck and cans of Miller. Tucked away in an office is Sage with his long black pony-tail." Sage told Stringfellow that he thought the "rampage" was influenced by Johnnie Cochran's speech on campus. Stringfellow then quoted one of the "rampaging" students, Xavier Davis, as saying he and his friends never went to the Cochran speech and weren't aware of it. Davis says the confrontation was caused by the brandishing of the shotgun. Sage also offered this other telling detail: "There was a long line that night, and one of the cars was a group of sorority girls with eleven different orders and wanting to pay with eleven different credit cards."

Davis and his buddies complained about the slow service. One of the Barn employees, Chris Montgomery, responded; they responded back; the verbal jabs escalated, culminating in Montgomery flashing the shotgun. Amazing no one was shot.

"It's not a black-white thing," Sage told the *Ledger*. "It's a school thing. If Ole Miss changed their name to the Chihuahuas, I'd be right here flying the Chihuahuas flag." Stringfellow pointed out that Sage's story and Davis', "differ greatly."

Sage: "They were the last car in line, and one of the guys in the car demanded they be waited on first. There was a car full of sorority girls that had eleven different orders and wanted to pay with eleven different credit cards.

"One of the guys said, 'Only at Ole Miss. Only in Oxford.' He said, 'If you don't wait on me now, I'm going to take this stick and beat your white ass.' My employees were scared to death. One of the guys went to get out of the car. One of the guys here went to get a shotgun out of the back. The guys left, but they came back. As far as I'm concerned, it's premeditated." Sage says about fifteen people returned to his store, circled two employees and waved fists in their faces. Some just watched and stood back. Then some of the guys ran around yelling racial slurs and tearing up the flags.

"Sage also said Johnnie Cochran should not have been welcomed onto campus.

"'It was wrong for Ole Miss to bring Johnnie Cochran in for that kind of speech. A lot of them heard the speech. I wonder if he is aware of what happened after he left?'"

Davis, as quoted by Stringfellow: "We were just standing in line. One of the guys from the Barn gave us a look. We gave the look back. Words were passed. He said he was tired and had been working all day. He went into the back and got a shotgun.

"We passed some more words. Then the supervisor came and asked us to leave. We left. I told my brother what had happened, and he was mad. The three of us in the car, my brother and another person, went back. There were some other people, and I don't know where they came from." Davis refused to identify others at the Barn or confirm reports that some were athletes. "Everybody that's black and tall is not a football player or a basketball player."

Davis said he didn't hear any racial slurs. "This was not about the flag. I've seen so much of the flag that I don't care. This guy pulled a gun on us over some words. We didn't threaten him. His actions were uncalled for.

"They tried to bring Johnnie Cochran into it," Davis said. "None of us went to hear Johnnie Cochran."

Stringfellow got a quote from a law student, Terry Harris, who was at the Cochran event and says Cochran spent all of thirty seconds mentioning the flag, and none of it was inflammatory. Harris even accurately noted that Cochran mentioned the courage of Khayat for taking on the issue.

Once again a real-life event, covered by a human press, illustrated just how elusive the truth can be. I think it also underscored the importance of words and their incredible power. It's scary to think how badly this ugly episode could have ended. Even in our little corner of Redneckville, a wrong word can get out over the airwaves and travel around the world — from the Stop and Go to the ten o'clock news — and get guns drawn.

Up in arms, indeed.

16

The next night, James Brown, the Godfather of Soul, played Sam's Town, a casino an hour and a half drive from Oxford in the Mississippi River town of Tunica, Mississippi, Tennessee Williams country. Sam's Town drew a racially diverse clientele, but the entertainment and furnishings were, as might be surmised from the name, western. James Brown was something of a break-through artist at this relatively new venue, which had previously booked the Hanks, the Haggards and the Barbara Mandrells.

Tunica itself raised the "Mississippi paradox." The poverty-stricken regions of the Delta metamorphosed into flatland dens of sin and neon desperation: slot machines, blackjack, all-night drinks and fishnet hangovers. Faulkner would have made great fictional hay of the Tunica casino scene. He would have known Tunica as a sleepy fishing village with a great diner, the Blue and White. He missed the town's devolution into Sugar Ditch, Third World America and now, most unlikely, a haven of loud legal gambling on fake boats sitting in a man-made puddle to satisfy the legislature's posturing that casinos could be constructed only on "boats" on "bodies of water." I can only imagine Faulkner's gape-mouthed reaction to the incongruity of a flashy, pulsating $3 billion-dollar industry sitting in the middle of what he knew as mosquito-infested swamp. What would he think of the all-you-can-eat buffet? And Lordy, Lordy, what would Faulkner have thought of James Brown?

I can tell you in one word what I thought of James Brown: power. Power in its most unadorned and purest form. Such force can be a surprisingly subtle and beautiful thing and therein, of course, lies the power. Much like the mighty river, it can be quiet and reflective, then suddenly rise up and take you and your life even while you are looking. This trip to Tunica gave a reminder of power's look, touch, smell, expression and mystifying thrall.

The dark roads leading to the Delta are redeemed by a pale glow on the skyline. To a hill-dweller who makes the trip and winds his way through the hills and piney scrabble to Senatobia then descends the final bluff into flat open expanse, it comes as a bit of a surprise. Everything is twenty miles apart. The sky has opened up and there is light. A variance in tone and texture but a bleakness to the beauty.

On a dark night with only half a March moon, the oncoming headlights became hypnotic. They came from an undetermined location for longer than expected. They kept coming and coming…and what? Still coming. On the narrow bridges your ass tightens. Outside of Tunica, the still darkness of what used to be narrow roads leading to the mighty Mississippi is dotted with convenience stores dwarfed by the thick five lane roads.

Off in the horizon, I could see the shimmering clusters of the gaming palaces. Sam's Town sports a faux-Western mining town décor and among locals is thought of as one of the "white casinos." But not this night. Tonight, James Brown was playing the complex in the

River Place Arena. The crowd turned out to be a 50-50 mix. In fact, it was one of the most integrated assemblages I had ever seen in Mississippi: young and old, black and white, grandparents to MTVers. A focus group dream. It was a tribute to the Godfather of Soul that his appeal crossed this many socially difficult lines in this racially-challenged state. I can't think of another event or personality who could bring together this kind of cross-section: rednecks with shotguns, smooth black dudes with jheri curls, older white seniors. James Brown was the first big-name black performer who could draw this type crowd in Mississippi in 1997, the Year of the Genius, for a measly $27.50 (plus handling).

Brown, despite well-documented bouts — and jail terms — with guns, drugs, fast women and even faster cars (hey, maybe that's why Mississippians love him — he's one of us!) strutted onstage, healthy, in full voice and presided over the show with authority and confident ease, smiling that smile. (His biographer, R.J. Smith, noted that Brown thought an entertainer needed two main ingredients: good hair and good teeth. Brown had both in fairly spectacular fashion.) His band was sizzlingly taut despite gray hairs at a couple of positions, indicating that some had been with the seminal entertainer through many years of triumph and tragedies and redneck breakthroughs.

Brown seemed like a funky Nelson Mandela as he gyrated and exhorted (yes, he really did "exhort") the women in the crowd to dance and "feel it." A generation ago, a black man exhorting white women, particularly a black man with a housewife's upflip hair-do, would find himself thrown in the river chained to a plow, not headlining the main lounge. The very idea that Brown was a hero to this breadth of people in the Mississippi Delta (not to mention the masses of the world) spoke to this man's power, not only as an entertainer, but as a survivor.

But could he make them dance?

"Music is the power!" he exclaimed during his two-hour show; two hours of kick-ass soul groove thunder with his smiling, beaming self wielding the baton. For the Godfather of Soul, the only magic wand is the singer's sassy butt. His tux butt, his pearly teeth and sweaty self-dripping polyester Badass. He looked just like you'd want him to look, and he could dance just as good as he wanted (maybe minus a few steps). Two hours of the Brown sound: crunching funk-phat bass, led by two full rhythm sections, two bassists, two drum kits and a full conga set. The groove pounded effortlessly: *Cold Sweat, Good Foot, Living in America, I Feel Good*, all life-affirming.

Brown was picture perfect in steps and stance — his groans and growls — leading the band one minute like a preacher, the next like Benny Goodman, signaling for solos. He commanded his guitarist to "play like Jimi Hendrix!" and then stood back while the band roared through several bars of "Purple Haze." The crowd seemed genuinely surprised at how good Brown and his band were.

He went to the cape bit fairly early, and why not? A factotum brought him a cape, prize-fighter style, as if to escort the sweating, emotional singer off the stage. The Godfather then feigned trying to leave before shucking the cape and racing back to the mike. This was Smithsonian material. Classic, time capsule stuff. It rightfully took its place among the classics of American popular entertainment along with "Who's on first?" Sinatra's raincoat, or Clint Eastwood's grimace, "Go ahead. Make my day."

Brown's history with women was a sorry indictment of violence and piggish behavior, but onstage it was a different story. Back-up singers have a long, important history in music, particularly in soul and R&B music. They are an integral role as point-counter-point to the singer and getting the song across. It's usually three black women lined up on a riser behind the band, background figuratively and literally. Ray Charles had four "Raylettes" who were so anonymous as to be instruments. Where Charles' Raylettes were elegant and fit for Carnegie Hall, Brown's four commandos, the Bittersweets, (probably an apt description for being a female in Brown's band), appeared ready to go toe-to-toe in any venue with any and all comers. They'd have to be the hardest-working women in show business. For two solid hours, they danced, struck sassy poses and sang their way in and out of songs effortlessly, all the while sporting to-die-for '70s-style shiny Pulp Bitchin' pant suits. The pimpiest, sassiest one was a little white singer, Amy Christian.

The crush of fans at the front of the stage meshed solidly as Brown worked his act: crystal clear, funky readings of a wide sampling of his many hits as well as showcase tunes for each of his band members including Miss Christian, who radiated confident stage presence, as well she should. After all, she was a white girl singer for James Fucking Brown, the Godfather of Soul, bucking it up here in Sam's Town, the Wal-Mart of gambling, right here on the banks of the Father of Waters in the most hateful state in America. Funkin' up de house with blue-haired blue bloods. Crazed dancing with the scions of the Delta, the planter aristocracy mixed with black funeral home directors.

I found myself right down front with the throng. Brown did the splits then took the mike by its cord and snapped the mike stand out into the crowd. It hung there between me and the black chick gyrating next to me for an instant before the Godfather snatched it back. It snapped back perfectly, wobbled once and returned to its original position. Brown approached all the dancers, spinning then high-fiving some of the crowd. As he came to my side of the stage, I waited then pulled out my camera and tried to focus in all the swirling, funky chaos. When he was right in front of me, I snapped the pic, which I still have. A dollop of his sweat squished onto my arm. It wasn't cold either.

For a moment, we were face to face, and it was almost like staring into the eyes of a machine (no, not a sex machine), but a show business machine. For a flash of a moment I was peering deep into the soul of funk, a portal of groove. I felt a surge right down into the base of my spine. I had read that he got his hair done three times a day, in the morning, at lunch and right before the show. It made sense now, because if his hair didn't have additives, it could never have held up to all the shim-sham shimming he was inflicting on it. In R.J. Smith's 2011 biography, *The One* (Gotham Books), he reports that Brown had taken physical abuse every day of his life as a boy and teenager. He was told daily he was ugly, even by his loved ones. He took a personal vow to show them all how beautiful he could be.

The casinos sit gleaming and rude amid the denuded swamp of the western Delta. This aggrieved land is now buzzing with slots and roulette where blood used to be the currency. The old blues men of this region inadvertently invented rock and roll, paving the way for Mick Jagger's children to go to private schools and have perfect teeth. Meanwhile, the blues men, the jism and the egg of the creation, wound up shot by a jealous lover, drunk or drugged to death like Robert Johnson, down on all fours, howling like a dog. Johnson didn't even live to make a second album. Most blues experts believe he was deliberately poisoned and dropped into a ditch, where he hunkered down before succumbing. Later, the coyotes gnawed his skull.

The eons have washed over the 200 miles of the Delta and its old road that is being widened to accommodate the idealistic gamblers, the Delta version of "the artery to the mall." The former death trap, Highway 61, runs the length of the Mississippi River and is the storied home to black migration during and after World War II, the setting for so many songs and legends about the blues. The Delta found cotton and catfish prices good and business up. The rest of the economy was government checks, minimum-wage menial gigs and, of course, casino jobs. The Delta economy was agribusiness and food stamps. The feds were the largest employer here, Uncle to the Old Man in this land of the land, the endless horizon.

On the last Saturday night of winter, 1997, the Godfather of Soul sprung forth like a blazing comet. Hale-Boppin' inside the faux-western confines of Sam's Town, the Duck's Unlimited, khaki-clad white crowd boogied with the black dressed-for-church crowd. I couldn't help thinking that during business hours, this same Ducks guy at his job at the bank could easily turn down one of his fellow dancers for a loan, or even foreclose on them on Monday. For this one night only, for this brief two hours, everyone was the same, safe from the suffocating strictures of race and class. Everyone was smiling and dancing.

As the show chortled to a conclusion, Brown's two emcees who had exerted some type of crowd control earlier, had given up trying to close it down and were boogying. The horn section was dancing with each other, the back-up singers doing the same. The entire audience was juking as one. Up front, a line of overweight black women shifted in time next to a prosperous-looking white man who could have been a captain of industry and his Junior Leaguer wife. Brown scanned the crowd, threw back his perfectly coiffed head and grinned enough wattage to run the casino.

Power.

17

Winter, like the rest of us, seemed to be losing its grip.

One sanctuary of sanity for Elizabeth and me was having supper once a week at her mother Betty's home. Betty's husband was Evans Harrington, the retired Faulkner scholar I called often for wisdom and Faulkner facts. Betty was a dynamo, albeit a five-foot one. She was a former English teacher, mother of five, terrific gardener ("She's her own bulldozer," Evans said) and always prepared a satisfying meal with salad, soup, entrée and veggies, all served on TV trays. We watched "Twin Peaks" or something on PBS most every visit. Afterwards, Betty cleared the dishes, and she and Elizabeth would sit at the kitchen table and leave Evans and me in the TV room where he would enjoy a pipe after dinner. I chuckled to myself how they adhered to old-school man-wife traditions despite being flaming liberals. Let it also be said that Evans was a pretty good shot with birds and a damn fine fisherman. With anyone else, being stuck with Dad might be a drag, but with Evans, it was always a pleasure. His conversation was always interesting and almost like a mini-seminar. He would start on one topic, digress, then digress from that digression, get stuck on a name or date — Betty would supply it from the kitchen — and he would keep talking. It was like night school, in a good way.

I also remember Evans as one of the most deliberate eaters I'd ever been around. If doctors say we're supposed to eat slowly for best digestion, Evans was golden. It took him thirty minutes to clean his plate. Carving into a pork chop evenly and unhurried. Telling a story before he speared the cut piece with his fork. Raising the fork to his mouth and — more story, the fork held in his hand in suspension. Thank God the meat was dead, or it would have been terrified, hung there, a pause before oblivion. Finally, a paragraph later, he would reach a pause spot in whatever his point (or points) were and move the forked food into his mouth and masticate the same way he spoke, slowly, surely, like the food had meaning.

I enjoyed his erudite conversation immensely, but I also liked watching him eat. I often attempt to follow his lead.

Evans' dad was the chaplain at the state prison at Parchman, an experience from which Evans wrote his novel, *The Prisoner.*

On this night, Betty was hurting fiercely in her back; Lena, the eighty-five-year-old grandma was wracked with arthritis, yet both insisted on doing the dishes despite our protestations and pleas to help. I didn't feel family enough to refute them. Evans offered his liquor cabinet, and Elizabeth poured up a rum and cranberry; Evans, a shot of Crown Royal and I, a Gordon's gin and tonic. We all gathered at the kitchen table for more talk punctuated by Evans lighting his pipe. Or emptying the smoked tobacco into a well-used ash tray and repacking, all the while deconstructing a verse of Shakespeare or discussing a particular bit of Faulkner criticism or telling a prison story. Betty hung on every word like she'd never heard the stories before. She really loved the guy. How could you not?

We happened to be over there on June 17, 1994, when O.J. Simpson led L.A. police on that surreal chase in his infamous white Bronco. I remember Evans saying it was all quite astonishing.

• • •

Belle survived her surgery, but the vet said it appeared the incision might have allowed some type of bacteria to get into her blood system. She began having a series of spasms, which graduated into full-blown seizures.

I had been keeping track of them so I'd be able to recount them for the vet when the time came. She had her third. These consisted of her suddenly walking around in circles for no reason then trying to maintain her balance before finally keeling over, paralyzed, quivering, watery eyes, scared, frothing, trying to get back up. I stroked her and tried to talk us both through it as if it were a nightmare, which it was. She looked me in the eyes as if to say "Help," but I all I could do was be there. It took several seconds, maybe over a minute though it seemed longer, before she finally came out of it. I wasn't taking her to the vet again just yet, with no money to pay the bill. There is no worse feeling. If she happened to die during one of these episodes, right before my eyes, I would never get over it.

"People have a very, very bad impression of Mississippi. But it's changing."

"Is it because of the writers?"

"The writing grew out of the dirt and this love of talk, talk."

V.S. Naipaul, *A Turn in the South* (1989)

18

The Faulkners were known to be a spirited bunch and capable of returning fire if they thought they were being threatened. There was dueling with guns in their not-too-distant past.

The first week in March, Jimmy Falkner laid down a pretty sobering threat: consent to moving the statue or Jill would pull all Faulkner artifacts from the university library, including — gulp — the Nobel medal. My story from that day's paper: "The University of Mississippi is in danger of losing all its Faulkner memorabilia — including the Nobel Prize now on display — following threats made yesterday at a closed-door meeting at City Hall, according to participants at the meeting.

"'They're trying to whip us,' said Jimmy Falkner, nephew of the late novelist, of the plans to erect a Faulkner statue on the grounds of City Hall. 'They've done nothing at our request. We feel like we have been used and ignored.' Faulkner continued, 'Jill is not happy. She's being pushed around. She owns everything in Rowan Oak and the medals, and she is thinking seriously of moving everything to Virginia and severing all ties with Oxford." Faulkner added he was all in

North Central Mississippi's Leading Daily Newspaper

THE OXFORD EAGLE

Serving Lafayette, Yalobusha and Panola Counties

VOL. 129, NO. 104 — *FRIDAY, MARCH 7, 1997* — *THIRTY-FIVE CENTS*

WILLIAM FAULKNER CENTENNIAL

Family threatens to pull Nobel Prize, other items

Rowan Oak artifacts could be taken if statue plans continue

Jim Dees
STAFF WRITER

The University of Mississippi is in danger of losing all its Faulkner memorabilia — including the Nobel Prize now on display at the John D. Williams Library — following threats made yesterday at a closed-door meeting at City Hall, according to participants at the meeting.

"They're trying to whip us," said Jimmy Faulkner, nephew of the late novelist, of plans to erect a Faulkner statue on the grounds of City Hall.

"They've done nothing at our request," Faulkner said. "Jill is unhappy," he said, referring to the author's daughter, who has lived in Virginia since 1953.

"She owns everything in Rowan Oak and all the (Nobel) medals and she is thinking seriously of moving everything to Virginia and severing all ties with Oxford," Faulkner declared.

Jill Faulkner Summers was unavailable for comment at press time.

At issue now, Faulkner said, is the location of the statue, which is contracted to be erected on the grounds of Oxford's City Hall. The Faulkner family has suggested alternative sites, such as Rowan Oak or at the author's grave.

Earlier, the family had also expressed concerns about the pose and height of the monument.

"Beckwith (the artist producing the piece) said it would be better if it was a seated pose and I agree," Faulkner said. "But Mayor (John) Leslie said there would be no discussion of options as to the location.

"We (the Faulkner family) feel like we've been used and ignored," Faulkner said.

Leslie was unavailable for comment. He has stated in the past, however, that family approval of the project is desirable, but not legally necessary.

Faulkner emphasized that the family has nothing against the sculptor, William Beckwith of Taylor, who is hard at work on a seated figure.

"I feel bad for Beckwith — we're all for him," Faulkner said. "He's under contract and he's doing the work, but he got hit when they cut the tree."

The statue of William Faulkner planned for the front of City Hall will have a similar pose as this statue of Mark Twain.

"We (the Faulkner family) feel like we've been used and ignored."

—Jimmy Faulkner

Faulkner was referring to the cutting of a magnolia tree this past January in front of City Hall to make room for the statue. The tree-cutting spawned local criticism and world-wide news coverage.

As to Summers' rights to the Nobel medal and the contents of Rowan Oak, one university official said today that Summers does indeed own it all.

"Well, I'm sorry the family is not satisfied," said Dr. Tom Verich, university archivist. "As far as I know she owns the medals and the materials at Rowan Oak. I hope this (the threat) is only a rumor. It's logical that these materials remain in Oxford — this is Yoknapatawpha.

"It strikes me though," Verich continued, "that the university is not a party to what the city is doing."

That sentiment was echoed by sculptor Beckwith.

"Sounds like they're punishing the university for what the city is doing," Beckwith said. "I don't want to see the university lose all that stuff. The piece I'm doing is nothing but to honor the man."

Beckwith added that he was indeed building a seated sculpture and had "bought the wood for the bench yesterday."

While all concerned await Summers' decision to pursue pulling of Faulkner materials currently on loan to the university, time is becoming a factor.

Beckwith said he has a May 15 deadline to deliver a clay model to the foundry, which will need a minimum of four months to do its work. The statue is set to be unveiled Sept. 25, the 100th anniversary of the Nobel laureate's birth.

The Oxford Eagle *headline from March 7, 1997*

favor of Bill Beckwith, the sculptor at work on the piece.

"'We're all for Beckwith, and I feel bad for him. He's under contract, and he's doing the work, but he got hit when they cut the tree.' Falkner added that if the statue is unveiled at City Hall on September 25, 'There won't be a Faulkner there.'"

Mayor John Leslie was quotable as usual, telling the Associated Press, "We didn't fix it to go in somebody's living room. Legally, we don't have to please them [Faulkners]."

"A university spokesman, Tom Verich, responded that Summers does indeed own the items she claims: 'We're sorry the family is unhappy, but the university isn't a party to what the city is doing. But it's only logical these items remain in Oxford — this is Yoknapatawpha.'"

There was very real fear in town these items would be removed.

Many Oxonians are proud of their link to Faulkner's legacy and the way the town itself is a character in his work. It's also widely known that Jill doesn't have fond memories of her time living in Oxford. Her parents could induce tension not to mention being the only child of a man many considered a "no count" drunkard. She has told interviewers that the one time she asked her father not to drink on a certain occasion, he replied with colossal cruelty, "Nobody remembers Shakespeare's child."

• • •

On March 17, two defense attorneys argued for a new trial for Byron De La Beckwith before the Mississippi Supreme Court. They claimed his 1994 conviction was a result of dead witnesses, fading memories and a new social climate. Beckwith, seventy-six, an unrepentant white supremacist, was convicted decades after the crime of murdering civil rights leader Medgar Evers in June 1963. He was serving a life sentence in the Hinds County Jail. In arguing against a new trial, Assistant Attorney General Pat Flynn said there was no need.

"Mr. Beckwith shot a man in the back and went out and bragged about the crime. We cannot say Mr. Beckwith got swift justice, but we can say Mr. Beckwith got justice."

To see this item in the paper might not resonate as much had I not stood in the same room with Myrlie Evers and seen for myself her dignity, bravery and grace. Ole De La was in the Hinds County lockup at age seventy-six, probably one of the few white faces among the Gen Pop. For him, it was karmic kickback of complete and total proportions, his ultimate nightmare. He was hearing rap music and seeing guys shower with corn rows in their hair. There must have been days when he first opened his eyes in the morning and, for an instant, forgot where he was until he remembered. Then, he thought he must have died and gone to hell.

The end of March saw a glorious orange full moon, the nightly flights of Hale-Bopp, Good Friday and Easter weekend. Spring came on the 21st and actually resembled spring, which isn't always the case. Unmerciful are the many years when a Mississippi spring lasts one day before going straight into ninty-degree readings…before lunch.

Nine tree-huggers were arrested for blocking construction on Jackson Avenue, the lifeline artery to the mall. The Rebel Barn incident was still a simmering memory. The front page of the March 25 edition of the *Oxford Eagle* provided a vivid time-capsule snapshot of what the little town was going through in the year of Faulkner: three Oxford bar owners were jailed for presenting an "obscene" 2Live Crew show back in December; students destroyed Rebel flags at the Beer Barn and the headline, "Arrests made as road work begins" complete with a color photo of a woman standing in front of a bulldozer, her hands behind her back, Tiananmen Square-style.

The top story reported that three bar owners were released from jail after serving four days for allowing "lewd and improper behavior" in their bar, the Lyric Theatre. The illicit behavior charge stemmed from a performance by the notorious rap group, 2Live Crew, in which nudity and simulated sex acts were displayed. Though this incident occurred in December of 1996, the sentencing and jail time were a 1997 story I was only too happy to cover. As the saying goes, you can't make this stuff up…

The next story reported possible criminal charges against the black students who tore Rebel flags off the wall and threatened Barn employees in the Rebel Barn fracas. In this follow-up story, Jonny Miles reported that it all started when three customers demanded service, were told to wait, and threatened to beat Rebel Barn employee Chris Montgomery with a stick.

The story continued, "When the driver emerged from his vehicle with a stick, Montgomery fetched a shotgun from the rear of the store and wielded it toward the driver. The trio left but only temporarily. Approximately fifteen minutes later, the larger group, some dressed in suits and ties, appeared with 'a lot of screaming and yelling,' Sage said.

"Montgomery, who was working at the store with twenty-two-year-old Eben Kirk, called police, who dispersed the crowd. Though no arrests were made, Sage said he expected charges to be filed today by both him and his employees. Police would not reveal the identities of the suspects but did say they were students at Ole Miss. Sage said he heard reports that counter charges were possible."

"The whole thing was very uncalled for," Sage was quoted as saying. "I think it's a racially motivated hate crime."

Here the story takes a turn for the juice, with Jonny and our intern, Caroline Blackwell, opening it up to other viewpoints. The story, which started burning as a small ember, flamed up with more oxygen.

"Oxford business owner John Crawford, who owns the Rebel flag-bearing Subway franchise on West Jackson, says confrontations over the flag are not uncommon at his restaurant. 'A flag was stolen last semester,' he said. 'They took it down during business hours and ran out with it. That flag has been part of my life for thirty-five years, ever since I first started going to Ole Miss football games. I didn't wave it as a racist then, and I don't wave it as a racist now.'

"Though corporate offices at Subway have requested the flag be removed, Crawford hasn't budged. As to the threats made at the Rebel Barn just down the road, Crawford replied, 'If they come in here and tear it up, it will be the last business they do that at. I'll never take it down.'

"'This is definitely not the way to go about this,' said Chaunte Smith, a black Ole Miss freshman. 'This whole thing has gone way too far.'"

Again, we were playing with fire as reporters. The last thing we wanted was for anyone to get hurt or worse. And we certainly weren't interested in flaming racial tensions in an environment where it didn't take much to do that. On the other hand, this was news we were (scarcely) paid to cover.

19

My lede on the tree hugger story: "When push came to dozer, the civil disobedience began. The plans to widen Jackson Avenue went from drawing board to reality yesterday as bulldozers began knocking down trees to begin work on the project, resulting in a spontaneous demonstration in which nine people were arrested.

"Police had issued a permit for demonstrators to lawfully assemble on the north side of Jackson Avenue, across the street from the road work. About thirty people had gathered at that spot at 3:30 p.m. yesterday. When the bulldozers set their sights on some of the larger trees, two demonstrators left their permitted area and walked across the street to sit down in front of the next tree in the bulldozer's path. At that point, according to eyewitnesses, police who had been trying to persuade protesters to return to the permitted area felt they had to act.

"'We had no choice,' said Oxford Police Major G.A. Lyles. 'Limbs and branches from the tree were falling down everywhere; you had big machinery out there. Traffic was very heavy — it was just a dangerous situation.'

Dave Dutton and Ann Fisher-Wirth arrested for protesting tree cutting on West Jackson Ave.

One of the protesters had a very eloquent and oh-so-quote-worthy take on the events: "This was Oxford's finest arresting Oxford's finest," said Dave Dutton — referring to PTA members, soccer moms and college professors also taken into custody.

The initial two arrests were followed by seven more, and all nine suspects were taken to the police station and charged with disorderly conduct. After being booked and fingerprinted, the nine were released on their own recognizance.

But, this being Oxford, the story then took a turn for the literary.

"'It was all spontaneous. There's something more important at stake than the particular law we broke,' said Dr. Peter Wirth, an instructor in English at the University of Mississippi who was one of the nine arrested along with his wife, Ann Fisher-Wirth, an associate professor of English. Fisher-Wirth was teaching a graduate cultural studies course called 'Writing Nature' when she and her students decided on a field trip — one that ended at the Oxford police station for her and three of her students.

"'We've been reading environmental literature like *Walden*, *Moby Dick* and Wendell Berry,' Fisher-Wirth said. 'Yesterday, we were discussing Gary Snyder's *Myths and Texts,* which deals with clear-cutting in the Pacific Northwest. I told the class that I couldn't discuss trees when they were cutting down trees on Jackson Avenue. It was not my purpose to coerce anybody, but the entire class wanted to go to Jackson Avenue.

"'I am very proud of them,' she added. 'They were not acting as my students when they were arrested. These students want to close gaps between the life of the mind and the life of decision-making.'"

Noble stuff.

But while the huggers were examining myths and texts, Oxford

Sand Company had a job to do. I spoke to the company president and got the classic other side of the story:

"'We've got a general contract to build a street through here,' Jerry White said. 'We're going to do our job and not get anyone hurt. I've lived here all my life, and I like trees, and I respect [the protestors'] right to their opinion — that's their privilege. We just don't want to see anybody get hurt.'

"With good weather, he expects to have the job completed in about five months. As for the protestors, they secured an assembly permit for today and were expected to be at the work site again this afternoon."

A previous edition of the paper, the February 28 *Oxford Eagle*, again provided a snapshot of the trials and tribulations of Oxford in the year 1997. The top story carried the headline, "City planner acknowledges growing pains" and the sub-head, "Jackson Avenue expansion plan under criticism." In the middle of the story was a small box: "West Jackson March Planned — Opponents of the city's plan to five-lane West Jackson Avenue will stage a march Saturday. A 'March for the Trees' will begin at 9 a.m. at the chamber of commerce building and will end at the Oxford Mall. The public is invited, and an escort by the Oxford Police Department will be provided."

That's right. The protestors were going to walk to the mall to protest a road being built to the mall.

My interview with City Planner Ben Smith was revelatory. In my brief journalism career, Smith remains one of the straightest shooters I've ever covered. He answered questions clearly and simply. After years as an engineer, he had the added benefit of actually knowing what he was talking about. I began the story with one of my whimsical ledes, but Smith quickly brought me down to earth: "The view from

Oxford City Planner Ben Smith's office is expansive. Through his window, he can see the city horizon and even out into the county.

"His view is above the trees but not above the fray.

"Last week after the board of aldermen moved to delay the awarding of a contract to five-lane West Jackson Avenue, Smith sat down to discuss growth, city planning and the 'unique' nature of Oxford.

Q: Opponents of the five-laning project have said that you can expect to hear from them on future projects. What's your reaction to that?

A: I think the problem is exaggerated. It's the growth we've had that makes the Square look as good as it does. If we weren't growing, people wouldn't spend $50,000 putting balconies in front of their buildings. They wouldn't have the money to do it. I think some of the problems are being blown out of proportion. Some of the problems may not even be real. Some may be imagined problems.

Q: What do you say to those who say, "We don't want Oxford to look like extreme West Jackson, i.e. strip malls, asphalt, pavement. We are losing what makes us unique."

A: I don't have an answer for that, because there's just as many people that like strip malls and they like to go to malls. That word "unique" is so overused. There are a lot of downtowns that could be classified as unique. Columbus, Mississippi, for example, has a very nice downtown. To have outlying areas develop into what a lot of the West Jackson opponents would want — you're going to have to have a much higher per capita income in Oxford, like Germantown, Tennessee.

Most people in Oxford, quite frankly, are more concerned about their day-to-day lives and making ends meet and what have you than they are some of the more unique things about Oxford. How they're going to make ends meet until the end of the month, that's their priority, not a tree every 50 feet down the street. Also there are constitutional limitations as to how far the city can go in regulating esthetics and beauty.

Then Smith went for the jugular:

This is Mississippi. This is not Massachusetts or Vermont. Mississippi has been last in everything ever since they started counting. I don't mean to be pessimistic, but there's some limit on how much of that burden the city of Oxford can carry and how far they can go to try to preserve this 'uniqueness.' Our primary function is to provide police, fire protection, paved streets, water you can drink, sewage services and picking up the garbage. That's basically why we (city officials) exist. Once you get past that, all those other things, quite frankly, are frills. Trees are a renewable resource — historic buildings are not. You can replant trees.

Q: Since you've been city planner are you more aware of beauty and esthetics than you were say, ten or fifteen years ago?

A: Oh, yeah. Things are changing around here, and changing rapidly. But traffic safety, access to property and flow of traffic far outweighs preserving the trees. Trees can be replanted. I admit it takes a long time for trees to grow back. But stop and think. If trees hadn't been cut down, there'd be no Lyceum, there'd be no University of Mississippi, there'd be no courthouse, there'd be no Oxford and we wouldn't be arguing about this. We wouldn't have this charming, cute, unique city if they hadn't cut the trees. It's a trade-off. Growth hurts. Growth can hurt you.

Sharron Sarthou, in protest, blocks a bulldozer

20

Elizabeth was embarking on a career in movies with aspirations to be a screenwriter (She had already adapted Barry Hannah's novel *The Tennis Handsome* and was working on an original screenplay.) I felt the book unfilmable; as with most of Hannah's work, the power was in the reading of his wonderful, Miles-Davis-meets-Hendrix, pyrotechnic prose. I kept my opinions to myself. Eventually, Elizabeth made the leap, flying out to Los Angeles and (miraculously, to my mind) securing a job as executive assistant to Lawrence Kasdan, writer of *Raiders of the Lost Ark* and the second *Star Wars*. He was one of the top names in Hollywood whose films had sold some billion dollars in tickets. She had the rare opportunity to learn the business at the knee of one of the true greats. I was happy for her and thought she was deserving just based on her intellect and tenacity. She was fighting Hollywood's prejudice against women, Southerners and people over forty. She was guilty on all three counts and yet had landed this remarkable position.

Meanwhile, I sat on the back porch of our farm house back in Mississippi with Belle laid up with a ten-inch incision on her shoulder/arm, chest hair and arm shaved, all stapled together with orders to not move much for two months. Bingo would lie next to her in full sympathy pain.

Somehow, we were managing to hang on. My small-town journalism job paid the bare minimum. Elizabeth's gig paid decently, but living in L.A. ate up "decently." Throw in vet bills, Volvo repairs and my pout house digs at Ewok, and we were stretched pretty thin. Still, since we were both following our dreams, it seemed worth it and even appropriate. We were starving artists, by God, albeit one, in my case, with a beer gut.

Bingo had arrived about a year after Belle. While Belle was discovered under the house following a storm, I found Bingo during an Ewok visit. He was about the size of a grapefruit, sitting perilously close to the road, crying his eyes out. He was solid white, which made me do a double take. Elizabeth and I had talked a lot about getting a second dog as company for Belle. With her designer's sensibility, Elizabeth had suggested our second dog should be white to complement Belle's dark coat. Here before me appeared to be a heaven-sent candidate. He was so young it would be like raising him straight from the litter. Ewok Village was home to clusters of Ole Miss students, and I had heard for years that at the end of the semester students would abandon their dogs or cats when it came time to go home for the summer. (Who knows why: afraid of what their parents might say, tired of feeding them, maybe simply because they're selfish, entitled little shits — who knows?) I doubled back on my bike and went to have another look-see. He was cute as cute can be — even while shrieking. It so happened Elizabeth was coming to pick me up later, and I knew if she saw this dog, she'd swoon. I figured I should do my own vetting before she arrived.

There was a thick pile of brush between my backyard and where Bingo stood. I went back there, some yards behind him and thought I would call him, clap my hands and see if he'd come to me. If he had enough puppy cojones to at least try to work his way through the debris to get to me, I'd certainly be given pause.

Weet, weet — I whistled, clapping my hands. "Come on, boy, come on! Come on!"

The little softball turned and tried to see with his small black eyes, crying then whimpering. He stretched his head. I called and clapped more. He looked at all the brush and cried. My heart sank. Poor little fellow.

"Come on, boy," I exhorted. "Come on!" Clap clap. "Come on, come here!" He regarded the brush pile again, which, from his vantage point, probably looked like Montana. Suddenly, he tore into it as if he were out to rescue me.

"Atta boy! Come on, boy, come on, boy. That's it!"

He worked his way through the thick pile, climbing over and under as needed, fear fraught across his puppy face. It took him a few minutes, but he made his way to my feet, screaming and crying, and I picked him up and stroked him, "Good boy. Hell yes!"

He reduced his screams to a whimper, and I took him inside and poured him up a bowl of water on the floor, and he had to reach his little head over it to drink, but drink he did. Finishing up, he looked up at me, and I poured some more, and he drank then stepped away from the bowl and panted, his tongue out, the heart of a lion. I was cool with Elizabeth seeing him. I was sold. I even started thinking how I'd have to hand-make some door tags to place on the front door of all the Ewok houses just to make doubly sure he didn't belong to anyone.

Elizabeth showed up, fell in immediate love. I made up a few dozen handmade signs with holes for the doorknob — like "Do Not Disturb" signs at hotels — and dutifully placed them at every house. After two weeks, no one had called and Elizabeth and I had our second dog. I came up with the wholly unoriginal name, "Bingo," and to this day cannot tell you why.

Besides providing love, companionship and all the other doggy attributes, Bingo indirectly precipitated my entrance into small-town journalism. All of this happened when I was at the end of my proverbial rope in the latter part of 1996 after being "downsized," and what rope that was left was tightening around my neck. Finances had dwindled, and push was coming to grovel… When the opening for a staff writer at the *Oxford Eagle* was announced, I swallowed my puny pride and sent in my resume. The *Eagle* was known as low-paying grunt work and perhaps a sign one's writing career was stalled. I later was called in for an interview, which went well enough, but I left feeling like they'd hire some twenty-something fresh out of journalism school, not a forty-something fresh out of nowhere.

As it happens, Elizabeth and I had worked on a Levi's TV commercial earlier in the year shot down in the tiny Delta town of Bentonia with ninety-five-year-old bluesman Jack Owens. We had made friends with many on the crew, including Debra, the casting director. The same production company came to Oxford in August of 1996 to film a commercial for TCI, a travel counseling service. The commercial called for numerous shots of down-home Americana (Oxford), culminating in a picture-perfect family cruising around in a Jeep, accompanied by their faithful man's-best-friend.

While the company was in town, Debra, an ebullient soul, came out to Taylor to see the countryside and Elizabeth's two-acre farm where we lived. While there, being a casting director and knowing the shoot called for a dog, she fell in love with our dog Bingo. Bingo was snow white with thick hair and some Labrador features but shorter. When I asked the vet his breed, he told me, "All I can tell you is both his parents were dogs."

Let it be said that Bingo wasn't over-endowed above the collar, but he had the sunniest personality and an almost human smile. His eyes crinkled, and he showed teeth. When he was really happy, which was most of the time, he had the blissed-out wide open grin of a millionaire stoner. Think Jack Nicholson as a miniature polar bear.

Debra whipped out a very nice Sony video camera and filmed Bingo hanging out on the back porch. We all petted him at once, and he broke out his biggest, widest Jack smile.

"He's adorable. You must bring him to the audition tomorrow!" she gushed. "Please, would you? Holiday Inn parking lot, nine a.m. tomorrow. I'd love to have that smile in our commercial."

I had the next day booked for sitting around brooding until it was mentioned that if he got the job, it paid $800 a day, and they'd probably need him for four days.

"We'll be there at eight," I assured her.

The next morning, we arrived a half hour early at the Holiday Inn parking lot, which had been transformed into a bustling shooting set, with a dozen-plus people scurrying around, all of whom stopped for a moment to greet Bingo. "Oh, he's so cute!" Rubbing both his ears.

"What's his name?"

"Bingo."

"Hey, Bingo! You are so cute."

Yeah, I thought. He's cute all right. About three large cute. All the attention only intensified Binger's smile, and I saw the two of us shit-grinning all the way to Union Planters Bank.

There would be competition, of course, with two other dogs. Pete, an almost-as-cute-as-Bingo male belonging to Beckett Howorth, Square Books owners Richard and Lisa Howorth's son, who himself was the quintessential all-American cute six-year-old. Pete had the inside track because Beckett had already been cast as the little boy who rides in the Jeep. Once you've hired the boy, only natural to use his real-life dog. But this is Hollyweird, baby. Why be real when you can be fake?

The other candidate was Jasmine, a female belonging to a buddy of mine from nearby Ecru, Scot Rorie, who, at the time, was known as Radar, maybe after the character in *MASH*.

When Bingo was confronted with Pete and Jasmine he immediately tried to hump Pete. Repeatedly. I pulled him off. "No." He panted for a moment, looked at me, forgot what we were talking about and immediately mounted Pete again. I pulled him off. "No!" He looked at me blankly as if a coherent thought never entered his brain, like he was as dense as the parking lot pavement. He remounted. This happened another five times, and I looked at Radar sheepishly. "Sorry, man."

"It's OK," he shrugged. "It's a domination thing."

I shook my head as I grabbed Bingo by the collar. "I'm afraid in this case, it's a stupid thing."

The director came onto the set and explained that the take called for Beckett to be seated in the back seat of the Jeep and call his dog to join him. The dog would jump onto the seat next to him, and the next shot would be the family driving off. Beckett and Pete executed the action flawlessly, as if they'd done this kind of thing countless times, which, of course, they probably had. They rehearsed a few more times, and then the director called for Jasmine. Radar led her over, and she refused to leave his side. He patted the seat next to Beckett.

"Come on, Jasmine, get in."

Jasmine climbed her way in rather tentatively, not even close to approximating the jaunty jump of Pete. When Radar backed out of the shot and stood with the rest of us, Jasmine leapt from the seat and followed him and again was too shy to leave his side.

"Thank you guys anyway," Radar said, putting a leash on Jasmine.

"OK, do we have one more dog?" the director said, looking at his call sheet. "Is Bingo here?"

"Right here," I answered and walked Binger over to the Jeep where Beckett was seated in the back seat.

"Ok, Beckett, let's rehearse this one. Call Bingo." Beckett clapped his hands and said, "Come on, Bingo, come on boy." He enthusiastically patted the seat next to him. Bingo paced nervously, wanting to comply, but he couldn't bring himself to make the leap.

"Come on, Bingo, get in!" Binger paced and smiled, clearly in a quandary. "Come on, Bingo," Beckett clapped his hands and again patted the seat next to him. Bingo circled the van nervously looking at the seat, looking away and finally walked over to one of the islands in the parking lot where the Holiday Inn had considerably thought to plant some nice ornamental shrubbery to enhance the parking experience of its guests.

It was there that Bingo went into a circular spin (I knew what was coming then), hunched down over the shrub and heaved out two textbook healthy turds, like potato logs, that looked just like the cheap dog food I forced on him. He then sauntered casually over to me and flashed his best Jack Nicholson grin. All was good in Bing World. I looked up, and the entire crew was looking over at me, some stifling giggles, others laughing openly.

I looked at the director and said, "I'm sorry, should he have saved that for the shot?" There was head-shaking and bursts of laughter. Pete jumped in next to Beckett, and I saw $3,000 turn, quite literally, to shit, right before my eyes. I looked over at Radar.

"Well," I said, "he's humped and now he's dumped. In dog world, it's like he's been to the Playboy Mansion." After we got home, satisfied that all my revenue streams had gone dry in a very real way, I called The *Eagle* and accepted the job as a forty-year-old cub reporter. I had earned my position the old-fashioned way: desperation.

21

Good Friday
Two Live Screwed

And on this beautiful day, Steve assigned me to cover the release of a "Treehugger Manifesto," at three o'clock at City Hall. I actually knew the two "huggers" personally, a couple of guys from the arts council who really had no environmental credentials but who over enjoyed the attention, just playing to the cameras and handing out platitudes. I "covered" the treehugger press conference from the balcony of Blind Jim's, a tavern across the street from City Hall that offered oyster po-boys and a decent gin and tonic. Fortified, I went over and took statements from the guys, accepted their press release and then returned to the balcony for follow-up cocktails. I could see they thought I was smirking a little, and maybe I was. From the balcony, I enjoyed seeing the Tupelo TV van pull up and watching them interview my tree boys, who straightened their ties and adjusted their hair. I had seen enough press events to know that when the TV camera light goes on, reality flies out the window. I inherently knew I wasn't missing anything.

It was a cloudless day devoid of humidity...a lazy wafting breeze tickled the hair on my forearm...It was after four o'clock; I had covered the news for the day; it was seventy-five degrees and breezy on the balcony. A friend at the bar invited me down to his truck. We left our fresh drinks sitting on the bar. "Right back," we assured the bartender. Once in the truck, my buddy pulled out a pipe and a marijuana bud the size of a banana — a sticky pine cone of green and orange hairs. Chillin' on a stick.

It smelled like Christmas. After three tokes too many, I had a Woodstock buzz or at least a half-Willie Nelson. I floated the 300 paces back to the office and grabbed my time card to see if I could clock out without laughing. The phone rang in the empty office, and I looked at it and knew better than to answer it at 4:30 on the Good Friday of Easter weekend. But, having left my mind at the bar, I picked it up. It was Steve Bramlett, the Oxford chief of police.

"I want you to come over and watch this tape," Chief Bramlett said.

"Tape?"

"Yeah. I've got a video of that 2Live Crew show, and I just want a public witness — you — to see that it's as bad — if not worse — as we've said it is."

Again, my better judgment had already clocked out. Somehow, my juice jones for a story kicked in and overrode my Willie Nelson head.

"Be right over."

I was as stoned as I'd ever been.

• • •

I felt like I was above myself, looking down, watching myself. I felt like I was the Wizard of my own Oz. On the way to the police station, I stopped by the convenience store and bought everything I could think of to cover my happy hour: Visine, cough drops, Binaca, even deodorant.

Lord, oh Lord, how long? How long would we remain helpless to the addiction of digging up the most salacious, scintillating or outlandish tidbit detail we could possibly uncover, even to the point of sacrificing friends and trampling any last shred of dignity for all involved… Is it really *that* Bad?

Uh, yeah. The juice goose is so over-powering it takes years of post-journalism civilian life to purge, to lose the sick need to tell everything you know and then some. And it wasn't like we were competing for scoops in a highly-contested media market. Our only competition back then, if you could even call them our competitors, was *The Daily Mississippian*, the Ole Miss student newspaper, affectionately known as "The Daily Mistake" owing to its continual rookie errors. And maybe the *Northeast Daily Journal* from Tupelo. Not exactly cutthroat.

The 2Live Crew show had taken place on December 4, 1996, at what was then called the Lyric Theatre. The hip hop band out of Miami was controversial for their obscene lyrics and song titles, which led to record stores being prosecuted for selling "obscene material" to minors. The band and their flamboyant front man, Luther "Luke Skywalker" Campbell, certainly relished their down and dirty image and played to it.

Under a headline, "Rap Group Gets Lewd, Nude on Local Stage" — now there's a headline — I spilled certain beans about this performance that could have very easily been left to rumor or urban myth. Instead, I interviewed Scott Caradine, co-owner of the Lyric, and, as it happens, a person I considered a friend. He also ran Proud Larry's — a bar on the Square across from Square Books — that I found a worthy successor to Oxford's anti-establishment past. Scott was quite forthcoming, and I could have down-played what he told me and still have written a story. Instead, I lunged to play the salacious card. Here's what I wrote:

"2Live Crew, the raunchy rap band known for court battles over their explicit lyrics and stage show, performed at Oxford's Lyric Hall Wednesday night to a packed house, but the show ended abruptly when the concert 'went too far,' according to some concert-goers.

"The band had tongues wagging after — and apparently during — the show as well."

It continues: "One concertgoer, Tad Wilkes, couldn't believe his eyes. 'It was hard to see. I didn't have my prescriptions on, but I did see the back-up singers expose their breasts. It was pretty outrageous.'

"Throughout the show, twenty to thirty audience members were on stage with the Crew, dancing on either side of them. The turning point came, according to eyewitnesses, when one male dancer moved to center stage and, in the words of one witness, 'dropped his drawers.' The crowd cheered even more when one of the randy female singers sprayed whipped cream on the man's exposed privates and proceeded to lick it off."

That's the money punch. "Exposed privates" and "lick it off."

Meanwhile, the photo next to the headline "nude" and "lewd" was a picture of a happy toddler on Santa's knee; the photo opposite "private parts" was the hospital presenting a check to the local food pantry. You can imagine the wicked glee with which Steve laid out the paper that day.

"'It appeared things could get out of hand,' said one Lyric Hall employee who requested anonymity. 'When dude dropped his drawers, that was it; we shut it down.' One particularly lurid rumor heard after the show was that the band had pulled a female out of the crowd,

North Central Mississippi's Leading Daily Newspaper

THE OXFORD EAGLE

Serving Lafayette, Yalobusha and Panola Counties

VOL. 129, NO. 41 — FRIDAY, DECEMBER 6, 1996 — THIRTY-FIVE CENTS

Santa visits

Rap group gets lewd, nude on local stage

'2Live Crew' show sparks controversy

Jim Dees
STAFF WRITER

"2Live Crew," the raunchy rap band knowe for court battles over their explicit lyrics and stage show, performed at Oxford's Lyric Hall Wednesday night to a packed house but the concert ended abruptly after the band "went too far," according to some concert-goers.

The band had tongues wagging — during and after the show.

2Live Crew's bad boy reputation preceded them to the point that the Oxford concert's promoters reportedly "underpromoted" the show to head off any possible protests.

The 2Live Crew fans who attended the show weren't protesting, but some were amazed at how far the band went with their stage antics.

One concertgoer, Tad Wilkes, couldn't believe his eyes.

"It was hard to see," he said. "I didn't have my prescriptions on, but I did see the back-up singers for the band expose their breasts. It was pretty outrageous but everybody there was a consenting adult.

"If you pay $15 to see 2Live Crew, you know what you're getting into. I don't think anybody saw anything that would send them into therapy," he added.

Wilkes and other eyewitnesses reported that the three female backup singers for the band wore skimpy costumes and periodically "flashed" their breasts to the crowd and simulated sex acts with each other.

Throughout the show, 20 to 30 audience members were on stage with the Crew at all times, most of them dancing on either side of the stage — for the most part.

Things got out of hand, eyewitnesses said, when one concertgoer off to the side of the stage moved to center stage and, in the words of one witness, "dropped his drawers."

The crowd cheered even more when one of the randy female

(See RAP on Page 2)

Lewd, nude headline opposite Santa Claus visit

stripped off her clothes and sexually abused her. Not true, said the woman in question, Katherine Miller, an Ole Miss student from Atlanta.

"'Oxford is a little town that likes to talk,' Miller answered when asked about the rumor. 'The only reason I was on stage was because I had met them earlier. They pulled me up on stage, so I just started dancing. I was not abused or violated in any way. It was no big deal.'

"When asked to comment, Lyric Hall co-owner Scott Caradine said, 'We did not expect what happened Wednesday. We knew the lyrics but not the nature of the stage show. We apologize for any discomfort.'"

As it happens, on March 20, 1997, in Oxford City Court, Caradine and fellow promoters Jeff Bransford and Mike Fishman were convicted on public indecency charges and wound up spending three nights in jail. Municipal Judge Glen Alderson refused to accept a plea bargain recommended by the prosecutor, Jay Chain. He called the performance "animalistic," despite hearing no testimony from the defendant's witnesses and not even viewing videotape of the performance. Bang, guilty, and the three were cuffed and immediately escorted to jail cells. He sentenced them to six months in jail (with all but one week suspended), a $500 fine and ordered them to pay all court costs.

In addition, the state tax commission revoked the liquor license of the Lyric and suspended for two weeks the liquor license of Proud Larry's. I didn't feel directly responsible, but, just as in the tree "riots," and rowdy aldermen meetings, I had somehow contributed, given spleen to the piqued. In the 2LiveCrew story, I did feel that had I not used the words "private parts" and "lick," in the story, my buddies probably would have merely paid fines. The chief of police and the prosecutor both recommended suspended jail time, but in what was viewed as a blatant political gesture, Municipal Court Judge Alderson fined them and took it upon himself to sentence them to jail.

This move inflamed many, including the threesome's fellow restaurateur, City Grocery chef John Currence, who wrote a lengthy letter to the editor of the *Eagle* about it: "What happened at the Lyric Hall in early December with 2Live Crew may be considered unfortunate but it was not criminal. Isn't it ironic that none of the unfortunate, and traumatized 700-plus in attendance filed a complaint? The official complaint against the Lyric bears the signature of [Oxford Police Chief] Bramlett. This witch hunt was orchestrated within the police department and the coffin nailed shut by Glen Alderson for reasons that no one seems to understand."

Our police chief took umbrage at Mr. Currence's letter and wanted a third-party witness to the Crew's performance. Again, it was Good Friday and spectacularly gorgeous, warm but breezy, all the blooms waving in place. On a day as beautiful as this, it would never have occurred to me to watch amateur porn with the chief of police in his office after getting high as a laboratory test rat. Driving to the police station, I felt like I was piloting a spaceship.

The Oxford police station is like most municipal buildings. It is lit in that sickly fluorescent light that bespeaks city money taking the lowest bid. The pudgy chief received me in his lair, another in a series of industrial drab, peach-colored cinderblock rooms. He got up, went into another room and came back with a videotape.

"I ain't providing popcorn."

The tape started, and it was readily apparent that it was the amateur of amateur videos. The cameraman would raise the camera whenever he took a slug of beer, which was often. The result was like a sicko strip show on a rollercoaster. The first questionable move hap-

Amateur video of 2LiveCrew in Oxford

pened early on. A 2Live Crew singer was swinging a young white girl around, and they were joined at the crotch. The singer then led the crowd in various chants: "Mother Fucker!" — "Chick sucker!"

Another comely Ole Miss coed was brought up on stage, and a Crew member in a furry top hat dry humped her to the whoops of the crowd.

During this sequence, we were joined by another officer, Andy Waller, who squatted on the floor next to us and looked at the screen.

"Unsullied Southern womenhood, ain't it?" he said disgustedly.

We turned back to the screen, and the 2Livers had the crowd chanting, "Kiss my dick, Kiss my dick!!" Then the Solid Gold 2Live Crew dancers came out and immediately made James Brown's Bittersweets look like physicists. They quickly stripped down to thongs and began spanking each other. This was followed by prancing along the lip of the stage, licking lollipops and, as the chief narrated, "Running them lolliops inside themselves and then tossing them out into the crowd."

Finally, a shapely Crewette walked across the stage completely naked.

"When Greg Oliver had it," Waller mused, referring to the venue's former incarnation as a garage, "my daddy used to get his oil changed there."

Meanwhile, onscreen, the women continued stripping, prancing, licking and tossing lollipops. I squirmed in my chair. After one or two lollipops, you've pretty much seen them all. Bramlett took note of my sigh. He leaned over and spat a partial chew into a cup.

"You still got bananas and dildos to go yet."

Meanwhile the 2Livers had the crowd chanting, "All women is a ho!" Then to the men, "All the fellows suck pussy!"

"Here's whipped cream boy," Bramlett said, motioning to the monitor with the remote. We looked, and a white male student was on stage along with what had to be thirty other people. Whipped Cream Boy suddenly had his pants pulled down by one of the Crewettes, and his member flopped out in all its ugly anti-glory. Some of the singers sprayed whipped cream on him, and, as the bad camera work tried to zoom in, the singer began licking it off.

"So she really did lick his privates," I said, marveling at my journalistic accuracy about an event I didn't attend.

The crowd loved it, and the Crew led them in a new chant: "They all be so horny, they show dey pussy!" The woman who licked Whipped Cream Boy was now naked. The dancers began strutting, bending over and showing the crowd the most private of privates. The lead singer looked around proudly then turned up his Heineken.

"It's a Roman orgy," I said to the chief.

"The Decline of Western Civilization right before our eyes," he replied.

Onscreen, a young woman was lying down on stage as the drunken camera zoomed in on one of the nude dancers, who sat down on what appeared to be a dildo.

"There! You see it? You see it?" Bramlett asked.

It was hard to tell if it was real or simulated, and I didn't want to sit there all afternoon while the chief rewound the tape endlessly and we tried to discern if we had seen "penetration of the vaginal canal," as the official affidavit read. We looked closer and saw a white male, lying on the floor, and the singers were man-handling him and others, spraying whipped cream everywhere. One of the Crewettes then crouched down on the young man's face, and again, it was difficult to know exactly what I was seeing.

"See that?" Bramlett sneered, "A damn Mustang mustache. You see it?" He saw me jotting notes. "Dammitt, don't quote me."

A wisecracking secretary came in. "Tape got you on your knees again, Waller?" she said in perfect Barney Miller sitcom fashion, before dropping some papers on Bramlett's desk and walking out.

"You see what I'm talking about?" the chief asked as he stopped the video and spat in the cup again.

"Yeah, I don't think that camera guy is gonna be in film school anytime soon."

"You have to agree this is pretty bad. We didn't just throw them boys in jail for nothing. We can't have all this nakedness and whipped cream shit going on like that, can we?"

I was thinking that maybe, in fact, we could, but I knew he didn't want to hear it.

"Yeah, that much whipped cream is definitely not good for you."

Bramlett looked at me expressionless.

Then he said, "Get the fuck outta here."

• • •

I ran from the police station to the safety of my truck. I cranked it, drove out of the parking lot and felt in vague need of a shower. The footage, however primitively shot, was disturbing and harrowing. I couldn't help thinking the whole riotous scene was a nightmare for the clean-up team after the gig: empty whipped cream canisters, fruit and vegetables not to mention the dreaded lollipops. We might be talking HAZMAT team.

But the whole vulgar, sexist scene was First Amendment-protected whether I thought it was cool or not. And yet, as Currence pointed out in his letter, no one complained. The Lyric Hall Three should have never gone to jail, especially for three nights and especially by a judge who heard no testimony, refused to look at evidence and went against the prosecutor's recommendation.

As I drove through the light traffic of a college town on break, I marveled that I had sat in the chief's office blindingly stoned and somehow didn't get the giggles or the sweats or have any sort of freak out. There were a couple of times I looked at him, and in my stony haze, it looked like his head had come swiveling off his body and zoomed in on me so close I could count his nose hairs.

"No, you idiot," I had to assure myself. "Sit tight. Don't react!"

During those moments the chief's eyeballs looked like dizzy, spinning globes.

Certainly the creepiest Good Friday of all time. I pushed in a cassette in the portable boom box I kept in the 1988 Ford truck, and the mesmerizing African trance of slide guitar on Ry Cooder's *Talking Timbuktu* came to life. It felt great to be rolling. It felt great not to be in custody.

And then I remembered I had a fresh drink on the bar at Blind Jim's.

"Memories haunt that vacant lot, hangin in the trees like patchy fog. Late at night, they whisper in the wind. No one listens to the trees and they'll be gone soon wait and see. Once they're gone they won't come back again."

Cary Hudson, Blue Mountain, *Hippy Hotel* (1995)

22

The front page of the March 28 *Eagle* contained a fascinating front-page story from the Associated Press on the Hale-Bopp comet. Scientists studying the comet issued a report on the material being spewed from it and concluded it was the very stuff of life.

"An analysis of the tons of organic molecules spewing out of comet Hale-Bopp supports a theory that such celestial visitors may have delivered to Earth the chemical seeds of life billions of years ago."

The story quoted Harold Weaver, a Johns Hopkins University astrophysicist.

"Hale-Bopp, like other comets, is an aggregation of ice, dust and chemicals, a 'dirty snowball,' that remains frozen in the deep cold of space. Only when a comet approaches the sun does the ice warm up and send geysers of material streaming away as the distinctive comet tail."

Weaver said what makes Hale-Bopp different from other comets is its size. It measures nineteen-twenty-five miles in diameter while the average is twelve. Thanks to new technology, scientists were getting their closest look ever at a major comet, and what they saw was unsettling.

"The surface of Hale-Bopp is an extremely violent place," Weaver told the AP, "with vents opening up as they are exposed to sunlight for the first time."

It didn't seem violent when I watched it late at night, but I suppose all that flash has to come at some price.

The Oxford Nine, the tree-huggers, made their initial court appearance in Oxford City Court April 4 on a spectacularly gorgeous spring day that saw the dogwoods, red buds and the wisteria all in bloom. Besides the invigoration of dashing across the Square, the court session afforded a rare opportunity to see city court in action, and I use the word "action" advisedly. After a hard day of newspaper reporting in city court, I can faithfully tell you: democracy is butt-ugly.

The courtroom was like a tomb. The judge sat up front amid the empty alderman chairs arrayed around him, with their name plates at each position. It looked like he had snuck in to hold court when no one was around, like Roger Corman filming a B-movie with other people's sets. The judge greeted a series of stricken souls, the first an old black guy up for DUI and reckless driving. The poor man was illiterate like you didn't think existed anymore. Court-ordered attorney. White boy thrown in the mix; sorority chick.

Judge closely questioned everybody, asked how much they made, determined if they qualified for a public defender. Most did, black and white. The judge peered over his glasses looking stern but with compassion. He gave people extended payment time, not a hard-ass at all. Thick-necked rednecks, sunburns, small black guys, big black guys, a sorority babe. He did have his stern side, telling several, "If you miss a payment and come before me again, you better bring your tooth brush." Then he called the tree-huggers up. Had them line up as a group, which initially struck me as strange, but I guess it was quicker. He asked the leader, the Corp of Engineers' Dave Dutton, how they pled. Dutton pled *nolo contendere,* but the attorney assured him that would be the same as guilty. They haggled briefly, and then Dutton said he would plead guilty but asked, "May I speak?"

"Go ahead, but if I think you're violating your rights, I'll stop you."

"I'm pleading guilty, but if there's anything I'm guilty of it's caring too much. I've put my job at risk. My little girl came crying to me, 'Daddy did you break the law?' I stood up for what I believed in. I stood up for what is right. I told my little girl that what you believe is pointless if you don't stand up for it.

"I plead guilty."

The rest did the same. The judge set sentencing for July 10, which brought a shriek from one of the defendants.

"Your honor, that's the weekend we're taking our kids to Disney World."

"OK, what date works for you? Tell you what, check your calendar and get back to me."

In fact, the judge's name was "Little," and after they left, it seemed they had been judged little. Any judge who accepts Disney World as a reason to reschedule a hearing is all right by me.

23

Rob Robertson, a Navy veteran who possessed more maturity and sense of subject than perhaps his younger, less life-experienced counterparts, was a former editor of the *Daily Mississippian.* In late March, he wrote a rather eloquent op-ed piece regarding the Hale-Bopp Comet and his trip outside of Oxford to our man-made reservoir, Sardis Lake, to view it. The same day, the student paper had the Rebel Barn "riot" on the front page and three letters to the editor regarding Old South symbols and "heritage." Here is a brief excerpt:

"I went out at about four a.m. last week to see the comet at Sardis. There it was, low above the horizon on a cool, moonless night, absolutely visible and spectacular without a telescope or magnifying aids of any kind, just hanging there.

"Seeing it gave me one of those introspective moments that every man gets at one time or another in his life, when problems and petty concerns really don't seem to matter much in the grandest schemes of things.

"It is a feeling that I've felt before, in the Navy, on many moonless nights at sea. On the open ocean in the absence of any man-made light, the sky literally stretches around you. It is easy to realize that between the vastness of the ocean and the vastness of space, you may not be so important after all. It is a reminder of one's own mortality.

"As we fuss among ourselves about flags and mascots, 122,760,000 miles away that twenty-mile wide ball of ice and dirt is hurtling through space, trailing gas and debris for thousands and thousands of miles behind it, giving the entire planet a glimpse of the earliest vestiges of the cosmos. While some 300 people gathered in the Circle at Ole Miss last Wednesday to argue over symbols and race, this rare, magnificent astronomic anomaly was nearing its closest approach to Earth on its lonely, isolated journey around the sun… The last time human eyes saw this sight was about 300 B.C., and the next time will be about the year 4397.

"Not that this has anything to do with Colonel Rebel or Dixie, and I'm certainly not suggesting that 'Comets' replace 'Rebels' as the official nickname for the school. It is simply that long, long after we are gone, perhaps after Ole Miss is gone, that very same comet will appear in the sky again, and whoever has inherited the planet some two dozen centuries from now will look at it again, and these last few days will be revisited.

"What will we want to be remembered for in 2,400 years? Will we want to be remembered at all?"

24

April
Catfish Crown is Passed

Mississippi loves the lowly, bottom-feeding catfish which is ubiquitous in state waters. Thus, there was much rejoicing at the re-opening of Taylor Grocery, a one hundred-year-old building down in Taylor, next door to Beckwith's sculpting shop. The building had been a general store for generations before being outfitted as what would become a prize-winning catfish joint. If this crazy year saw the rise of fears that Oxford was "losing its small-town charm," the re-establishment of this anti-establishment proved that all was not lost. A true bit of funk was on the horizon…

Here's what I wrote then:

"The catfish crown has been passed. Mary Katherine Hudson, owner and proprietor of Taylor Grocery and Restaurant since 1980, has sold her acclaimed business. The new owner is Lynn Hewlett, a former Taylor resident who hopes to have the eatery re-opened and running by summer. Hudson, who cites health reasons for the sale, ends her seventeen-year run on top of the catfish world — The Catfish Institute recently rated her preparation of pond-raised catfish one of the ten best in the country. Although selling the business was 'one of the hardest decisions I've ever made — I prayed and prayed over it' — she is also grateful for the national recognition.

"'It's nice to go out on top,' she said with a shy smile.

"Hudson's national ranking was all the sweeter because she was self-taught. 'I had never fried fish of any kind before I started this,' she told me. 'I learned by trial and error.' I asked her how many fish have hit the grease in her seventeen years. She grimaced.

"'Thousands,' she said with weary assurance."

The business, overlooking the town's old railroad and Taylor's once-bustling downtown, had also served as a general store, with a smattering of groceries, piles of romance novels and a cold drink box stocked with pop and root beer. The town was founded by John Taylor in 1832 following his purchase of the land from the Chickasaws. The store where the catfish place operates was thought to have been built in 1899 and served as a dry goods store until 1930, when it was refashioned as a general store. The store evolved into a catfish restaurant in the 1970s.

Perhaps the building hasn't aged gracefully, but with its benches out front, the folksy restaurant served as a gathering place where no one put on airs — except for the smell of frying catfish which clung to every customer like humidity on the Yocona. Exposed electrical wires running along the ceiling like the long fingers of a skeleton added to the charm.

Aside from its award-winning catfish, Taylor Grocery was famous for having signatures of its customers on the walls. Now a dizzying collage of the unintelligible, in 1997, you could still make out the signatures of everyday folk and others such as Jimmy Buffett and the great Willie Morris — who may have presided over his meal without touching it. Hudson said the easy atmosphere came the hard way.

"I'd put in ninety hours some weeks," she said ruefully. "Work so hard I'd just go home and cry afterwards and say, 'That's it.' I had nightmares about the parking lot being full and being out of fish. I'd work all night in my sleep." But the work paid off, not only in national recognition but in letters and friendships from all over the world.

"I think people liked the idea of going to an old, beat-up store and getting some of the best fish they ever had. We were like family."

Mary Katherine Hudson was Taylor-made. She was born there and lived in a spacious house across the street from the restaurant.

"My granddaddy was the town doctor. I was born in the house I live in now."

Taylor, like so many small farming communities, took a hit during the recession of the 1980s. Before that, Hudson remembered a busy store where farmers bought their groceries, where field hands and pulpwood cutters gathered in the morning to purchase lunches of bologna and soda crackers. The new owner — and current proprietor of Dixie Creek BBQ — vowed to maintain the catfish quo.

"We're going to keep it just like it is," Hewlett said. "We'll just add barbeque and ribs and a few more steaks." Besides a little painting and central air, Hewlett also planned to build a new kitchen in the back and add a couple more tables. He said the store will serve the community. "I want you to still be able to come in and get you a bologna sandwich for lunch."

There was a certain symmetry to Hewlett's taking over the store. His grandfather, C.H. Carr, operated a store next door for years.

"Pappy used to dip ice cream cones at that store, and I'm thinking about doing that."

Catfish, ribs, ice cream, celebrity customers, and moon-pie a la mode. After you sign the check, you can sign the walls.

The re-opening of Taylor Catfish, despite being seven miles outside of Oxford at the end of a curvy road, was an immediate hit and to this day attracts carloads of diners who make the drive to step back into a world before fast food. This is slow food at its best. People drive out and wait sometimes two or even three hours for a table. They cool their heels on the old wooden front porch, replenishing their drinks from their cars. Sitting on the porch and visiting. It's a throwback to another era.

And Lynn Hewlett intended to be right there with them, sitting on that one hundred-year-old front porch, sipping mash and working up a catfish appetite by talking philosophy or maybe picking at a dobro. Watching traffic go by and feeling sorry for the people who are in their car and not on the porch.

Lynn Hewlett put his money where his memories are.

• • •

By April 7, five candidates — including two current aldermen, a former alderman, a school board member, and the former owner of the Hoka Theatre — had qualified to succeed retiring mayor John Leslie in Oxford's top municipal post. The filing deadline passed Saturday at noon, leaving voters with the following lineup: Republicans Dr. William C. Baker and Pat Lamar; Democrat John W. Bounds and independents John "Jay" Eads and Ron Shapiro, the former Hoka owner.

That Monday morning, we covered a story of local interest from the weekend. On Saturday, an accident left a local writer with a broken pelvis and other injuries, and his well-known, curiously-shaped dog was killed. Shortly before seven p.m. Saturday, Scotty Ray "Chico" Harris was struck by a car driven by Derek Arrington, a twenty-three-year-old law student from Hattiesburg. Harris was tossed into the air and his dog, Wayne, run over. The pair were Oxford characters and could be seen walking around town together most every day. Wayne was particularly noticeable for his long frame and short ears.

"I'm lucky to be alive," Harris told me from his hospital bed, still groggy from painkillers. Oxford Police Chief Steve Bramlett agreed.

"You can have the right-of-way and still be dead."

Meanwhile, silly season raged on over Ole Miss Chancellor Robert Khayat's announcement that the university was conducting an "image survey" regarding Old South symbols. Two local publications, *The Daily Mississippian* and *Oxford Town*, printed full-page stories quoting the school's athletic coaches on their reaction to the survey. At the same time, letters to the editor continued to pour in, including one in the *Clarion Ledger* that referred to Khayat as "Chancellor Scalawag."

It was mind-boggling that such Civil War terms as "scalawag" were still being employed by old racists only three years away from the millennium.

In an April 24 *Mississippian* story under a banner reading, "Heritage or Hindrance?" the headline read, "UM coaches on the flag," and beneath that, "A good time now to be forgotten."

Each coach said the flag had kept them from getting one or two desirable players each year. Then-UM Athletic Director Pete Boone weighed in with this observation: "…it's just hard for me to understand why they're yelling for the team with one hand and then doing something with the other hand that's keeping the team from reaching its potential."

The coaches also stated that sometimes athletes already had their mind made up about Ole Miss based on reputation or press and wouldn't even come visit the university to check it out.

Rob Evans, the head basketball coach who would win SEC Coach of the Year honors and who also happened to be African-American had this to say: "Across the country, Mississippi has somewhat of a tarnished image, and a lot of it is because of the past, and some of it is because of a lack of knowledge, but there is definitely an image problem. Is it used in recruiting? Absolutely."

Then there was the "Brad Lott debacle." In fall of 1996 at the annual Ole Miss-Mississippi State football game, or Egg Bowl as it is known, an Ole Miss alum was heard screaming racial epithets at a black State football player.

Brad Lott was a former state senator from Pascagoula who had been involved in the unsuccessful recruiting of the player, Eric Dotson. Lott, who was seated behind the State bench, let fly with his vitriol. His rampage made headlines across the state and even made the national wire.

One Internet poster offered this eyewitness reaction: "I was right behind Brad Lott as he stood behind the Mississippi State bench and hurled racial slurs at Eric Dotson. He kept telling him he couldn't wait to get his nigger ass back to the 'Goula (Pascagoula). I honestly could not believe what I was hearing. I'm guessing Lott had paid Dotson to go to Ole Miss, and Dotson took his money and went to State. Eric Dotson was Mississippi's version of Albert Means. Anyway, it takes balls, or idiocy, to stand behind that bench, with nothing more than a chain link fence separating 6'6", 330 from 5'10", 200 and yell the things he was yelling."

Ole Miss head football coach, Tommy Tuberville, said the incident couldn't have come at a worse time.

"The chancellor had talked about the (image review) before then, but that (the Lott incident) happened in the fourth quarter of the recruiting season, just two months before signing day. It certainly put us in an awkward bind."

Van Chancellor, the much-respected women's basketball coach, was blunt in his assessments: "In my nineteen years at Ole Miss, my greatest problem has been the flag. It is just a symbol that generates mixed emotions, and it is a shame it does," he said. "To the Ole Miss faithful, it is a symbol of pride, a symbol of spirit, and it is a symbol of everything that is right about Ole Miss. To another segment of people, it is interpreted in a whole different manner. It is just unfortunate."

The eminent historian Dr. David Sansing told *The Daily Mississippian* that he saw a common thread between Ole Miss sports and the flag.

"I concluded that every time the Ole Miss Rebels take the field to the sounds of 'Dixie' and the waving of the Rebel flags, it's the charge of Gettysburg all over again."

One can certainly understand why a black athlete would want no part of such a scene.

"Everybody needs a dream to keep from waking up so mean."

Duff Dorrough, *Where's the New Land of Dreams?* (2012)

25

Missing Charlie

Once the door of middle age is breached, death becomes raw reality. I pushed the button on the answering machine one day and puttered around as the beeps and mostly routine messages filled the air. Then the voice of my friend, Tom Rankin.

"Jim? This is Tom. Charlie Jacobs is dead."

The curt news kicked my gut so completely I can still hear Tom's disembodied voice all these years later.

Charlie was from Cleveland, Mississippi, a son of the Mississippi Delta and one of those white boys who could belt soul/blues music with a growling fervor that made you assume he was black if you heard him without seeing him.

His best friend and fellow musician, guitarist Jerry "Duff" Dorrough, recounted their first meeting in a small Delta roadhouse: "Charlie, nervous for the last time, approached the stage with his harmonica. The place was packed with wild, screaming kids and drunks, and the kid was fixin' to make his local debut. He had a ragged harmonica, which he played fairly out-of-tune, but that didn't matter. He was pure energy once he started the song.

"I still have a tape of this night somewhere, and it is no exagger-

Charlie Jacobs

ation to say that he killed 'em. He wasn't that good of a singer (although that would swiftly change), and his harp playing was rough, but he killed 'em with sheer energy. This performance was not lost on me. I said to myself and the band that night, 'This guy would make a great front man with a little work.' The crowd screamed their approval. The kid had found his thang. That was Charlie Jacobs."

Charlie and Duff would soon join forces in a band called The Tangents, a band Jonny Miles called "The best band you never heard."

Charlie played harp and sax for the group, a hard-charging R&B outfit that barnstormed Mississippi and beyond from the mid-1980s until the late 1990s. The Tangents were also cultural hybrids: White boys with a keen Delta capacity for total blues assimilation, right down to the bloodshed and tears.

Their resulting white/negro sound was variously referred to as "punktry," or as Charlie preferred, "Cajun heroin music," or, after midnight, "niggerbilly." The Tangents masterfully wove Otis Redding with Hank Williams and a dash of John Lennon and Duke Ellington when needed. Truly a cultural hybrid. I once wrote that Charlie's gravelly, cigarette-hoarse, whiskey-laced vocals rumbled like "a bullfrog in coitus on the dark side of the levee."

"We left him with the maid too long," was the Jacobs' family joke. Charlie turned away from his Delta genteel lineage in favor of the life of a bluesman, complete with a heroin habit. We used to joke, "He gave up tennis for racket."

The Tangents were the first white rock band in Mississippi to go au natural onstage, and I don't mean they performed in the nude. Rather, they dressed in street clothes, which in Duff's case was dicey indeed: pajama tops and paint-splattered khakis over cowboy boots wrapped in duct tape — the only guy I ever saw who could pull off cowboy boots and shorts.

The Tangents were Oxford mainstays who loved our town, and the town certainly loved them back. They exuded a sincerity, a love of Mississippi, a realness onstage that included their joking with the audience, letting us in on it. They were fearless, and they rocked with energy, some anger and tasty chops.

The trip to Charlie's funeral would be a jarring ride. The ride from Oxford to Tunica for James Brown wasn't really a Delta trip. Tunica, while geographically in the Delta, has been so transformed by the gaming industry, it's more like driving over to Disneyland if it were built by meth heads. Driving to Cleveland, especially for the funeral of a contemporary who should have lived for decades more, was a blues song in itself.

It takes a long time to get nowhere down there. The towns are strung out twenty miles apart, giving ample time to consider the big sky of sad history that rolls past the window. The Delta looks too bleak to be true. Some of the little towns like Alligator, Winstonville or Benoit seem to sag haplessly against the wind.

Driving from Oxford over to Clarksdale, then south on fabled Highway 61 by Duncan and Shelby, where cotton is still king, was to drive back in time. Emmett Till doesn't seem so ancient. The landscape could be the 1930s or the '60s. Certainly, it didn't look like 1997. There's Mound Bayou, the little all-black town founded by freed slaves and now gone bankrupt. Once-proud John F. Kennedy High School has weeds growing up through its abandoned sidewalks. Then there's Merigold with its one red light. Then Renova, desolate, forlorn. On a blustery spring day, a few nights before the second full moon of the season, the place looked like the windswept set of a movie; *The Last Picture Show* maybe, or *Children of the Corn.*

Charlie's burial would be held outside of Cleveland, the home of Delta State University, in a tiny hamlet several miles south with the Biblical name of Beulah. Cleveland at least looked like it was part of the 20th century, albeit the homogenized franchise food and asphalt aspects of it.

Charlie's funeral in Cleveland was held in a chapel so small most of the 200 or so were left to mill around the church yard. Some tried to listen in to the church proceedings, while many of Charlie's old drinking and drugging buddies shuffled around outside and tried to figure out how it had come to this. I was glad I missed the open casket.

"He couldn't have looked any deader than he did in life," one said, pulling a beer out of his suit pocket. Another asked from behind massive fishing sunglasses, "Are we going over to the house afterwards for the open casserole viewing?"

Finally, the service was over, and the people inside started filing out, including Charlie's bereaved parents and closest friends.

Charlie's mother came out of the church, beautiful and classy with a stoic beatitude despite the devastation. She hugged Duff and comforted him, smiling faintly and looking, publicly at least, like she was going to weather this like a warrior. Her husband, however, was having none of that. He wore the shell-shocked look of a man who was about to bury his only son.

We all stood there after the surreal proceedings that seemed to have little to do with Charlie and in which his name was, strangely, seldom spoken by the preacher, who obviously didn't know him. He hardly seemed represented at his own funeral.

Another of Charlie's large-living buddies leaned over to me and whispered, "He's probably going through God's medicine chest right now." Then the casket was rolled out as pollen played through the spring air. It was loaded into the hearse as the throng milled around and greeted each other.

Someone said, "The graveside is eighteen miles, flip on your lights and get in the procession. Old family plot down by the river. Duff's gonna play a couple of farewell tunes." We ran to the car.

The towns in this area, some twenty to thirty miles from the Big River, are some of the most Depression-era looking on the map; Duncan, Shelby, Mound Bayou and those that sounded like they were named for some long-dead planter's black mammie: Malvina, Renova.

I was struck by how the oncoming traffic pulled off onto the side of the road in what seemed a disappearing piece of respectful Americana. We continued on to Beulah, past the rusting water tower with the town name barely visible. But we didn't stop, continuing on farther still towards the family cemetery surrounded by willows and long rows of cotton near Lake Beulah. There across the dirt road from a prolific pecan grove rose the only hill in the county, an Indian mound.

As the dozens of cars parked, and the mourners disgorged from their vehicles, our mutual friend Semmes appeared.

"I hate they're burying him here," he whispered. "This is the spot where they said Charlie missed seven deer one morning. Seven!"

Semmes shook his head as we took in the vast acreage and the wind and the sound of air through the trees. In the distance we weren't sure if we were hearing the steady churn of the nearby Big River or the mother tears for the lost Choctaw.

"Missed seven of 'em from sunup to mid-morning," Semmes repeated, straightening his Ole Miss cap as we headed to the graveside.

"Shot all around 'em… had good shots at all of 'em." He paused. "Course, he was on that epilepsy medicine."

Charlie, it should be noted, didn't have epilepsy.

We left our vehicles and walked to the Indian Mound where Charlie was to be buried. It seemed impossibly dramatic; almost unreal, especially for a character so full of life and music as Charlie. The gathering of mourners was large and younger than most funerals. Under any other circumstances, a gathering of this group would have been assembled to hear the Tangents play.

It was a long, windy walk up to the gravesite. As we got out of our car, car after car pulled in behind us to park. Walking up the gravel road, looking at the surrounding cotton fields, you got a sense of how back-breaking the work must have been fifty years ago. There was just so much land, very little shade, and I could only imagine what August and September must have been like out here. It was as Delta as Delta gets — the river, cotton, the Indians, the endless land and Big Sky.

A group of Charlie's musician friends, Jim Ellis, Billy Marquis, Sam Toller, Duff Dorrough, George Allen and Carl Massengale huddled around his grave and waited until each mourner arrived from their parking spot, and it took a while. Cars were lined up as far as the eye could see. The group sang gospel numbers as some 200 friends and family looked on. Duff stepped forward and announced he would play one of Charlie's favorites. The tune was Stevie Wonder's "Heaven Is A Zillion Miles Away." It seemed such an un-Charlie song. He was surprising even in death.

Fish Michie told the *Clarion Ledger* newspaper afterwards, "The '80s were such a fun time for us. It was a magic carpet ride. When Charlie joined the band, he was some of the rawest talent I had ever seen, but he learned, and you could tell the music came from the toes on up when he played."

The long drive back was sad and sobering. Charlie burned bright, white hot, then out. I met him at the start of the "magic carpet ride" in the 1980s when he and the Tangents first started playing the Hoka where I worked in the deli. He would often arrive in the late afternoon for their gig that night. At three or four o'clock, the place was deserted, and we could take a breather and really talk. I found him passionate about blues and soul music and extremely knowledgeable. After music, it seemed, his go-to mood was pissed off. Business slights, personal crisis, band woes. In that gravel voice, his complaints sounded particularly heavy. However, when his heart was lighter, he could be wickedly funny — profane and profound.

I remember fishing with Charlie at Sardis once and being startled at the change in his demeanor as soon as he had a hook in the water. Quiet, purposeful, the anger washed from his countenance. No chit chat. He assumed the fisherman's stoic quietude. I remember thinking if I were around him more, I would see the layers peeling, and I'm sure I would often find myself being surprised by him.

When the Tangents broke up in the mid-1990s, Charlie took his sax and sass to New Orleans, a seemingly perfect fit for a man of his funk. I was in Oxford trying to learn to write and didn't see Charlie as much. I'm sure he growled his way through his New Orleans life. One story came back to us that he had gotten into a fight with one of his fellow musicians at a gig and taken a bar stool to the head, requiring dozens of stiches. Who knows the origin — probably one of the usual suspects: money, drugs or a woman.

Bluster was a front for a sweet but perhaps tormented soul. One of his best songs is called the "Rhythm of Spring":

I feel the blood pumping through my veins,
my heart's thumping like a railroad train.

Sun shining through my window pane,
asking me can I come out to play.

Charlie left family. They will hear stories of their kin, cut down so early in life, and all they will know are the tales and the tunes. They will miss him without having known him. Perhaps he will be a ghost to them, or maybe a spirit that occupies their heart when they feel mischievous or when they feel love.

The great Oxford writer Larry Brown wrote this about his old fishing buddy Charlie: "I remember the music and the hot Mississippi nights when he stood pouring sweat on the stage and let it rip, playing his heart out because the people were screaming for it and because he loved it so much. I'm glad we had the quiet times as well as the loud ones, and I hope he's finally at peace out on that Indian mound, overlooking his beloved Delta, the land of his blues."

Amen, brother. Miss you, Charlie.

26

On April 19, Motee Daniels died. He was known in Lafayette County as a small store owner, farmer and famously, though whispered, as "Faulkner's bootlegger." Mississippi didn't legalize whiskey until 1966, four years after the author's death. So common was the practice of illegal whiskey that the Mississippi Legislature put a "black market tax" on its sale and collected revenue. The old joke was Mississippians would "stagger to the polls and vote dry" on any liquor referendum.

Motee ran for various political offices in his time, including coroner. His campaign card featured a head shot on the front, and the back of his head on the back, inscribed with the words, "Vote Motee Daniels — He's the same coming and going."

At a courthouse political event, Motee appeared on stage with his campaign manager, a dog named Buster. Legend had it that Motee had taught Buster to say "Momma." The sign on Buster's back said, "Motee Daniels for Coroner-Ranger. Buster Daniels, Campaign Manager."

By the 1970s, any national correspondent who came to town to write a story on the town's Nobel laureate sought out Motee. This was true of Roy Reed of the Associated Press who filed a memorable dispatch in 1974:

"Motee Daniels came in from the pasture in his suit, necktie and cloth hat and scraped the red mud from his shoes as he stepped into his little grocery store. He disappeared for a moment among the shelves and came back carrying a bottle in one hand and a bottle of Coca Cola in the other. He drank twice from each bottle, and then the ritual began. He handed the whiskey to the guest, and the guest turned the bottle up and drank twice, and after each swallow, he turned up the bottle of Coca Cola and drank from that. Then the host took the bottles and drank twice from each, and they were ready to sit down at the back of the store and talk.

"Daniels' store is the only business establishment, and he is the most substantial citizen of a tiny, diminished community called Dutch Bend. It is about fifteen miles south of Oxford, where William Faulkner lived and wrote. Some scholars think Dutch Bend is Faulkner's fictional Frenchmen's Bend, the hamlet where he began his trilogy on the Snopes family and Yoknapatawpha County.

"Daniels, who is sixty years old, knew Faulkner most of his life. If it were not for a lingering anxiety about the law, he would admit that he was the bootlegger who sold whiskey to Faulkner before liquor was legalized in Mississippi.

"He remembers Faulkner with some affection, but he has never read any of the books in which Faulkner sketched the mythical Yoknapatawpha County (which closely resembles the actual Lafayette County) and coupled it with men and women similar to Motee Daniels and his thin, jolly wife, Lucille, and hundreds of others, black and white.

"'I thought he was a damn fool,' Daniels said of Faulkner, chuckling and shaking his head to indicate a confession of error. 'He had a frame of mind that you could walk right up in his face and, hell, he wouldn't pay no attention.'

"'We used to drive from right over here to Oxford with a mule and a wagon, leave way before daylight,' Daniels continues. 'We didn't buy nothing to eat. My mama would put something in a dishpan. We didn't have enough money to buy a Coca-Cola. We'd drink water out of the water fountain.'

Enduring such poverty, it's perhaps no wonder that Daniels jumped on the relatively easy money that came from selling whiskey. He scoffed to Reed at the low ambition of his 1970s neighbors.

"Fact is, you can't hardly get enough men today hardly to dig a grave. They're just too damn lazy to do anything. Nobody out here milks a cow; nobody goes out and picks up eggs and all that kind of stuff. And back then, why, do you think they'd go to the store to buy a quart of milk or a dozen eggs?

"Before his guest left to drive back to Oxford past the new brick houses and the brittle, tin-skinned mobile homes and past the sullen old unpainted wooden houses that stubbornly affront the prospering green hills, Daniels got the two bottles from the chair and repeated the ritual."

Daniels later told Columbus, Mississippi, reporter, Berkley Hudson, that Faulkner never came and bought his whiskey directly but sent someone. Daniels also noted his primary economic concern was "supplying the Lafayette County sheriff's deputy with free whiskey and with keeping the sheriff's illegal slot machine in good repair."

In his story entitled "Bootlegger Contributes to World of Literature," Hudson wrote, "Motee started his bootlegging business after it became apparent to him that his juke joint just wasn't going to make him any real money. He would buy label whiskey in Batesville and sell it at his place, usually doubling the price. In trouble with the law off and on, Motee was finally drummed out of the 'corn likker' corps in the 1940s when his place was raided in a county-wide assault on bootleggers — the feds were doubtless having a slow month. After that, he took on a number of jobs and 'even lived with a preacher one year.' He couldn't stay completely away from whiskey, though, so he ended up working for nine years with the Calvert Whiskey Company's public relations department in Memphis. After that, he returned to farm and run a grocery store just southeast of Oxford, Faulkner's hometown."

Hudson continued, "Motee Daniels was enjoying the greatest fame of his career as 'unofficial host to Faulkner devotees.' Since he made a significant contribution to Southern literature by providing whiskey to William Faulkner, who admitted that he had to have it to produce, and since his grocery store was located fifteen miles southeast of Oxford in what surely must have been the Frenchman's Bend setting for much of Faulkner's fiction, Motee was for a while a celebrity sought out by literary scholars and journalists and tourists from all over the world. His one gasoline pump [grocery] on Highway 334 has become one of the tour stops of the University of Mississippi's Faulkner Symposium, with Motee and Lucille entertaining hundreds of symposium visitors at the store in their nearby cabin."

Daniels discussed his bootlegging days with a reporter from the *Washington Post,* telling of how the police sometimes arrested students with carloads of beer: "We'd tell the police to treat the students like everybody else, and the police would have to load the beer back into the cars. They'd get mad as hell." He also introduced the subject of his "jukehouse"— a roadside tavern.

"Those ole country girls would chop cotton and corn all day, and juke in there all night. There were fights. My head would feel like a sack of walnuts the next day."

With so much national press written about Motee's past exploits it would only seem natural that his obituary in the *Oxford Eagle* might include a passing reference to his entrepreneurial skills regarding spirits. Jonny Miles, as senior writer, was given the task of writing Motee's obit. In it, he listed Motee's past occupations as "farmer, store owner, entrepreneur and bootlegger."

When our Southern Baptist publisher, Mr. Jesse, read that, the whiskey hit the fan. He summoned Jonny into his office for a Christian tongue-lashing, what we in the news room referred to as "he got shared with," as in he shared with Jonny his displeasure. Jonny was already on shaky ground due to a negative story he had written about local industry titan, Caterpillar, among other affronts. Mr. Jesse let him know that sullying Mr. Daniels' name in his *Eagle* obituary was the next-to-last straw, that his job was on the line.

We actually ran a "corrected" obituary the next day, identical to the previous day except the offending word, "bootlegger," was dropped. Mr. Jesse wanted the family to be able to clip and save the *Eagle* obituary for future generations of Daniels to cherish without Motee's character being besmirched, never mind that Motee himself regularly besmirched it.

Jonny was about done with the *Eagle* by this time and resigned shortly after this episode. He made his way to New York, telling the Yankee editors he had been fired from Faulkner's hometown newspaper for revealing the name of the great man's bootlegger. It wasn't quite one hundred proof true, but the editors lapped it up. We were ecstatic for him but, at the same time, missed him terribly in the newsroom. Steve and I continued on, but it was tough with no one there to spit on the floor.

It is worth noting that the Center for the Study of Southern Culture at Ole Miss instituted cash awards named for Motee and Lucille Daniels. The awards are given to Southern Studies students who write the best papers and thesis.

Not bad for a bootlegger who never read a word of Faulkner.

"These white people will accept another civil war knowing they are going to lose."

William Faulkner, *London Sunday Times*, (1956)

27

May
Gonzo Hot Summer

In mid-May, with the spring semester completed and summer school still two weeks away, Oxford reverted to the sleepy Southern town it had been for generations. This two-week respite was among the favorite times of year for locals, who happily noted the reappearance of "parking places and bar stools." During this interim in 1997, even with school out, the Rebel flag issue stayed in the news. A state senator from central Mississippi in Brandon, Mike Gunn, apparently with political aspirations, thought he could use the flag fracas to his advantage. He came to Oxford and gave me a good shot of silly for our editorial page:

"Mississippi's tragic history and surviving Old South trappings, continues to be fertile field for writers, movie-makers and politicians. Whatever it is about the land of cotton, old times here are certainly not forgotten. This week in Oxford, with the university at ease until summer school, the ongoing chronicle continues.

"Tuesday, State Senator Mike Gunn, R-Brandon, came to campus as part of his campaign to 'save' Colonel Rebel and the song 'Dixie' from an 'image enhancement' study the University is conducting.

A staged beheading of Colonel Rebel led by State Senator Mike Gunn with actors posing as Robert Khayat (in black) and a Confederate soldier.

Today, author Nadine Cohodas arrives to discuss — and defend? — her book and its intriguing title, *The Band Played Dixie: Race and the Liberal Conscience at Ole Miss.* Both Gunn and Cohodas are using Mississippi's troubled past to peddle their wares. In Cohodas' case, a book; in Gunn's case, he is soliciting contributions to a direct-mail campaign to 'save our heritage.'

"Cohodas' book is well-researched and reports the history of integration at Ole Miss without bombast; the horrifying facts alone provide the drama. As for Gunn, his supporters are fond of saying their feelings are based on 'Heritage not Hate.' Given the bizarre nature of Gunn's presentation Tuesday, that explanation might well be changed to, 'Heritage not Hilarity.'

"Gunn arrived at University Circle in a Ford Escort with three assistants who popped out of the small vehicle like carnival workers and began busily setting up props and costumes. One donned a Confederate soldier's uniform, and the other wore a black hood and carried a huge fake sword. He was meant to represent a medieval executioner, except he had the name 'Robert Khayat' pinned to his shirt.

"An American flag and Mississippi flag were set up at the base of the Confederate statue, but the Mississippi flag fell repeatedly into the dirt. As the flag fell a third time — winds of change? — the executioner scrambled around with duct tape.

"'He's all wrong for Khayat,' one of three reporters present told Gunn as the executioner huffed and puffed with the tape.

"'Khayat never carried that much weight, even in his playing days,' said another.

"Gunn began reading his statement. Those assembled included the reporters, two cameramen from Tupelo and Columbus, a young black woman who had happened by and two Dutch tourists who watched bemusedly while thumbing their Fodor guides.

"'I am convinced,' Gunn said, 'that Khayat is doing the bidding of the political left to wipe out all remnants of the Old South. If he gets his way, here is what will happen to Colonel Rebel…'

"At that point the faux executioner put the long sword to Colonel Rebel's neck. Gunn continued on, bemoaning, 'left-wing conspiracies,' 'fund-raising machines well-oiled with contributions from naïve egalitarians' and 'revisionist propaganda brainwashing our children.'

"In thinking of past Mississippi politicians who have resorted to the use of gimmicks, Gunn's hyperbole and corny props would seem to be the last refuge of the unelectable. In 1995, he ran unopposed in the general election to win his state senate seat in District 20. Prior to that, he ran for U.S. Congress twice and failed to make the run-off each time. Although still boyish at age forty — his pre-packaged earnestness and dark suit suggest Howdy Doody grown up to be an undertaker — losing campaigns take their toll on a political life. For Gunn, the flag issue would seem to be the perfect horse to ride to keep alive whatever political fortunes he may still have.

"Unlike racist firebrands of Mississippi's past who lured voters with redneck vernacular and homespun folksiness, Gunn is slick with TV-ready sound bites. When asked why he didn't allow the university to conduct its image survey and then attack the conclusions if he disagreed with them, Gunn clicked into cliché mode.

"'Sometimes when leaders feel the heat, they'll see the light,' he intoned, looking straight into the cameras. After the beheading and the prepared statement, Gunn and his posse prepared to climb back into their dusty Ford Escort for the ride to the airport. They were scheduled to decapitate Colonel Rebel in Biloxi on the Gulf Coast at

3:15.

"The young black woman who had listened quietly asked to speak to Gunn. Standing in front of the statue that bears praise for 'Lafayette Countians whose bravery and valor made glorious many a battlefield,' Gunn turned away, telling the woman, 'Sorry, gotta catch a plane. I'm sure the media here will take your statement.'

"The woman, Brenda Foster, a university employee with the artist series, regretted Gunn's early departure and then gave her assessment of the 'symbols study.'

"'We're moving in a direction at the university of a community where we can feel love. We can feel equal love and respect for one another,' Foster said, while behind her, Gunn and company tried repeatedly to load their sword in the Ford, but it wouldn't fit. They pulled it out and tried again. 'We're moving toward harmony,' Foster continued as Gunn and his cohorts continued to grapple with the sword, doing their best Three Stooges. I could only hope the news cameras were getting it. Finally, the sword was stashed, the senator buckled in, and the compact car pulled away. Ms. Foster concluded, 'The Civil War and the years following it destroyed a lot of lives, and we should be careful and respectful when talking about it.'

"Ms. Foster then took her leave, and the small media contingent did likewise, leaving the Confederate statue to resume his lonely vigil. A slight rain began falling with the sun still out."

"Beauty is dimly perceived terror."

Rainer Maria Rilke (1875-1926)

28

Heat and Horniness

The summer of 1997 was election year in Oxford, with the mayor's office open for the first time in twenty-five years and all alderman seats up for grabs. The primaries were held in early May, runoffs two weeks later and the general election in early July. This meant the candidates had to go door-to-door in ninety-degree heat, day after day, sunburned, fake smiling, sore-handed. Throw in the tree issues and the Faulkner statue saga, and there was a special mojo hanging in the humidity.

With trees falling and tempers rising, a concerned group of voters banded together, some 500 strong, and organized a series of candidate forums featuring pointed Q and A. Along with candidate forums, the group of 500 ("the Cult," the old timers called them) organized fundraisers and phone banks.

Ron Shapiro was in the running in early May as an independent for mayor. The affable Shapiro ran for most offices that came up: state representative, public service commissioner, even U.S. Congress — where he received forty-plus percent of the vote despite spending most of the campaign tramping through Mexico. He was the Last of the Freakos still giving it a go.

He was what they used to call a "long hair." A bonafide hippie, who was nonetheless embraced by Oxford. He had cred as an Army veteran, (desk job in Korea during Vietnam) and small business owner. There he was at candidate forums and debates in a cream-colored suit and white bucks, a bow-tie and a straw hat out of which spilled his Wavy Gravy hair. Haight not Hate. A native of St. Louis and former ski bum, Ron took to Oxford and, through his talents and work, became the town's de facto Minister of Culture. His story is the end of the Sixties come to town.

Shapiro managed three movie theaters spread out over Idaho, Montana and Wyoming. Over one summer he met a passel of visiting girls from the South and became smitten with one in particular, Sara Jane Foster of Memphis. At summer's end, when Sara Jane returned home, Shapiro found himself visiting Memphis. Once down South, the wanderer, who had lived in locales as disparate as Mexico, Italy and Korea, liked what he saw.

"On those Memphis trips, we'd always drive down to Oxford," he recalled, "and I'd look around. Sara Jane kept saying, 'You ought to move down here.' It took me about a year and a half or so, but I came on down."

Once in the South, the relationship with Sarah Jane, as he put it, "never worked out," but his relationship with Oxford did.

"I fell right in. Plus, I wanted to write. In fact, I wanted to write a book about women." Oxford is certainly the ideal place to do research on that subject; the town is a Disneyland of Southern beauty, a veritable theme park of horniness. But for the itinerant ski bum, theater manager and would-be-writer, something was still missing.

"I was in Oxford, hanging out in the evenings, and I got bored. I wasn't big on the bar scene much. I found out that after having that

Mayoral candidate Ron Shapiro talks to a reporter.

theater in Wyoming all those years, that I really was at a point where I really liked movies. I started looking around Oxford to get a building going, you know?" While looking for the appropriate site to launch a funky movie theater, Shapiro moved in with Willie Wallace, who ran the town head shop, Local Color.

"I had met Willie in Aspen a few years before when I was there visiting Semmes [Luckett]," Shapiro said.

"Willie and some people were staying with Semmes. I met Willie, and he said, 'Well, if you get to Oxford, look me up.' And boy, I did. He was the only one I knew in town. Willie's head shop was right downtown. The store was downstairs, and we lived upstairs. It was located a hundred yards from the police station. That's how cool Oxford was."

If the head shop was a stoner's throw from the cops, the only bar in town was just around the corner. That bar was the Gin, a large tin edifice that had been converted from the town's unused cotton gin into a tavern.

Being the first bar in town, at least, non-hotel affiliated (the Holiday Inn had recently opened) the Gin was an immediate hit. The social scene was so narrow, spread out over only a couple of blocks, that everybody knew everybody, particularly among the freaky, long-haired element.

Meanwhile, the search for a building, one suitably condemned, continued. Several possibilities were investigated, including an old church on West Jackson Avenue known as the Belfry. Shapiro worked on securing the Belfry for a couple of months, even going before the Oxford Board of Alderman. Ultimately, the board denied conversion of the Belfry because of a lack of parking. (In 1996, the Belfry became the office for mega-selling author John Grisham during his Oxford tenure.)

After more false starts, the site for the Hoka finally presented itself, and in true Oxford fashion, it was close by — a small tin building next door to the Gin. Originally, the little hut served as a cotton warehouse where cotton was stored as it waited to be ginned at the old gin, now tavern. When Shapiro found it, it was being used as a mechanic's garage for auto repair by another Oxford impresario, Greg Oliver.

"Oliver kept cars in there, and it was perfect for a theater because he had the floor slanted. He hated the Gin so much he was going to open a drive-thru window at the far end of (the tin building) and give away free beer." Instead, Oliver decided to open his own restaurant, Oliver's, which operated briefly. (Oliver eventually moved to the Caribbean.)

Shapiro took over the garage/warehouse, and he and his roommates ponied up $11,000 to turn the place into the Hoka Theatre.

"The building was just a shell with no wiring and no plumbing. We'd work during the day, then stop and smoke a reefer and go hear a band at the Gin and then go back and work some more. It only took us six weeks to get the place open."

That such an earthy edifice existed right downtown in Oxford, just a block off the main square of the Lafayette County seat, is testament to how somnolent and unhurried Oxford was, even as late as 1977. By this time, Local Color had moved from its spot near the police station to a shady enclave behind the Gin. Next door was a still-operational blacksmith shop. (Proximity to police continued for the head shop: the blacksmith was Andy Waller, the Oxford police officer who watched the 2Live tape with me. For a couple of years, he practiced his ancient art next door to an unabashedly hippie establishment that saw a daily, unsteady parade of freakazoids, tripsters and just plain bong trash.)

The Gin had rather immediately blossomed into a bustling bar known for its tasty plate lunches and beautiful waitresses. All of this made for a nice neighborhood: you could snag a beer, buy rolling papers and get your horse shorn, all during lunch.

Such wacky incongruity made Oxford a tolerant oasis in a somewhat fundamentalist North Mississippi landscape. The town was surrounded by buckles of the Bible Belt like Batesville, Pontotoc and Water Valley. Fine towns, to be sure, but perhaps not locales where one might assemble a hippie army to mount a movie theater, intending to name it for LSD. (More about that later.)

Oxford was surrounded by miles of dry counties and tiny hamlets with numerous churches sporting marquees with pithy aphorisms like, "Come out of your dark room, and see what develops." Thus the Hoka-Gin-Local Color scene made for a comfortable work environment for the freako carpenters who built the Hoka. Over the six weeks of construction, they installed a stage, seats, ticket area and a nice, spacious lobby.

Kevin Robie of Jackson, Tennessee, was perhaps the brains behind much of the actual design and construction. Robie brought in his buddy, carpenter Sammy Freeman. Ed Godfrey from Natchez was another roommate who lent a helping hammer.

"After he got up," Shapiro said. "Godfrey was one of those Natchez late sleepers. He'd roll in at two in the afternoon and work until two in the morning."

Emmitt Moore of Holly Springs, now a highly respected carpenter in Austin, Texas, put in sweat and beers. Robert Malone (now a beloved painter and teacher) and "Skinny" Kenny Vaughn of Oxford (now an Arizona tennis pro) were helping hands. Some ten to twelve people pitched in at various times over the course of the month and a half.

And, of course, the Southern women. Cool chicks like Jani Locke, Beth Cocke and Cindy Yancey offered broad support. Those three have gone on to leave their substantial marks as a potter/lawn artist, attorney and legal assistant, respectively. However, back then, in their boisterous days of bohemia, this winsome threesome was on hand to work hard and keep the construction of the Hoka on an appropriately uneven keel.

The guys brought in stacks of rough-hewn wood for the walls. Space was cleared, and one hundred or so seats were scavenged from old theaters and even a bank. A few reggae posters were hung up. The coffee was spiced with cinnamon, and a weekly hour's drive to Memphis provided the films. A fickle pair of ancient projectors (circa 1934) noisily cast images onto a far wall slathered with white paint.

Shapiro didn't name his new enterprise after LSD (The Crystal, the Sunshine) as his predecessors out West had done. But he did name it "The Hoka Cinema," with the acronym nicely referring to the active ingredient in marijuana. Hoka, by the way, was the name of the Chickasaw princess who was screwed out of her Lafayette County land in 1832 for a fraction of its worth, *ala* Manhattan. Ironically, the word means, "I agree," or translated literally, "OK."

"Yeah, they took everything she had, and she was on the Trail of Tears, like, the next day," Shapiro said, ruefully shaking his head. Perhaps the karma had come full circle. Keep in mind it was a "chick he saw," who brought Shapiro south on his own trail of tears. Unrequited love sent him head-over-headdress for his new Indian mistress, Hoka.

After a couple of years of showing movies, the roommates realized there wasn't enough income from the theater to support the entire posse. The group slowly scattered, and Shapiro emerged as the sole owner. A new movie, *Star Wars*, was a big hit, as were revival showings of Chaplin, (a Shapiro favorite) and W.C. Fields. Fellini, Bergman, Herzog and other European fare, rarely offered to a Mississippi audience.

College kids crammed the theater on dollar night and brought their beer-laden ice chests with them. Still, Shapiro looked at the spacious lobby and saw a lot of unused space. He decided to put in a cafe that would sell sandwiches and other late-night munchie food to the inebriated. Stew for the stewed, if you will. The Moonlight Café was an immediate hit.

The ensuing scene that sprouted around the movies, literary conversation and camaraderie constituted graduate school for me. Authors such as Willie Morris and Barry Hannah gave the Hoka a literary sheen that prompted our patrons and staff to delve more thoroughly into Southern literature. Square Books and the Center for Southern Culture on campus provided in-the-flesh views of Eudora Welty and Alex Haley.

Part of Willie's job with Ole Miss was to book his writer friends to come visit, so during these years, we were treated to visits by the likes of William Styron, John Knowles, David Halberstam and Peter Mattiessen. Abbie Hoffman, Allen Ginsberg and California Governor Jerry Brown passed through. Even Ralph Waite, TV's "Daddy Walton" from *The Waltons*, came to Oxford to show his film, *On the Nickel*, a bittersweet (and, he told us, biographical) story depicting a group of alcoholics in New York. (The title is also the opening theme song by Tom Waits.) Waite, at the time ten years sober, ending up staying a week. We showed his film every night he was there. (Very good, by the way.)

The theater was all "handmade" with a small stage at the end of the tilted floor. Bands of every genre played, sometimes until the wee hours. Inevitably, on occasion, the police would arrive, and Ron would grab the cash and flee into the night. He knew they wouldn't arrest an underling, and he could later just pay the fine. The Hoka showed three movies a night, programmed like a good indie theatre, everything from current films to classics (my first experience with *Casablanca* was there) to adult fare. Midnight porn movies were solid moneymakers.

Simply attending a movie could also be an adventure. There was Barton, the grumpy, film savant ticket taker, and King, a Labrador retriever that had the run of the place. There was a certain row of scavenged seats that weren't properly secured to the ground and often would send an entire row of moviegoers crashing on their backs, popcorn flying, feet in the air. I never heard a complaint.

For the first ten years, there was no air-conditioning, and determined patrons were known to strip down to watch a particularly hard-to-get classic that Ron had booked. There were also poetry slams, full-length plays, even wrestling — but for only one night after the flooring in the ring broke and the main attraction, a name lost to the haze, fell completely through.

The small town of Oxford could often shine like an intellectual oasis in North Mississippi or, as Willie Morris called the vibe, a "boondocks avant garde." The town became a seat from which to experience the very best in literature and progressive thought. It's no wonder many of us adopted Oxford for all of our adult lives without really meaning to. I worked at the Hoka for ten years, my longest tenure at any job.

The rustic appeal of the Hoka lasted twenty years. Think of a barn with every available bit of wall space plastered with cool posters, a great stereo, mismatched tables and chairs, tapestries tacked on the ceiling, overhead fans, a screen door. A funhouse for freaks. Yet, Ron's personality was so inviting — he can make small talk seem large — and the interesting movies and music he offered brought in the bookish weirdos as well as the sorority girls, retirees, skateboard punks, laborers, students, righties, lefties, Bible study groups and *Debbie Does Dallas.* That was his gift to Oxford, and in return, Oxford gave a home to the wandering ski bum, the Merry Prankster who missed the bus.

So, sure. Why shouldn't he be mayor?

29

On May 12, Ron Shapiro officially dropped out of the mayoral race. He had a letter hand-delivered to the Oxford City Clerk's office to that effect. When contacted in St. Louis, where he was on family business, Ron stated, "I have definitely withdrawn from the race and hope to make an endorsement of one of the remaining candidates next week."

City Clerk Virginia Chrestman said Shapiro's withdrawal would become official that day after the city election commission met.

"The ballots haven't been printed yet," she noted. "They'll probably print the ballots and leave his name off."

On May 20, a run-off took place between Buddy Faulkner (great-nephew of the author) and John Mistilis (son of one of the most beloved restaurateur families in town). It was widely whispered that Buddy was running to get on the Board in order to spearhead a vote to have the Faulkner statue moved to Rowan Oak. It was intimated that Jill Faulkner Summers would be a substantial donor to such a project. The day was cool for late May, with clouds skidding by before the sun finally did a late peek-a-boo. I shot hoops with my dogs for a bit out in Taylor then drove in to the local gym — one of the town polling spots — to await the results.

Upon arrival, I immediately saw a friendly face among those with note pads or sitting in lawn chairs, Ron Borne. Borne was a longtime University professor, amateur baseball historian and a favored raconteur in town. On this day, he was seated at a card table and indeed was wearing a poker face. With only 2,500 voters registered and a fraction of those actually voting, plus this was a run-off in one ward, the results could be expected within an hour.

I asked Borne how it was looking.

"Tight," he replied, looking around.

"This race?"

"Tight."

"This race is tight?"

"Tight."

"Tight?" I played along.

"It's tight."

In the gathering twilight, we stepped outside, and there was an all-white Little League baseball game in progress on the field in front of us and a pick-up game of hoops (all-black) raging in the parking lot. I watched for a few moments, trying to decide if I thought it was a bad thing that the two seemed so segregated. Suddenly there was an inside-the-park home run, the youngster churning around the bases and his teammates shrieking as he crossed the plate. This was followed by slashing drives to the basket, elegant, airborne ballet resulting in the sweet swish. Nope, I thought, this is okay. It's sports, and no one is being shot.

One of our civic leaders, Queenie Barnes, came out and said there were affidavit votes still out, and the results would be announced the next day at nine a.m. She did, however, have partial results: Mistilis,

177; Faulkner, 165.

"Tight," said Borne.

The next morning, it was official; Buddy lost his alderman seat to Mistilis by seven votes. It remained to be seen what the Faulkner family would do now. The long, hot summer of the statue had begun.

• • •

Another Oxfordy quirk appeared in the late spring of 1997: *The Blind Jim's Radio Hour*, a one-hour bluegrass show broadcast from my po-boy bar, Blind Jim's. The bar, by the way, was named for a blind man, Jim Ivy, from the early 1900s, who had been blinded as a teenager while working with tar on the Tallahatchie Bridge. Jim was known as the "Dean of Freshmen" and sold peanuts at the Student Union. He became a much-beloved figure the day his fervent cheering rallied the Ole Miss Rebels in a heated football game against their hated rival Mississippi A&M. After that improbable victory, Blind Jim became a fixture and unofficial mascot at all Rebel sporting events.

"I've never seen them lose," he would quip. The Ole Miss News Service reported Blind Jim lived happily ever. "In a whirlwind courtship, he married Blind Rosa Sanders and lived across the street from the church his mother founded, the Second Baptist Church." He died in 1955.

In the spirit of its namesake, the bar was warm and welcoming, with peanut shells on the floor. The food at Blind Jim's was exemplary and the spirits cold and sturdy. Still, an unlikely spot for a live radio show.

The show had begun in April, left the air due to a lightning strike on its tower and then regrouped to begin its summer season.

Modern listeners might use *A Prairie Home Companion* as a comparison, but in reality the only similarity between the two was both were on the radio. The Blind Jim's show was all music, although there were some comedic pronouncements made by Ed Dye, an elfish dobroist from Alabama who had had a journeyman career in show business — and the Santa Claus beard to prove it — including a stint as a stagehand on *The Ed Sullivan Show* and a thirty-year career as a Nashville bluegrass sideman.

"I grew up with radio shows," he said, "It's not such a novel concept."

Each musician took a turn leading the band through a tune. On the first show after the lightning strike — "I don't know what to think about that," Dye told the *Eagle*, — the band was Bryan Ledford on guitar and banjo; Caroline Herring on guitar and vocals; George Sheldon on bass; Laura Weber on fiddle and Charlie Cushman on banjo. Guests included Luther and Cody Dickinson and George McConnell. At one point they all came together for a ten-minute reggae version of "Blue Moon of Kentucky," led by Dye wearing a frilly tux shirt with orange suspenders and Blue Mountain baseball cap.

"The performing arts is a high and holy calling," Dye told the *Eagle* after the show. "They are as important as doctor, lawyer or Indian chief." The show continued and morphed away from the bar and set up shop in a local bookstore, Off Square Books, the funky remainder bookstore in Oxford. The band called themselves The Sincere Ramblers.

At the suggestion of bookstore owner Richard Howorth, they renamed the radio show, *The Thacker Mountain Radio Show*. (Howorth thought the name adequately expressed what he felt would be the amateur nature of the show). There was, of course, no mountain in the area, but there was a fire tower on a hill out in the county called Thacker Mountain. Midnight visits by carousing teens were common. Visitors would climb the stairs of the tower at night and do teenage things while basking in the vast, darkened vista. Some visitors were, uh, older than teenagers.

Oxford slowly embraced this new old-fashioned radio enterprise. It seemed to fit the community; sit in wooden chairs in a former furniture store and listen to literature three blocks from Faulkner's house, then rock out to music from the ever-burgeoning Oxford music scene that included John Stirratt of Wilco in his earliest bands. One resident referred to Oxford's "cheerful embrace of eccentricities," and that would seem to fit Thacker Mountain Radio. There were empty seats at first. The show continued for one, two, three years. Five years. Thanks to Square Books, authors from every corner of the world came through with their books, some so often they became friends. Soon, the bookstore was overflowing with audience, and this curious little radio experiment expanded to twenty-four shows a year.

What other small town has its own *Grand Ole Opry* of literature?

30

War and Whiskey

Cynthia Shearer, the curator of Rowan Oak (and herself an accomplished novelist), called the *Eagle* to say there were a couple of older gentlemen touring Faulkner's home, and we might be interested in their memories of Oxford during WWII. Mullen dispatched me to go get their story, and I interviewed them sitting on the front steps of Rowan Oak, where it was white hot.

The two looked like veterans in that they both wore unfashionable dork glasses and plaid shorts. One of them had a comb over that was at best, optimistic. I guess when you faced down death in the Great War, nerd glasses and disappearing hair are the least of your worries. Their memories were worthy, including the wonders of whiskey in the woodpile and coeds frolicking in the snow in their swimming suits. Color me intrigued.

The two were Bob Daniels, seventy-three, of Bellingham, Washington, and Frank Roach, seventy-two, of San Francisco. Both had spent 1942-43 taking engineering courses at Ole Miss as part of the Army Specialized Training Program. The ASTP accepted only the Army's best and brightest, and those who gained entry not only had to perform their Army duties — drilling, marching and obstacle course running — but complete college-level courses in physics, calculus and science. Daniels remembers taking twenty-eight hours one semester.

"It was a load," he said, shaking his head. "They knocked off about half the kids after that first semester, because if you got an 'F,' — Whoosh — you were gone."

Enduring the rigors of Ole Miss Army life gave the young soldiers a zest for living when it came time for weekend furloughs.

"When we had a chance to play, we'd play," Roach said.

"We'd split a cab — 50 cents apiece — and go out into the county to a fellow's house — a Mr. Gibbs," Daniels recalled. "He had two woodpiles out there," he said as Roach nodded his head in agreement, "a five-dollar pile and a six-dollar pile. We'd give him five dollars, and he'd pull a bottle of whiskey out of that woodpile," he said laughing. "We went out there a lot, but we never tried the six-dollar pile."

Roach recalled the two would take their whiskey to a beer parlor on the Square and drink whiskey with beer chasers. "The bar was called the Green Fern," he said, smiling at the half-century-old memory of cold beer. "It was run by two women, one of them a Miss Dorothy Odum. That was strange for those times — women running a bar."

"We'd sit there and talk to the locals," Daniels added. "This one guy bummed a couple of beers off of us, and I saw him later riding in a car, and I said who the hell *is* that? Somebody said, 'Oh, that's William Faulkner.' I remembered him from the bar. He didn't say much, just mostly listened."

Newspaper accounts of the war years in Oxford paint a picture of a small farming community sacrificing much-needed tools and men for the national effort. A photo from a June 1942 *Oxford Eagle* shows the result of a scrap metal drive — 80,000 pounds of metal piled up in front of the courthouse. The same edition reported that "nearly one-tenth of the men of military age in Oxford and Lafayette County are already in uniform."

Everything imaginable was rationed using coupon books: one pound of coffee per person every five weeks, "meatless Tuesdays" and the requirement that everyone register the serial number of the five automobiles that were allowed. Farmers were asked to produce more food with less equipment and manpower. Farming programs sprung up with morale-building names like "Food For Freedom," "Plant for Peace" and "Soldiers of the Soil." Even free time was rationed. Able-bodied men seen loitering were questioned and later, following aldermen degree, subject to arrest. However, community sacrifices weren't the biggest impression left on Daniels and Roach who, as impressionable eighteen-year-olds suddenly found themselves in the Deep South. Even fifty years later, they recalled the culture shock of strange accents and unfamiliar mores of 1940s Mississippi.

"The Ole Miss dean of women, a Mrs. Hefley, as I recall, she was a tough old bird," Daniels recalled. "The first two questions she'd ask were, 'Are you married?' and 'Are you Catholic?'"

"The center for young people in Oxford back then was the USO dances at the community center (now the park commission building).

"I remember somebody asking one of the Oxford girls, 'What do you think of all these soldiers,' and she said, 'We find them almost human.'"

"I found Oxford clannish," Roach said. "A totally different culture. I didn't think of it as a negative, just hard to understand. I was a Yankee, and it was hard to break into… so, you know, your family became the Army."

"The first time I walked down the street in Oxford and the blacks stepped off into the gutter, I was shocked," Daniels added.

"And of course, the main item was the speech, how else could I get tricked into getting married?" Roach laughed. He was married to the former Helen Burns of Oxford (University High School Class of 1942). Despite the language barrier, Oxford did its best for the thousands of soldiers who passed through town during the war years.

"Leave three things off your menu when entertaining Yankee soldiers," the *Eagle* advised readers in 1943. "Turnip greens, hominy and black-eyes peas."

Roach agreed.

"The deluxe dinner back then," he said, "was the chicken-fried steak at the Mansion." Cuisine and culture aside, the soldiers did endear themselves to their hosts by giving something back to the community that had been lost after 1942 — football.

"Ole Miss didn't field a team in 1943," Daniels said, "so the ASTP played a game in Hemingway Stadium, Company A versus Company B."

Company B was coached by Eddie Khayat of Moss Point.

"Our regular quarterback couldn't make it, so I was quarterback by default."

The game must have not gone well because he quickly changed the subject.

What about coeds in bathing suits in the snow? I ask.

"Mississippi had a very severe winter in 1942, a lot of snow," Roach recalled. "I just remember some of the gals coming out of the sorority houses in their bathing suits. They had a frolic in the snow."

We both let the image hang in the air. The idea of young coeds frolicking in the snow wearing swimwear was bracing as we sat there in the ninety-degree heat. Mr. Roach had the advantage; he had actually seen these girls; I could only conjure my own image. His was fifty years old, but it obviously stuck with him.

Daniels and Roach had a special fondness for Oxford, and why not? They experienced more in a year than most locals ever will: sharing a beer with William Faulkner, suiting up and playing a football game in Hemingway Stadium, and for Daniels, falling in love and marrying a local girl. After war and remembrance, did they enjoy their return trip?

"Absolutely," said Roach. "it's quite a bit like family, returning to Ole Miss."

"He did a lot of traveling in the front yard."

Jimmy Faulkner, speaking of his uncle

31

June

Comedy of Fools

Beckwith loaded up the Faulkner statue on a trailer, secured it, and drove it to Lugar Foundry on Highway 64 in Eads, Tennessee, outside Memphis, an hour and a half drive. I spoke to him when he got back to Taylor.

Beckwith: "I left the hands off. It was a last-minute decision, but it turned out to be the right decision, so I was proud of that. Once I got up there, we took them off for the molds, and I had little studs built where they could slip in, and it would be a lot easier to cover all the surface area that way."

Me: "How long will they have him?"

Beckwith: "I don't know. They're working on Elvis. He's right in there. They're probably a little parallel."

History was made on June 3 as Oxford elected its first female mayor and Republican as well. Patricia Chadwick Lamar defeated her Democratic opponent, John Bounds, by more than 700 votes and her independent opponent Jay Eads, a Navy veteran, by seventy-seven votes, out of 872 cast.

The sunburned Lamar told the *Eagle* that "Oxford is ready for a new direction, a new vision for moving into the 21st century."

Nothing against Lamar, but over the course of the campaign, I became numb to this type of "vision speak" of platitudes. It had a nice ring to it, but if I had a dollar for every time I had heard it over the six months, I'd be writing this from some secluded island where cold cocktails would be fetched by the fetching while I lounged.

Jonny Miles had been replaced by Kristin Harty, who turned out to be such a pro, we couldn't bring ourselves to fart or make up headlines about oral sex or spit on the floor. In other words, our boys club had been breached, and Steve and Bruce and I were being forced to act our age.

Harty was a consummate reporter. Her election story quoted the defeated John Bounds, the only Oxford native in the race. When asked about his post-election plans, he gave one of the best answers of all time: "I've got a bush hog in the barn."

Harty's report on Lamar's historic night including the news the new mayor had a "cellular" phone: "Wearing a green hat and carrying a cellular phone, Lamar sat in a chair toward the back of the crowd that gathered in front of a blackboard at the Oxford Activity Center Tuesday night, where election workers tallied votes from each of the six wards. In an agonizingly-suspenseful delay, election workers spent more than an hour counting votes from two wards, leaving the race between Lamar and Eads wide open. Lamar maintained a lead over Eads, although at times marginal, throughout the count."

Lamar had been elected alderman of Ward III in 1981, again, the first woman to do so, and served for twelve years. Now on this warm Mississippi night, the warm and gracious former homecoming queen made history again, not only as Oxford's first female and Republican mayor, but taking the reins when there was much civic drama in the air.

"I'll be ready to go from day one," she assured her hometown paper.

• • •

Dean Faulkner Wells was Faulkner's niece, who the author raised after her dad (Faulkner's brother, Dean) was killed flying an airplane that Faulkner had provided. Faulkner treated his niece, Dean, like his own daughter, hosting her wedding at Rowan Oak and giving her away, and providing for her boarding school years in Sweden. Over the years, she proved herself to be worthy of her lineage, producing a handful of books, including a re-telling of some of her uncle's favorite Halloween stories (*Ghosts of Rowan Oak*). She inherited more than her family's literary prowess. Slight in stature, she had her uncle's haunting, dark, sad, eyes; his fierce loyalty to loved ones and his twinkling, mischievous spirit.

Dean and her husband, Larry, were patrons (and nearby neighbors) of the Hoka and best friends (and publishers) of Willie Morris. Their friendship provided an inside look at the Faulkner family. We became friends with Dean's mother, Louise "Weesie," and aunt. Perhaps when we first met them, we were a tad intimidated by their literary stature, but any discomfort was quickly dispelled by their accessible manner and the joy with which they lived their lives. They fit perfectly with the gonzo milieu of the Hoka. Willie, Dean and Barry Hannah led the charge of the "South End Zone Rowdies," a loose group of thirty or so who took in all the Ole Miss Rebel home football games in probably the worst seats in the stadium.

Dean loved her hometown of Oxford deeply and was particularly incensed at the rampant changes taking place in 1997. It was in front of her house where the one hundred-year-old oak trees had been unceremoniously cut years before that set in motion the current unrest. And yet, she kept her own counsel, not appearing publicly at any of the statue hearings regarding her beloved uncle. But that's not to say she didn't have strongly-held, heartfelt opinions.

One night, I interviewed her off and on the record. "I'll be your Deep Throat," she told me chuckling. "So far, it's been a comedy of fools. Out back at Mammie Callie's (servant's quarters at Rowan Oak) is where the statue should go, near the east garden. I had thought it should be at the stables. He did sit out there where the wisteria is."

Her husband, author Larry Wells, chimed in: "Pat (Lamar) came up to our door and asked for our votes. We told her we are supporting her because we feel like Oxford is right on the cusp. Do we want to be Tupelo or Natchez? We agree with Barry Hannah, there are too many people tearing up the woods to make money. That's who's trying to shape Oxford. Pearline [a beloved housekeeper who worked for many families in town] was offered a quarter million dollars for her lot and turned it down. These developers are the kind of people who go to their kids' Little League games and sit behind home plate and yell, 'Spike 'em, son!'"

Dean then expressed her fears for the statue at the City Hall site: "Those Square sitters (bored teenagers who gather at night) could clown around, and something could happen. Maybe not vandalized, but he would certainly be vulnerable to mockery." She then summed up her feelings: "Either they want to honor Faulkner, or they don't. Do they want Pappy (Faulkner's family nickname) for a tourist attraction, or is it genuine? Oxford has a chance to say the most glorious soul came from here. It's time for people to get over this. Put him where he will be the most comfortable, which is down home with the wisteria."

In a June 12 editorial, I covered statue controversies of the past that had similarities to what Oxford was experiencing…

"Statue controversy is nothing new, and Oxford is in good company when it comes to quarreling over bronze likenesses of heroes. The recent debate over a memorial in Washington, D.C. for Franklin Delano Roosevelt (at issue: whether or not to portray him in a wheelchair) occasioned press articles on other statue debates in history. One of the most infamous, as profiled in the May issue of *Smithsonian* magazine by Andrea Gabor, was the Jefferson Memorial.

"According to Gabor, the Jefferson Memorial debate devolved into a 'showdown' on the floor of the U.S. House in 1937 over the cutting of cherry trees in D.C.'s Tidal Basin to make room for the huge memorial. The trees became a 'cause célèbre,' she writes, 'as people chained themselves to the trunks in protest.' According to Gabor, then-President Franklin Roosevelt eventually lost patience with delays and pushed through a $500,000 appropriation to begin construction. His wife, Eleanor, Gabor writes, 'had publicly written, in what was certainly an act of defiance, a paean to the trees in *Reader's Digest*.'"

"The positioning of bronze lions to grace either side of the entrance to the New York City Library is another granite dust-up Gabor describes.

"'Theodore Roosevelt,' she writes, 'who loved hunting big game, made it known that he favored elk or moose as guardians of the library. Another group lobbied for a pair of industrious beavers.' When the artist Edward Clark Potter's lions were finally unveiled in 1910, smarty editorialists — glad they don't exist anymore — heaped derision on his pieces.

"'Mealy-mouthed and complacent,' one sniffed. 'Stuffed,' opined another, and, my favorite, the lions 'bore a likeness to the dour Norwegian dramatist Henrik Ibsen.'"

Closer to home, Joseph Blotner wrote in his Faulkner biography that a monument to the University Greys, Ole Miss's Civil War unit who later suffered one hundred per cent casualties, enraged Faulkner's grandmother, Sallie Murry Faulkner. In 1910, the huge sentinel was erected on campus on University Circle (where it still stands), but Mrs. Faulkner, angered that the campus location seemed to exclude all the county boys who had also served, "took the most drastic step she could think of: she resigned from the United Daughters of the Confederacy."

Blotner further reports that the "United Confederate Veterans later voted to erect another monument in the courthouse square, but she would not live to see it."

"Yesterday won't be over until tomorrow and tomorrow began ten thousand years ago. For every Southern boy fourteen years old, not once but whenever he wants it, there is the instant when it's still not yet two o'clock on that July afternoon in 1863..."

William Faulkner, *Intruder in the Dust* (1948)

32

July
Fear and Watermelons

July 3 was a high-water mark for Oxford. It was swearing-in day on the Oxford square for the new mayor and board, an event that would kick off the town's Fourth of July weekend. I wrote this of the historic day:

"Oxford's new mayor, Pat Lamar, took the oath of office with a bang Thursday, kicking off her new administration and a long Fourth of July weekend. The three days of events included a parade, a twenty-one-gun salute, a street dance, and — of course — fireworks… The ceremonies had all the color and pageantry of small-town Americana. City Hall was festooned with red, white and blue bunting, and blue chairs were set up in the street in front of City Hall to accommodate the several hundred spectators.

"The celebration culminated today with Lamar quietly assuming her duties as Oxford's first new mayor in a quarter-century and its first woman mayor ever. Thursday, she was joined by her sister mayors, Betsy Aloway of Abbeville and Jane Rule Burdine of Taylor, the first time all three incorporated towns in Lafayette County will be governed by women.

"In the spirit of cooperation, Burdine said she and her small town were "always ready to help Oxford." Alluding to the controversy over the Faulkner statue, Burdine offered a solution.

"'The town of Taylor wants you to know we'd be happy to take your statue and put in front of Taylor Grocery,' she said as the crowd applauded."

On July 7, the new mayor's first day on the job, I gleaned this little nugget: "One of Pat Lamar's first official acts as mayor yesterday was turning down tickets to the circus. A caller from Tupelo offered Oxford's new mayor a visit to the Big Top, which Lamar graciously declined. Instead, she arranged for seventy residents of the North Mississippi Regional Center to attend.

"'OK, call me back if you need me,' she told someone at the Center. 'The number here is 234-'

"'-2340,' came a helpful voice from down the hall.

"And so it was for Lamar yesterday at her first day on the job — a new phone number, and soon — a new office. Lamar spent her first full day as mayor in a temporary office across the hall from the actual mayor's office, pending alterations.

"We've pulled the carpet up in there, and we're just gonna sand the floors down and just have the hardwood floor."

• • •

On July 18, the results of the controversial "image survey" — that led to death threats against UM Chancellor Robert Khayat, an avalanche of letters to the editor, teeth gnashing and wringing of hands — was released and was more notable for what it didn't say than what it did.

Old South symbols such as the Rebel flag, Dixie and Colonel Rebel were deliberately left out of the questions to see if respondents mentioned them, according to Harold Burson, head of Burson-Marsteller Public Relations, the firm which conducted the questionnaire. He spoke at an athletic building on campus before a crowd of about 150 students, faculty, administrators and media. He explained that a telephone survey was conducted that questioned 1,000 adults nationwide. Of those who knew about Ole Miss, a favorable opinion was expressed about the school by a 3-1 margin. However, eighty percent of those who responded didn't know enough about the school to have an opinion.

That led Burson to declare, "Ole Miss is the best-kept secret in the South.

"You've just got to do a better job of selling yourself."

The Old South symbols were mentioned by only four percent of respondents, but Khayat recognized the pulsing community interest in them — did he ever — and he brought up the subject in his remarks.

"Let me make this very clear, and I'll try not to be emotional," he said before pausing to compose himself. With tears welling in his eyes, he continued, "The Confederate flag is not a symbol of this university. Chancellor Fortune in 1983 and the Alumni Board of Directors in 1991 made that clear. People who love Ole Miss need to know that the hate mail that many in this room received in the past year was not sent by Ole Miss people but by others with their own agenda who do not care about this university.

"That flag is part of our history, but not a symbol."

Khayat went on to say that the symbols "would go through an evolutionary process. Ultimately, they will be in the hands of the students." Then the old former law professor turned downright eloquent.

"The most enduring symbols of Ole Miss are, and always will be, the lives of our graduates as they make their mark in the world."

I left thinking that this was a very astute man. Certainly no one could accuse him of being a dictator. What kind of total asshole would threaten his life?

Speaking of total asshole, I have my own sad history as a Rebel flag terrorist. In the summer of 1971, I was seventeen and a functioning idiot. My school district in Greenville, Mississippi, underwent a sweeping, federally mandated integration. My high school went from having one or two black students in the spring of '71, to being sixty percent black in September, seemingly overnight. When we ended our junior year white students were the overwhelming majority. When we came back from the summer, it was a bold new world. Suddenly, the athletic teams were all black, ditto homecoming court, all student-elected offices, most of the student body, like a flipped negative.

My buddies and I were solid middle-class shitheads and were on our way to Ole Miss after graduation so we weren't too concerned. We befriended several of our new classmates. We also loved black music and grew to love black culture and, as is the case historically with white suburban kids, adopted black slang, black mannerisms, etc. And yet, we also maintained a perverse love of all things Rebel, the flag, the song "Dixie," Southern culture in general. We weren't racists, we weren't even rednecks; we just practiced a senseless dichotomy.

As our senior year started, we — a core group of about five: myself, Sonny, King Rat, Mad Dawg and Ghetto — plus a wider circle, began to chafe at what we perceived as political correctness and uptightness. The five of us shot hoops together and smoked cigars at lunch while listening to Skynryd's "Free Bird" before it was a cliché.

We collectively consumed an ocean of beer. I don't remember any of us ever having a date, with the exception of Sonny. With his crystal blue eyes and curly locks, the boy had game, even then.

By the time second semester rolled around, we were high-rolling seniors. We could smell freedom right around the corner, the so-called "first day of the rest of our lives." Somewhere along the line, we began to formulate a plan to run a 3' x 5' Confederate flag up the flag pole in front of the school. Our goal wasn't to intimidate our black classmates, but rather to stick it to the man, in this case, our straight-laced principal, James Young. Young wore baggy suits, had an 1890s hair cut, parted in the middle like Ichabod Crane and droned on in old-school cadences that cried for ridicule.

We fancied ourselves a rag-tag, underestimated group like we had seen in cool war movies like the *The Great Escape* or *The Dirty Dozen*. We doled out assignments to bring our plan to fruition. Mad Dawg, as the smallest and most agile, was selected to climb the pole with the flag and affix it to the ropes, which he would then cut. Sonny and I would be look-outs, posted up in dense trees on either side of the school, armed with walk-talkies. If we saw the police, we would squawk to Ghetto, who had a third walkie as he hid in a bush close enough to the flag pole to holler to Mad Dawg.

Sonny and I took our positions a few nights before the actual caper for a dry run to time how often the cops drove by the school. Not very often, as it turned out. If the plan could be executed flawlessly, there would be no police to even hide from. Ghetto and King Rat would man the getaway car.

We chose a Thursday night so the flag would be flapping on the pole to greet students on Friday. It just so happened that day was also the day of an assembly when our buddy Hilton was slated to play the national anthem on his electric guitar, Jimi Hendrix-style. In the midst of his shredding he was going to sneak in a whacked out, barely discernible version of "Dixie." We were hardcore, I tell you.

On Thursday night, (I forget now what story we used to get out of the house, no small feat on a school night) we all took our positions. After getting the go signal from Sonny and me, Mad Dawg looked straight up and began his shimmy up the pole, the flag folded into his waist band, a Bowie knife clenched in his teeth, Tarzan-style.

Sitting in the tree, I couldn't see Mad Dawg's progress and was left in blind faith. After a couple of minutes, I saw headlights approaching.

"Gotta car coming," I whispered into the talkie. "Tell Dawg to cool it." Mad Dawg, they told me later, held tight to the top pole and ceased all movements. Cars passed the high school all the time. What driver would think to look over to check to see if someone was clinging to the top of the pole, especially at night? Dawg held on and willed himself to be invisible. It helped that he probably only weighed 150 pounds. The car passed uneventfully.

Mad Dawg, all wiry strength plus guile, moved farther up the pole until he reached the top, an incredible feat when I think of it now in my fat adulthood. He clipped the Rebel flag to the rope, pulled off another three feet or so and cut the rope. For good measure, he spread Vaseline all over the pole as he made his descent. King Rat and Ghetto picked us all up, and we sped home. None of us slept that night.

The next morning, we all tried to hide how excited we were to go to school. Once there, the reaction was exactly as we'd hoped — the whole school was abuzz. The police came, and finally a fire truck was summoned, and a cherry-picker was deployed to remove the offending banner.

During that day's assembly, Hilton wailed on "Dixie," and it was a little too recognizable, and he was summoned to Mr. Young's office. As I recall he wasn't disciplined much. Our group got away with it completely, something at which I still marvel. Some of our classmates knew it was us, but no one ratted. No bragging. We kept our mouths shut. I suppose the statute of limitations has run out. It is strange to imagine that were we to pull such a stupid stunt today, it could possibly be a felony hate crime or even be considered an act of terrorism.

I went on to college at Delta State, near my hometown, and during my freshman year, actually took in a young, black, homeless kid and put him up in my dorm room for several weeks, again, without getting caught. Nixon ran against McGovern that year (1972), and Nixon reminded me so much of our high school principal, my lefty politics were solidified.

I recount this sordid tale now to illustrate what a patchwork of thoughts and emotions that can be wrapped up in the Southern psyche, what the band Drive-By Truckers calls "the duality of the Southern thing."

In the intervening years, skinheads and hate groups have co-opted the Rebel flag and turned it into a symbol of evil intolerance and celebration of hate. I went from owning several and climbing a tree to fly one to actively opposing the flag.

The great Shelby Foote (from my hometown of Greenville) wrote *The Civil War: A Narrative*, a 2,800-page, three-volume account of the war that he spent twenty years researching. According to the *Atlanta Journal Constitution,* Foote "visited more than 1,000 battlefields, traced almost every campaign by walking it or riding it on horseback and plowed through every reference source available, including the U.S. government's 128-volume history of the war on land and its thirty-volume history of the war at sea." In 1990, he became the reluctant star of the eleven-hour PBS show *The Civil War*, directed by Ken Burns. Foote later decried the flag's appropriation by dumb rednecks: "Klansmen who have appropriated the flag: 'I tell them to their faces that they are the scum who have degraded the Confederate flag, converted it from a symbol of honor into a banner of shame, covered it with obscenities like a roadhouse men's room wall.'"

"It's still mainly abused and absurdly defended. And I understand blacks' feelings when they see the Confederate flag. The real villains are Southerners who knew what that flag truly stood for and allowed yahoos to carry it. We should have stood up and said that those people ought not be allowed within one hundred yards of the Confederate flag, let alone use it as a symbol for all they were doing. But we didn't."

As a middle-school student, I kept a Confederate flag on my wall. The small flags were passed out to the crowd at Ole Miss games. My brother and I used to write the score of the game on the stick and then file the flag into a container, a large cylinder wastebasket that itself was in Rebel flag colors. Racism never crossed our minds. It was all about the Ole Miss Rebels. Our dad had season tickets starting in 1957, and after we got old enough to go, he took us to football games our entire lives. At some point, we eventually threw the flags away. By 1997, my high school antics of 1970 were an embarrassment, and all I can chalk it up to is being a not particularly bright or worldly teenager — and, of course, being a total asshole.

33

On July 24, the call came in late, just before quitting time on a Thursday when Steve and I were about to clock out and head to the Upstairs Bureau. We were laughing when the phone rang, but that ceased when Steve reached for a pen while cradling the receiver between his neck and shoulder. With a furrowed brow, he repeated the info as he jotted it down: "Four o'clock, mayor's office, right. A mural with a guy eating watermelons, right, right." He continued scribbling. "Okay, thanks. Bye." He looked up at me. "A group of black citizens in Water Valley is meeting with the mayor this afternoon to complain about a mural that's being done on Main Street that shows a black guy eating a watermelon." He tore his note off the pad and held it out to me. "You wanna check it out, or do you wanna get a drink?"

"Loaded question," I said.

We both decided I should go check it out. As I headed out, it occurred to me, at the very least it was a good way out of the office. I thought about how it was indicative of how these bizarre stories just kept coming, Faulkner's birthday or not.

Water Valley is a former railroad town some twenty miles south of Oxford. Legendary engineer Casey Jones is said to have died there.

As befits its name, the town throws an annual watermelon festival each year, complete with a Watermelon Queen and, in recent years, lawn mower races, watermelon eating contest, music, a carnival and an array of food — in other words, a pretty typical small-town festival.

When I arrived at the mural site on Main Street, I decided to remain in my truck for a few moments to take in the scene before I jumped in asking questions. It was definitely a rough, unfinished painting. There was the black guy, kneeling down in shabby clothes, handing a piece of watermelon to a small boy. I tried to be offended by it, but couldn't get it up. It had been a long week, a tough news cycle, as we say. I had just finished an op-ed piece on bream beds, hadn't shaved and felt like I had done my work for the week. Having to deal with a Water Valley mural at happy hour on a Friday seemed like the gravy on my shit sandwich of a week. As I sat there, I peered around the downtown area and noticed they are really fond of churches in Water Valley. A cluster of them dot the horizon, anchored by the granddaddy of them all, the First Baptist Church. On this day, it was undergoing renovation with myriad scaffolding and a massive new cross being put in place like God's Own Jumbotron.

I walked over in the scalding heat and snapped a few shots of the mural. Further on, I noticed a historical marker identifying the site as the "cradle of Methodism" of North Mississippi. I continued walking, checking my notes, and almost walked into an antique cannon displayed at the Baptist Church, which seemed weird amid all the churches.

I headed over to the mayor's office, and Mayor Hart was there with the Water Valley Chamber of Commerce president, Steve Thompson. Both seemed a little taken aback by my disheveled appearance and whiskers. We did the intros, and the mayor seemed to give me the stink eye.

"We're waiting on Luther Folsom of the Yalobusha NAACP," Hart said, drumming his fingers on his desk. "How are things at the *Oxford Eagle*?"

What a non-starter as a conversation device. I thought about how we sat around laughing and waiting for happy hour and made up filthy headlines and spat on the floor, but finally just said, "Fine. Fine. We're rolling in dough down there." They both looked at me like I'm an escaped mental patient. Hart decided to use the down time with a "journalist" to sell his town.

"Well, we've got a lot of great things going on in Water Valley," he exclaimed, the snake oil starting to rise in his voice. "We have only two empty store fronts here, and we're getting calls from folks in Oxford saying the rent's too high to live there anymore. Yeah, getting calls from Oxford." He went on for another fifteen minutes and I was so out of it, I actually wrote down some of what he was saying, knowing full well I'd never print it. Thompson, the chamber president, was closer to my age, and I actually remembered seeing him in the bars in the old days. He was checking my eyes and trying to keep from giggling as I humored the mayor. After a half hour we discussed whether or not we should wait any longer. Fifteen more minutes went by. I was facing the mayor, and behind him on the wall was a large color painting of a pastoral scene of a lake in the woods. After staring at it for nearly an hour, a subliminal message appeared, and I did a double take — a huge white cross had emerged. It was a very uncanny visual. It was so big and prevalent, it was a miracle I didn't notice it before. The effect was somewhat creepy.

I'd had enough. Being with these two was like sitting in the waiting room of purgatory, and the only magazines were in large print.

We said our goodbyes, and I walked out into the harsh sun and headed to my truck, which I knew would be roasting like a baked potato, the cab like aluminum foil. Looking across the street to the mural, I saw that it was now a crime scene in the making. About one hundred fuming young black people were milling around and pointing at the painting. Five Water Valley cops, including the chief, were across the street in a Junior Food Mart parking lot monitoring the situation. A bona fide Mississippi racial situation in the making (and, boy, we've had plenty of practice making them).

I waded into the melee.

The crowd was all black, mostly female, poor-looking and with a strange, deranged look. Not Down syndrome exactly, but many in the crowd exhibited some sort of mental affliction. They were sweaty in their anger. One woman, maybe a teacher or a counselo, had obviously talked to Steve Thompson and was giving the crowd the party line.

"It's unfinished. Let the artist finish his work."

A guy in a tank top saw me writing notes and told me he was the vice president of the local NAACP.

"I just spent forty-five minutes waiting on your boss," I told him. "And believe me, that's forty-five minutes I'll never get back."

I continued, "The mayor tells me the artist had to interrupt his work to run to Memphis for more paint. He's nowhere near finished."

He nodded with skepticism. The crowd moved in around me and had me surrounded. I shot a couple of glances at the cop nearest me. He had a bemused look as if to say, "Who's this joker?" I thought I was speaking privately with the vice president, but suddenly, I had an audience and was inadvertently breaking the "fourth wall," stumbling over the line from observer journalist to participant.

As I stood in the middle of the seething sweaty mob, I had to admit I was actually happy to see the cops. Right or wrong, I felt like they had my back. Even though the mural was obviously unfinished, this wasn't an art crowd, and they were convinced the mural was done, and it made fun of black stereotypes.

"Yeah, he through. It's finished," said a member of the crowd to much agreement. "Yeah, look at that. What's that supposed to mean?" he said, pointing at the half-finished image of the black man eating a watermelon.

Another gave her name and agreed to be quoted. "I'm Katherine Brown of Water Valley, and my first impression when I saw it was I felt like I had been slapped in the face."

Before I had time to think, my mouth was working. "No," I said, as heads swiveled my direction. "You can tell it isn't finished. Look at Casey Jones."

Indeed Casey Jones, sitting in the engine, was just an outline, and the rest of the mural was rather hazily sketched in. Most any objective observer could immediately tell it was only half-done, but, as I say, we weren't dealing with connoisseurs on this day.

The crowd looked at me with what I can only call disdain, and I couldn't blame them. My stubble and glassy eyes gave me the appearance of someone passing by on their way to the liquor store. But I did have my notebook and tape recorder, and I was wearing baggy Dockers, so I probably looked poor enough to pass for a newspaper reporter.

Steve Thompson showed up and huddled with the NAACP veep and the police chief and a representative from the crowd, and it was quickly decided they would sit down and agree to an arrangement. There was a gas station/convenience store across the street, and the group began moving that way. Thompson came over to me.

"We're going to talk it over in that Junior Food Mart. You're certainly welcome to sit in," he said.

Actually, I'd had enough for the day, but knew I had to sit with them. It was sort of my job. Then I remembered it would be air-conditioned in the Junior Food Mart, and I could get a break from the stifling, take-no-prisoners heat. It seemed to wave up from the pavement and beat down from the sky at the same time. It's hard to appear professional when your shirt has turned to puree and your armpits are drooling down in black rivers of goat. I followed them in and grabbed a water and peered out at the crowd of maybe a hundred or so.

The four huddled in a small booth while I hovered. Thompson spoke first: "Y'all, let's just paint over the black guy eating the watermelon and let Kermit [Kroll, the artist] change it, paint something else in there. The city commissioned the mural, so I think we have the authority to change it. Really, no big deal."

And just like that, they agreed to paint over the offending image — with white paint no less — and let the artist deal with it when he got back. Someone was dispatched immediately, and the little child enjoying a watermelon was soon white-outed like you would a mistake in typing. I couldn't help thinking these guys, well intentioned and full of heart, were backwoods art gods, and I, a lowly redneck scribbler, watching them wield their power with a ham hand.

There they were — among the huge jars of hard boiled eggs floating in a mysterious purple goo; the paisley ball caps clothes-pinned on a rope that also contained bandanas made in China, looking down on plastic tacos, artificial tattoos, fake silver keychains, Vienna sausages, spinning hot dogs and three rows of stale coffee, crammed into a little booth there — ordering up a white-washing. I had just spent the better part of an hour watching a white cross, and now I was witnessing a literal white washing of history, in this case commonly agreed to by black and white.

When the little figure was painted over, the crowd was placated and dispersed. This in itself seemed some type of victory. In years past, a public dispute of this nature would have easily escalated into the familiar ugliness. I applaud Water Valley and the leaders for what they did that Friday in the over-heated moment. It was yet another reminder of the importance of symbols and public art and history to the people of Mississippi. These things matter and are taken to heart.

"The purpose of the painting," Thompson said, as he walked me to my truck, "was to promote our history and the unity of black and white people in the area. We saw how they took offense and came to the conclusion that if it bothered them, we should paint it over.

"The Bible says if eating meat offends your brother, you don't eat meat."

As I cranked up my truck for the ride back to Oxford, the whole day seemed wonderfully wacky and enough reason to drive down to this quaint little village and cover this story, even if it was on a scorching Friday at five o'clock when any reasonable man would be clocking in elsewhere.

"[Man's] moral conscience is the curse he had to accept from the gods in order to gain from them the right to dream."

William Faulkner, interview *The Paris Review*, 1956

34

August
Humidity Has Its Day

August in Mississippi separates the homies from the visitors. The heat and humidity seem unreal if you're not from here — and often if you are. The heat starts early — actually, it never really leaves; it's eighty degrees at midnight, ninety when you're having coffee, ninety-nine by lunch. Such searing blasts cook the very air itself. Faulkner's wife, Estelle, famously remarked to her novelist husband, "There's something about the light in August." Faulkner biographer Joseph Blotner reports Faulkner immediately stood up and walked into their house (they were on their east gallery taking in cool cocktails away from the blazing sunset) and changed the title of the book he was then working on from *Dark House* to *Light in August.*

Faulkner abhorred air conditioning and never owned one in his lifetime. He reportedly said of it, "They're trying to do away with weather."

Estelle was said to have installed a window unit the day after his death.

The late great novelist William Styron (*Sophie's Choice*) was dispatched by *Life* magazine to cover Faulkner's funeral in July 1962. He wrote then of the heat, "The heat is like a small, mean death itself, as if one were being smothered into extinction in a damp woolen overcoat. The feeling on this Saturday forenoon is a hot, sweaty languor bordering on desperation."

Keep in mind Styron grew up in Virginia and thus was no stranger to Southern summers. When he later encountered Shelby Foote at the wake at un-air-conditioned Rowan Oak, the Mississippian offered the Virginian advice on how to deal with it:

"You've got to walk through it gently; don't make any superfluous moves." Foote then added depressingly: "This is just beginning to build up pressure. You should be around here in August."

Indeed, August may have something to do with the southern drawl, as if talking too fast might cause a person to spontaneously combust.

Even with the brutal temps and oppressive air, August 1, 1997, saw the publication of *Fortune* magazine's list of the five best places in America to retire, and there was Oxford in the top five. It was almost laughable on a such a blazing day.

Finding itself on such lists was becoming commonplace for Oxford but this '97 designation was front-page news in the *Oxford Eagle* that day. The magazine noted in its cover story, "Towns such as Chapel Hill, North Carolina, Lawrence, Kansas and Austin, Texas, already receive their share of retirees… but the town we recommend is Oxford, Mississippi. Here, retirees can take advantage of a rich cultural life — and cheaply, to boot. The prime real estate market is tight within walking distance of the Square, but when available, a three-bedroom house can be had for $150,000."

Fortune also took note of retirees being exempt from income tax on certain investments, as well as the positives of SEC sports, quail hunting and "Barry Hannah, John Grisham and Willie Morris living in Oxford, an impressive writer-to-citizen ratio for a town of 10,000."

Never mind both Grisham and Morris had moved away years before, and none of them would relish being used in real estate brochures. For the record, the other towns joining Oxford in that 1997 Top Five towns for retirement were Beaufort, South Carolina; Carlsbad, Caliornia; Sequim, Washington, and Ocean County, New Jersey. Random though it seemed, it was part of the portfolio Oxford was slowly amassing as one of the most noteworthy small towns in America.

On the same week as the *Fortune* announcement, in the same edition of the paper that day — the Faulkner family once again made the news…

"A special exhibit of paintings by Maud Butler Falkner, the writer's mother, has opened at the University Museums on the Oxford campus."

The article by Linda White of the University News Service (using Falkner without the "u" that William invented) stated that "thirteen paintings from the collection of Dean Faulkner Wells, the artist's granddaughter and the writer's niece, will be on display through October 5 at the University Museums on the Oxford campus.

"Nannie could not not paint," said Wells. "I tried to pick paintings that represent all of Nannie's work. She did still-lifes, florals, landscapes and portraits, with everything from oils and pastels to watercolors. And she painted on everything. There's one painting in this collection of a child's toy that's done on a window shade."

White wrote that the mother of the great Nobel Laureate was herself immersed in the arts.

"Mothering a house full of rambunctious sons didn't leave much time for painting, but it was Falkner's sustenance — as well as reading. She never tired of the ancient writers Plato and Aristotle, but she was just as interested in the current writers of the day. She read every evening before going to sleep and was reading *Lady Chatterly's Lover* the night she died [in 1960]."

"Nannie always wanted an exhibit," said Wells of her grandmother. "It matters so much that's she's having one now."

Coincidentally, the first weekend in August, Water Valley held their annual Water Valley Watermelon carnival without incident. Kermit Kroll came up with a nice mural, adding a group of white and black Water Valleyians enjoying what one hopes was cool, crisp and sweet watermelon. It brought to a close one of the more bizarre, down-home events of this wonderfully whacko year…

And speaking of whacko… In August 1997, along with the myriad issues it was dealing with, the University of Mississippi dissociated itself from a conference on Elvis Presley it had hosted the previous two years. Saying the school could spend its "time, energy and money on more rewarding efforts," they broke ties with the two-day event and its organizer, Dr. Vernon Chadwick. Chadwick, who happened to be the brother of new Oxford mayor Pat Lamar, was miffed but re-located the conference to Memphis.

The *Oxford Eagle* reported that many thought the cancellation might have been caused by the 1996 conference, that featured a lesbian Elvis, Elvis Herselvis. *Eagle* reporter Humphreys McGee wrote of her performance: "Elvis Herselvis, the self-described, 'atomic-powered lesbian,' opened her long-anticipated performance dramatically as her band, the Straight White Males, belted out their music from behind a curtain that parted to reveal 'the hardest working drag King in show business' with her back to the audience, frozen in an admirable, authentic pelvis-centered pose. She broke into 'C.C. Rider,' and the crowd of one hundred responded enthusiastically."

In the follow-up story, McGee wrote of the conference's demise under a huge headline that read: "Ole Miss Kills Elvis." He quoted Chadwick, an assistant professor of English at Ole Miss, in a front-page story: "This is backwoods, backwater lack of vision. This administration is intolerant of sexual diversity to begin with and class diversity as well. When will this trouncing of civil liberties stop? After all, the study of Elvis is the study of our national prejudices."

In one year, the university had killed the Rebel flag and now Elvis too. These people were asking for it.

Elvis Herselvis, the self-described "atomic-powered lesbian" at the 1996 Elvis Conference.

35

Ole Miss further showed their liberal/cultural uppityness on August 20 when a professor from the school, Dr. Bill Ferris, was named by President Bill Clinton to become chairman of the National Endowment for the Humanities. Ferris was director of the school's respected Center for the Study of Southern Culture. The Humanities Council was under fire during this time by conservative lawmakers who wanted to end funding to the council, PBS and many other supposedly liberal government media/arts programs. The *New York Times* and others speculated that Ferris' appointment might blunt some of that criticism because Mississippi Senator Trent Lott, then the powerful senate majority leader, supported Ferris.

For the first football game of the year on August 30, the university announced changes in the look of Colonel Rebel, the school's on-field mascot. Heretofore, the mascot was outfitted like an old Southern gentleman or plantation owner, with a hat and three-piece suit, a white beard and cane. Think Colonel Sanders without the chicken. From the *Mississippian*: "Instead of his traditional garb — blue coat, red pants, grey hat and vest — he will be sporting a football uniform and helmet. We're not really changing Colonel Reb; we're upgrading him," said one official.

These baby steps to "upgrade" Colonel Rebel rather than get rid of him outright was the university's way to not offend the fan base and donors, but it all smelled of desperation. It seemed to me if they were intent on keeping the old man mascot, they should have a second mascot, also dressed in a three-piece suit, and he could be a lawyer ready to file suit when the old man collapses. What opponent is going to fear a mascot that is an elderly gentleman with a white beard and walking cane?

News from the international front rocked the world on August 31 in a story from Christopher Burns of the Associated Press from Paris: "Princess Diana, 36, whose storybook marriage captured the hearts of the world and whose divorce shook the royal family, was killed along with her companion, Dodi Fayed, in a car crash early today as they were being chased by photographers, police said. The crash, which also killed a chauffeur, happened shortly after midnight in a tunnel along the Seine River at the Pont de l'Alma bridge, while photographers followed her car, a police spokesman said on condition of anonymity.

"Prince Charles and the princess were divorced in August 1996 after 15 years of marriage."

"After taking several readings, I'm surprised to find
my mind's still fairly sound."

Willie Nelson, *Me and Paul* (1985)

36

September
Small-Town Giant

Working for a small-town newspaper, while filled with undeniable drudgery, also had its perks. In addition to the "juice," gossip and inside info one stumbled across, there were free books and concert tickets that made their way to our offices. The *Eagle* had an excellent entertainment supplement during this time called "Oxford Town." It was a twenty-four-page tabloid featuring music listings (Oxford has always maintained a bustling music scene), book reviews and feature articles written on the cheap by the town's teeming flood of young, aspiring scribes. The editor was Jamie Kornegay, a brilliant writer from nearby Batesville.

I've been a Willie Nelson fan since the mid-1970s, when "the Red Headed Stranger" emerged from Texas with his honky-tonk blend of redneck hippie soul. Bought his albums as they came out. When we received a press release announcing he was performing at the casino in Tunica (again, Sam's Town), the wheels in my sweaty lunk-head began grinding. I figured this was one of the few opportunities I might have to meet him and interview him. Like millions, I had been a fan for years. Pretty much everything about him appealed to me:

not only his songs (I've seen an interview where he says he wrote "Crazy," "Funny How Time Slips Away" and "Hello Walls" in a single week.), but also his bio: from giving up the biz to try pig farming ("How hard can it be?") to surviving his Nashville home fire (he famously raced in for his guitar, which held his reefer stash), returning to Texas to reinvent himself from suave turtleneck crooner to freaky-deaky, outlaw, ponytail, pot daddy. And, of course, that voice… twangy like a rusty screen door that needs fixing, but still sounds like home.

Using *Oxford Town* letterhead, I wrote up an official interview request and sent it to Willie's public relations firm. After a couple of follow-up phone calls, to my surprise, I was actually granted an interview with Willie to be conducted after the Tunica show.

I was given instructions to meet Willie's bus after the show and contact his road manager, Dave Anderson. I had already met Willie's longtime head roadie, Poodie Locke, a barrel-chested Texan with shoulder-length Willie hair. He handled Trigger, Willie's battered guitar that is so legendary, it's had a documentary made about it. The guitar is a Martin N-20 nylon-stringed classical guitar that, over the years, developed a second hole after decades of furious strumming by its road warrior owner. Back in Poodie's skinnier tequila youth, when he walked on stage carrying the guitar to set it into its guitar holder, audiences would often burst into applause, thinking he was Willie. Most of Willie's crew had been with him for decades.

Poodie became an Austin celeb and even had his own night club, Poodie's, outside Austin. The logo was a profile silhouette, ala Hitchcock, of his ponytail and monumental beer gut. I met Poodie through Semmes Luckett, a legendary Ole Miss alum who had such a curious thirst for knowledge, he had academic credit hours in five different decades. Semmes went on to a career in the hospitality industry in Aspen, where he would meet and provide crafty counsel for mountain crazies like Hunter Thompson, Jack Nicholson and notorious surfer trash Jimmy Buffett. I knew if I spotted Poodie I could drop Semmes' name.

For once, I was prepared. I had actually come up with about 30 questions. The last thing I wanted was awkward dead air with Willie. I had a large notebook with me and filled a page and a half. We may think we know our idols because we read so much about them and pay attention. But the idea of actually sitting across from Willie Nelson… for some reason, though I knew I would be star struck, I felt an odd serenity. I thought if I could just make him laugh once, it would break the ice and we would just be two dudes kicking it…

After a two-hour and twenty-minute show at Sam's Town, in which Willie had to be the only country music performer to ever segue from Jimmy Cliff into Hank Williams, the audience started filing out and I headed toward the stage. I immediately spotted Poodie, who had his back to the house, doing roadie stuff. I called out, "Poodie."

"Yeah," he said, not turning around.

"I was looking for Dave Anderson. I got an interview lined up with Willie. I'm Dees, old friend of Semmes Luckett." He took hearing Semmes' name in stride and didn't look up from his business until he was ready and done. After more brief fiddling, he turned and walked toward me and shook hands. "We met in Biloxi a while back," I said. "How are you?"

"Good, man," he rasped. I could tell he didn't remember meeting me but I was good with that. After decades of shows, thousands of miles in hotel rooms of forgotten cities, not to mention funny cigarettes, I can imagine a certain blur sets in. He led me over to Willie's tour bus, the Honeysuckle Rose II.

"Hey, Dave, this guy says he's set up with you?" Dave and I shook hands, and within minutes I was seated across from Willie in that diner booth, a picture of Willie and Keith Richards staring out on the wall behind Willie.

"How ya doing?" Willie said, holding out his hand.

We shook hands.

"Doing great, Willie. Thanks for talking to me."

In that instant, I made up my mind not to be freaked by his large, radar-like eyes, the fact that I'd been a fan for twenty years or the picture of Keith Richards. During the drive over, I knew I wanted to start the interview with a jolt, a flash that would let him know this wouldn't be the same old *People* magazine shtick. I went weird immediately.

"You have a reggae album coming out and a blues album… Are we seeing the Nigger Willie?"

He looked at me and then broke into a big laugh, his faced creasing like a bloodhound. "Well, I hope I have some nigger in me. (*Laughter*). I know I've got some Mexican in me…but I've done blues all my life."

"It was weird out there tonight watching housewives from Senatobia dancing to Willie Nelson singing 'The Harder They Come.'"

(*Laughing*) "Yeah, they might have thought I was talking about the IRS for all we know…"

"You made your name as a writer with Patsy Cline, Ray Price, Ferlin Husky, all having huge hits on 'Crazy,' 'Night Life,' 'Hello Walls.' Now you're on a bus surrounded by people all the time. Tell me about your writing."

"Well, I don't do as much writing as I did back in the 'hungry

Willie Nelson on his tour bus

years,' as they say, when you were writing to pay the rent, or you were writing for this artist or that artist, and you had a lot of things to write for… Now I write when the mood strikes me."

"What about marijuana? Does that help you write?"

"Well, for me it's good medicine. It keeps me calm and out of trouble. (*Laughs*). And that in itself gives me more time to write songs. On the other hand, when I used to get in a lot of trouble, I wrote more songs about it. So it's a toss-up."

I laughed. So did Willie. "Right."

"Kinda like Prozac, you know, I've seen guys take that and just don't give a shit anymore. They kinda doze off." Willie chuckled. "What the fuck… get 'em back on weed, at least, you know, they go.

"At least go get something to eat…"

"That's right! On that fucking Prozac, all of a sudden they're zero."

We laughed together, and I was taken by the way he had of putting a person at ease. In listening to the tape later, I could hear my laughter was relaxed in the way I laughed with my buds. The radio up front squawked in the background, as roadies, drivers and techs geared up for a drive to St. Charles, Louisiana.

"Got just a couple more questions, Willie. I puffed a little on the way over" — putting my hand to mouth with an imaginary joint — "and thought up a bunch of stuff to ask you."

Willie looked over at his road manager, and in a request I'm sure Dave had heard thousands of times, said, "Light one up, Dave."

I tried to act nonchalant as Dave pulled a joint from his front pocket.

"You ever write a song on the golf course?"

"Not one I remember," he replied to laughter all around. Then he added, "Except maybe this one—

It was just an old Titleist II. But it did what it was intended to do. We met in the fairway, balled in the stairway, thanks to the old Titleist II.

Again we cackled like old stoners. Willie laughed deep and long.

I shuffled through my papers. "Thanks for talking to me. Not gonna keep you here all night…"

Dave lit up a joint and handed it to Willie, and Willie took a nice long draw on it and handed it to me, and just like that, I was smoking dope with Willie Nelson on his bus. I was conscious of thinking that later when I was on the way home, I would scream and dance a jig. This was, after all, a true bucket list moment and one I never necessarily wished for, but here it was. For the moment I was all business, or at least as all business as you could be smoking dope and sharing laughs with Willie. As much as I poo poo my job and miniscule salary, it was paying off right now.

"You've sung some of your songs night after night for twenty-five years. Do you ever put it on auto-pilot or think about your laundry when you're onstage?"

"You'd think I'd get tired of singing 'em, and the ones I get tired of singing, I don't sing every night. But I don't really get tired of singing 'Crazy,' 'Nightlife,' because I don't have any arrangements; I sing 'em different every time. I don't really have an act. When I do get tired of one, like I say, I'll drop it for a week and come back to it. A lot of times, I get in trouble; there's some songs I can't drop. I can't drop 'Always on My Mind' or 'On the Road Again' or 'Crazy.'

"Looks like you're busy with movies lately, *Wag the Dog* with DeNiro and Hoffman —"

"Yeah —"

"*Gone Fishin'* with Joe Pesci."

"Right. And I did one in Canada called *Half-Baked*… Doing one in October with Woody Harrelson—"

The weed was breeding over-familiarity, and I found myself saying, "Yeah, he came to Oxford recently." I blurted it out, interrupting my host — "and shot for three days on a movie about Larry Flynt."

"Did you meet him?"

"I did briefly. He had a big Rasta body guard with him who would go jogging at five a.m. with his shirt off, dreadlocks bouncing off his back, circling around the Oxford Square before dawn. You know, it wasn't too long ago in Mississippi a black guy could get in trouble fully-dressed —"

Willie laughed and coughed. "That's funny."

"Speaking of movies, I brought you a book. (I held up *Father and Son* by Larry Brown). This is by one of our writers in Oxford, Larry Brown… It's 'peckerwood mayhem' kind of stuff. It's country people stabbing and drinking…"

"Fuckin' and fightin' — " Willie chimed in.

"And then after lunch…" We both laughed. "But Larry's a good guy…and they're making movies of his stuff."

I handed the book to Willie. "He signed it to you. Read the first twenty or thirty pages or so and see if it grabs you. It's a hot little story. Kind of a country thriller. I don't know if you read much fiction…"

"That's great," he said quietly. I got the distinct impression he could give a shit. His daughter, Lana, was standing nearby. She wrote Willie's online newsletter, the *Perdernales Poo Poo*, which I'm a big fan of. Her writing echoes her dad's love of puns and silliness. I got the idea she might at least give Larry's book a look-see.

The joint had made several rounds, and I was now the opposite of nervous. I suddenly began to sound like part of his management team.

"Might be somebody in there [Larry's book] you want to play." I looked over my notes for any unasked questions. "Willie, you continue to keep up quite a touring schedule. When you gonna cut back on some of these dates, you're doing 200-250 a year?"

"I don't know," he said, taking the joint from Dave. "I seem to fare better when I'm working. I usually get in a whole lot of trouble on days off."

"What about Beck? You recently did a video with Beck?"

"Yeah, his dad is an old friend of mine, David Campbell. I did an album called *Healing Hands of Time,* and David, Beck's dad, did the arranging on that. That's where I met him. He brought him to the studio one day. And then this video thing come up, and he called and wanted me to come in and do that. And we're also gonna do the *Tonight Show*, uh, when that is, one day next month... He just won a bunch of awards last night [1997 MTV Music Video Awards]. He's a hot little kid."

Stoned journalist switched on the babble button: "He came through here, came through Memphis and played with Jim Dickinson in North Mississippi; his sons play drums and guitar. Dickinson's a producer. Beck came through, and they were doing this blues thing, and Beck got right in there with 'em. They cut a few sides right there in Memphis, and the Dickinson boys were very impressed. California kid who's just copping these blues licks, just immediately. They said he was a very nice guy too, very good in the studio, very professional. I don't know how old he is... What is he, twelve?"

Willie laughed. "Around the waist."

Laughter all around. Dave, incredibly to my glassy-eyed horror, lit another joint and sent it around. Sweet Mother of Moses, I was dealing fairly well with my current orbit. I wasn't sure I needed to fire the booster rockets and see the edge of outer space, but I also wasn't going to nerd out and tell Willie, "No thanks, I'm good." The joint came to me, and I held it while I asked my next question.

"What's it like having young sons now, Willie (Lukas and Micah, seven and eight), at this stage of your life?

"They're great," Willie said, a calm seeming to come over his already ultra-calm. "They keep you young, keep you moving. They're really a good thing to have at this stage of a guy's life. I really appreciate the kids more. Back when I was first having kids, I was still a kid myself. It was hard to be a kid and a parent. But now, I've had two or three different families, now… three or four, who knows? But each one is different. It's a comfortable thing now."

"How do you keep touring?"

"I enjoy it. I quit work a long time ago. I'm retired now. I don't do anything but play golf and music and run around, and that's not really work. I used to make it work. I used to make it really hard. You know, do everything you can do between one show and the other to try to keep from showing up for that one, you know?"

I definitely felt him on this one. Our entire staff had shown up for work in various stages of sobriety, the combo of wine and grind. Playing with pain.

I asked Willie about Farm Aid, and he said, "It's a blight on our country that we still have to have Farm Aid. We're losing 500 family farms a week. We had 8 million farms, now we're down to less than a million. That 500 a week is still clicking off; they're not on the front pages anymore, but we're still losing 'em."

I had seen a photo of Willie in top hat with Prince Charles and thought maybe he had a Princess Diana story. "Willie, I've seen a cool picture of you and Prince Charles, just wondering if you ever had the opportunity to meet Princess Di?"

"No," he said and looked genuinely hurt, as if I'd asked about a deceased family member.

Neither Willie nor Dave ever hurried me or gave an indication they were indulging me. I suppose their unhurried vibe emboldened my chatter.

At last, I looked over my notes and realized I had asked all my questions. Willie seemed to pick up on this. He reached over to the side of the table jumbled with a telephone, folded chess board, papers, cards, ash tray and pulled out a cassette. "I've been working on a new song if you'd like to hear it."

"Please, please," I said; the smoke hung in the air above us like dialogue clouds in the cartoons. I was now in a Willie Nelson cartoon.

"This is a Christmas song I'm working on called 'El Nino'. Everyone talks about El Nino as a negative thing, but it actually means 'child' as in a rebirth, a renewal. It's perfect for Christmas."

He put the cassette in, and we listened as we passed the end of the joint.

He is born. There's a reason now to carry on. Toot your horn, write another song. Love is here, seated at your table now, not living in a stable now. Love is here. So let us sing, let us sing. Love is King, Love is King.

He looked at me. I nod my head.

"Beautiful," I said. How many hours have I spent listening to Willie Nelson music, and now I was listening to Willie Nelson music with Willie Nelson. I told myself to freak out later, or you know, write it all up in an over-priced book.

Seated at your table now. Not living in a stable now. I found myself commenting on the song, "Oh, I like that," "Oh, that's good," as I would with a friend.

In the interest of politeness, I felt compelled to wind up the interview and thank him. I had thought this a couple times throughout, but made myself sit a little longer, soak it in. I had been here an hour, smoked weed with the man, and he had played me his new song.

I'm not going to compare Willie to Faulkner or 2Live Crew to neatly tie in my theme of race in America, but in his own peculiar way, Willie has been a civil rights activist. In the 1970s (about the time his cover of "Blues Eyes Crying in the Rain" crashed into national consciousness), he brought country music audiences together with the hippie youth of the day, both deeply suspicious of the other. Willie would eventually incorporate a rainbow of music into his: reggae, blues, gospel, New Orleans jazz, Tin Pan Alley, bluegrass, Texas swing. It is hard to think of a major recording artist he hasn't played with.

Willie has lent his name and time to a wide variety of social causes besides family farmers. He has promoted preservation of wild horses and bio-degradable fuels and has been one of the few country stars to support same-sex marriage, saying, "Everybody should have the chance to be miserable."

In fact, some years after my visit, Dave Anderson came out as a gay man, after road managing Willie for years. Upon hearing the news, Willie deadpanned, "And all those years, I slept alone."

It was time to leave the cartoon. I felt like Willie had won the life lottery. If you had to spend your time "playing golf and music and running around" at least Willie used his position to spread a gospel of alternatives and cheerful hope, not to mention great music. I was convinced, more than ever, of his worthiness not only as a writer and artist, but also as a human being. If only more people entered the Willie cartoon. As Texas singer/raconteur/politician Kinky Friedman called him, "the Hillbilly Dalai Lama."

We shook hands, and the front door of the bus opened, and the dream bubbles dispersed. I stepped out, and there were probably one hundred people waiting in line for an autograph. After several moments, Willie stepped out and walked over to the autograph line. It was well after midnight, but you just knew he was going to sign an album or photo, or a CD, or old magazine or even just a ticket stub, but it would be something the person would keep for the rest of their lives. That is a certain kind of power, the power to induce joy, and Willie wields it well.

As I left the bright lights of Tunica, I wondered if what had happened had really happened, or had I really been in a cartoon. And if it was a cartoon, could I take it to work on Monday to the *Oxford Eagle*?

"To live in — in this country, anywhere in the world today, and to — to — to be against giving a man what equality — cultural, educational, economic — that he's capable and responsible for, is like living in Alaska and being against snow. You've got snow. It's — it's foolish to be against it. You've got it."

William Faulkner, University of Virginia (February 20, 1958)

37

The N-Word: A Contradiction in Slurs

I had begun my interview with Willie Nelson using the word, *nigger* to throw Willie off guard a bit, to get a laugh (thankfully, he sensed I wasn't a racist asshole) and to signal this wouldn't be a boring, paint-by-numbers interview. I didn't use the word lightly, but I have to say, I felt more comfortable using it in 1997, than I would now. The word has been used in literature in non-vicious ways by Mark Twain and William Faulkner and, more recently, by the late, great Barry Hannah. A decade later, filmmaker Quentin Tarantino would dine out on repeated uses in his work. In 1997, I thought it had an edgy, even jazzy quality to it. It's sad to note that as I write this, twenty years later, race relations have regressed so precipitously, I would never use the word even in a faux-hipster vein trying to get an edgy laugh. With the deterioration of race relations in America, the climate is so fraught with frayed nerves and bruised feelings burned to raw, combustible endings, the word is verbal dynamite.

Richard Pryor, who spewed the word repeatedly during his career, famously repudiated its use in his 1982 film, *Live on the Sunset Strip,* following a soul-searching trip to Kenya. With the later explosion of hip-hop culture, the word once again found favor among many artists.

In a 2005 *New York Times* op-ed piece, Derrick Z. Jackson wrote: "In 1993, Snoop Dogg said he used the word because 'it's me.'"

In 1996, Def Jam founder Russell Simmons said, "When we say 'nigger' now, it's very positive."

Actor and rapper Ice Cube claimed the word was a defiant "badge of honor."

In an interview on NBC's *Today* show, rapper 50 Cent said of his incessant use of the N-word: "I'm not using it as a racial slur.... It's just slang."

Back in 1997, I certainly would pick my spots in saying the word out loud. In 1996, the highly-acclaimed NBC television drama *NYPD Blue* caused a national stir when a character uttered the word in anger, perhaps a first for American television. That episode and the resulting editorial clamor, plus the Ole Miss image review of 1997, caused me (as a liberal Mississippian) to delve further into its use. After interviews and a bit of pre-Google research — Heaven forbid, I actually had to visit a library and photocopy book entries — here's what I wrote that year:

"A recent front-page story in *USA Today* proclaimed, 'NYPD Blue Tackles the N-Word.' The episode, the first for the show written by a black screenwriter, dealt with the repercussions of a white police officer calling a black officer a nigger. The show's content was considered newsworthy and demonstrated once again the power of the dreaded N-Word.

"After 200 years of racial turmoil and even war, America still hasn't retired this word. From Jim Crow to 'gangsta rap,' from Mark Twain to *Pulp Fiction*, this country has juggled this epithet like no other. Just last year (1996), all the complexity and undercurrents of this slur were once again brought to the fore by Detective Mark Furhman's use of it during O.J. Simpson's 'Trial of the Century.' Suddenly, 'nigger' became national breakfast conversation.

"Two simple syllables. Yet, so explosive, so vile, Dan Rather and others couldn't even bring themselves to say it. It was reported as simply 'the N-word.' As with most epithets, those being slurred have no such hesitation. *Nigger* has long been used among blacks as an endearment or greeting. Langston Hughes, during the height of the Harlem Renaissance in the late 1930s, was quoted as saying of Zora Neale Hurston, 'She is certainly the most amusing of all the Niggerati.'

"Today the word raps forth from urban radio formats day and night and is played for laughs by numerous African-American comedians on *Def Comedy Jam*.

"Indeed, Bondie Gambrell, a black community activist in Los Angeles was quoted in that city's newspaper as saying, 'Yes, I use it privately in my conversations with my friends. There is such a contradiction in how it's used by so many different people, including blacks, that sometimes you cannot come up with a clear, concise stance on who should use it and who shouldn't use it and when.'"

So what is the status of this word that won't go away? Is it a greeting, a term of endearment, comic fodder or is it, as [O.J. Simpson murder trial] Judge Ito assessed, "perhaps the single most insulting, inflammatory and provocative term in use in modern-day America?"

For answers, I went to the Ole Miss library, a notion that now seems charmingly quaint in our online, on-demand, finger-touch world. The librarian asked if she could help me, and I told her I was researching the origins of a certain word.

"Very well," she said in her sweet Southern accent, turning to her computer terminal, "What's the word?"

I looked from side to side then whispered, "Nigger."

She froze momentarily, grimaced and began typing. Another librarian walked past and overheard. "What's the word?" she asked helpfully. The first librarian looked around, covered her mouth and said, "Nigger."

"Oh, my."

The three of us huddled over the computer as if to contain deadly nerve gas from seeping out. I could've sworn I heard a police siren off in the distance. The librarian quickly handed me the printout of various reference books, five pages of listings on over-sized computer paper with the holes running up and down each side. She shuddered with relief, and I walked out as if I was carrying kryptonite. (I wasn't immune to the discomfort either. When it came time to name this story on the computer I hesitated to call it "nigger." Just didn't want to see that word at the top of the page and listed in my documents. Or discovered if the FBI ever busted in and sacked my hard drive.)

The word "nigger" seems to have derived from the Latin "niger," for black, and was used in the British slave trade around 1587 as "negar" or "neeger" in an attempt to pronounce the Spanish word "negro." Other scholars believe it could have evolved from the French word, "negre." At any rate, it's current spelling and usage appeared in 1786 by Robert Burns, "How graceless Ham laugh at his dad, Which made Cannan a nigger," and by Lord Byron in 1811, "… the rest of the world — niggers and what not." Though still racist, the word was used rather benignly without its overt rancor in the years surrounding the Civil War.

"Steam nigger" was a power-propelled lever for adjusting logs at a sawmill. "Niggerhead panther" referred to a hard-rock mining formation. "Niggerheads" were the drums of a steam capstan and "nigger heaven" was a widely used term for the upper berth of a passenger train sleeping compartment or the balcony in a theatre. President Woodrow Wilson used the common phrase, "nigger in the woodpile" (denoting a defect or flaw) in public in 1911, as did the *Cambridge Daily News* as late as 1930. H.L. Mencken wrote of "nigger-lice" in 1940.

Exactly when the word was outlawed by polite society is hard to pin-point, but certainly it catapulted into rancorous use on May 17, 1954. That was the date the Supreme Court ruled "separate but equal" schools were unconstitutional in the famous *Brown vs. Board of Education* case. In the years following that ruling, white people could be divided into two distinct camps by whether or not they used the word. Some even developed the hybrid "neegra" to straddle the fence, depending on to whom they were talking.

In recent years, the word, while firmly forbidden like an obscenity, seems to have made a "comeback" and has morphed into a catch-all for most any race. In the aforementioned *Pulp Fiction* (1994), Samuel L. Jackson's character says he is going to "chill them niggers out," and he is pointedly referring to white characters. Queen Latifah, a prominent rapper-turned-mainstream TV star, was quoted in *Newsweek* referring to the U.S. federal government: "Those niggers don't know what the fuck they doing."

So just who is allowed to say it and to whom? In September 1997, soon after my smoky, wondrous encounter with Willie Nelson, in which I had sprung the word on him rather abruptly, I interviewed a classroom of black college students, young men and women born in the late 1970s for whom the civil rights movement and even Richard Pryor ("That Nigger's Crazy") were the stuff of history books. What was their take on this word? They used it, heard it on all their favorite songs and in comedy clubs. And yet, I suspected that few, if any, had ever been called a "nigger" with malice by an angry white person.

I called on English professor Doug Branch, and he graciously allowed me to meet with his freshman class at Rust College, a historically black college in Holly Springs, Mississippi, some twenty miles north of Oxford. I met them on the third floor of the Doxey Building to discuss "The Word." The students, all black, were a perfect geographical mix, hailing from Chicago; Cleveland, Ohio; Clarksdale, Mississippi and Kenya, Africa. It was still hard to say the word in front of them at first. There was an undeniable strangeness, sitting in front of a group of black people, in the teacher's chair, no less, saying "nigger" repeatedly.

After the first time (and no one flinched), I found myself saying it a few more times than necessary in some kind of embarrassed attempt to neutralize it. Finally, when I was comfortable, the students really opened up.

"When one race has experienced injustices from the other race," Antoya from Cleveland said, "and they call you that, it's not humor anymore."

Cheryl, also from Cleveland, added, "A nigger is a stupid person, so it really doesn't affect me."

"There's too many other words in the English language," Keith of Chicago pointed out. "Like homey, my black man, my brother. What's up, man?"

"But you call each other nigger, don't you?"

"We say, 'nigga' G-A, not nigger, G-E-R."

"Ah, nigga…"

"You know like, "Niggaz With Attitude. NIGGAZZ!"

"NIGGAZ, NIGGAZ…" several chanted.

"Wow, a differentiation between 'nigger' and 'nigga.'"

"Yeah," Antoya continued, "Tupac has that song, '**N**ever **I**gnorant **G**etting **G**oals **A**ccomplished', it's on his album, *Tupacalypse Now.*

"Nigga is like the word 'bad,'" Cheryl explained. "The meaning of it has totally changed and now 'bad' means good."

"Yeah," I said, "but 'nigger' and 'nigga' — come on, we're splitting Afros here, aren't we?" I waited. They didn't get the reference.

"I mean where's the difference?"

Keith (pointing to his heart): "It's what's in here and where you're coming from.

Cheryl: "I had one white friend who could say it, and I would just laugh because I knew where he was coming from."

Baron, from Kenya: "In Kenya, the white people there don't really think of us as 'niggers.' They think of us as Africans. I've never heard a white man call a black man a 'nigger.'"

"Okay," I said. "Let me pose this one. Have any of you ever been called a 'nigger' by a white person in anger? Who was saying it in a racist, threatening way?"

The class mulled the question collectively, many shaking their heads and finally, there were no hands raised. Well, I thought, at least one of my pre-conceived notions held up.

I forget how much energy you get by osmosis hanging out with young people. I left feeling good about the future of the country. Still, I didn't feel I'd satisfied my quest to find the true meaning of the word, to put to bed the myth, but, nonetheless, my visit with the class was instructive. I had never heard the "niggas" versus "niggers" distinction, for example, but I still didn't feel like I had reached any concrete conclusions regarding the word. I have to admit I laughed when it was used in *Pulp Fiction,* and I still think the word possesses power, even positive power, if used effectively in literature and art, even by white people. John Lennon's "Woman Is the Nigger of the World" comes to mind. There's a rap song by Umar Bin Hassan called "Niggers Are Scared of Revolution." (Note "nigger," not "nigga.") The point of the song seemed to be that people who care only for crack or gangs will never be able to fully affect their freedom from oppression.

So what's the answer? Is a slur simply a slur? Or is racism in the eye of the beholder? Perhaps it's like the Supreme Court's ruling on obscenity; i.e., "I can't define it, but I know it when I see it." Maybe white people will never fully understand this word any more than they understood why black people applauded the O.J. verdict. Or perhaps it's simply as Keith of Chicago said: "It's what's in your heart, where you're coming from."

• • •

On the drive back from Holly Springs, I pulled into a rural beer store and put a six pack on the counter. A congenial black man rang up my purchase. I had been to the reference books; I had gotten the international student's perspective, so I couldn't resist an everyman-on-the-street take.

"Sir, I don't mean any disrespect," I said, starting before I could stop myself. "I'm a writer working on a story on race relations. I was wondering if you would mind telling me what the word 'nigger' means to you?"

He glared at me momentarily, shifting a cigar from one side of his mouth to the other. His brow furrowed as my anus tightened.

"It don't mean nothing to me, but I can tell you what it means to you," he said raising his finger, leaning in closer.

"OK."

"It means yo' ass."

"Right," I said, taking the beer. "Thanks a lot."

Thus endeth the lesson.

38

On September 11, one of the most lovable characters of the Civil Rights era made a comeback when the Reverend Will D. Campbell was finally invited back to the Ole Miss campus after being chased away in the 1950s for his liberal views on race. He spoke at the Student Union ballroom under the title: "Looking Back: Religion at Ole Miss."

In my research before I met him, I determined that he was truly a man of God but also a man of goats…and whiskey.

As historian Charles Engles wrote, "Barely three months after the U.S. Supreme Court ruled against school segregation in its May 1954 *Brown v. Board of Education* decision, Will Campbell became director of religious life at the University of Mississippi. The thirty-year-old Baptist preacher would later become a maverick, unofficial pastor to the civil rights movement, an outspoken prophet to Southern Protestants and a popular author."

Campbell proved to be a maverick, all right. It is difficult to grasp, so many decades now removed, how much courage Campbell and others of the era displayed in being sensitive to Negro rights in the 1950s and '60s, and being called the dreaded "nigger lover." People were killed as a matter of common practice during these years, almost a decade before the case of the three civil rights workers ambushed and shot near Philadelphia, Mississippi, brought the heat of national revulsion. It was simply a very vicious, mean time.

For all his humor and grace, Campbell would soon become one of the most despised men in the state of Mississippi. So reviled, he was actually removed from his position as director of religious life at Ole Miss and more or less obliged to flee the state of Mississippi under extreme duress. And what was his crime? He invited a speaker to campus who announced he was donating part of his recent quiz show winnings ($32,000 on *The $64,000 Question*) to the NAACP.

Longtime Southern journalist Curtis Wilkie wrote that it was even more comical than that: "Before I enrolled at Ole Miss, Will had been run off as school chaplain for playing ping-pong with a black man."

As usual with Mississippi and race, the truth was simple and complicated, tragic and hilarious.

Eminent Mississippi historian Dr. David Sansing explicates the details in his first-rate *The University of Mississippi: A Sesquicentennial History*: "The white power structure's determination to cordon off Mississippi's college campuses from the outside world was manifested at Ole Miss in the fall of 1955 when Will Campbell, director of religious life at the university, invited Reverend Alvin Kershaw to participate in the annual religious emphasis week. Kershaw's invitation was part of Campbell's larger plan to engage the issue of racial injustice in Mississippi. Reverend Kershaw won a large sum of money on a popular television quiz show and announced that he would contribute part of his winnings to the NAACP. The announcement that the university invited a speaker for religious emphasis week who praised and financed the work of the NAACP prompted, as Campbell anticipated, a stormy debate and a demand that the university withdraw the invitation."

Indeed, as Sansing further points out, the incident led to a speaker's approval bureau being set up by the governor's office to have a (racist) bureaucrat approve any speakers invited to campuses, not just at Ole Miss, but across the state. Writers took on censorship during this era in their own ways. Years earlier, in his novel *Sanctuary*, Faulkner named the Memphis whorehouse madam Reba Rivers' lap dog "Mr. Binford" as a salute to the head of the Memphis board of censors, Lloyd T. Binford.

An interesting side note is that Reverend Kershaw won the quiz show money due, in part, to his expertise in jazz. He later became chaplain for the George Lewis New Orleans Jazz Band and wrote a Bach cantata into his services in the 1950s.

Campbell's liberal leanings (and for 1950s Mississippi, he was radical) led to his being denounced and then shunned. In 1957, he escorted the "Little Rock Nine" as they integrated Central High School in Little Rock, Arkansas. Later that year, he was the only white person invited to the founding of the Southern Christian Leadership Conference at the Ebenezer Baptist Church in Atlanta with the Reverend Martin Luther King, Jr. He eventually moved into an old farmhouse outside Nashville and wrote some twenty books and became an in-demand lecturer, activist, and "bootleg preacher." Not bad for a poor boy born on a hard-scrabble farm in Liberty, Mississippi, Amite County.

Campbell died in 2013 at age eighty-eight.

It is worth noting that Campbell's troubles took place in 1955. The Meredith crisis (that left two dead and hundreds injured) was in 1962. Other dust-ups concerning the Confederate flag and racism continued until 1997, when the UM Chancellor received death threats over his study of university symbols. When battles run one hundred years without resolution and cross a century, it begins to feel Biblical, almost like the Middle East. Burning, but never quite burning completely out until a gush of wind kicks up the flames again.

The *New York Times* obituary, as is often the case, published a poetic summation of Campbell's character: "A knot of contradictions himself, he was a civil rights advocate who drank whiskey with Klansmen, a writer who layered fact and fiction and a preacher without a church who presided at weddings, baptisms and funerals in homes, hospitals and graveyards for a flock of like-minded rebels that included Johnny Cash, Willie Nelson, Dick Gregory, Jules Feiffer and Studs Terkel.

"Most of his scattered 'congregation,' however," the *Times* continued, "were poor whites and blacks, plain people alienated from mainstream Christianity and wary of institutions, churches and governments that stood for progress but that in their view achieved little. He once conducted a funeral for a ghost town, Golden Pond, Kentucky, where the residents had been removed in the late 1960s to make way for a Tennessee Valley Authority project."

Campbell told late author John Egerton: "I never took it all that seriously. I always thought it was better to reach out to people with humor than with erudition — or fear, which seems to be the weapon of choice of the electronic soul molesters, otherwise known as TV preachers."

Campbell was serious — and seriously funny, but he was also a scholar. After earning a degree at Wake Forest, he attended graduate school at Tulane University in New Orleans, then entered the Yale University Divinity School, earning his doctorate in 1952. After his Ole Miss tenure, Campbell spent ten years working with the national Council of Churches as their Southern liaison before falling out with them. He began freelancing and officially split from the Southern Baptists.

"I consider myself a 'Seventh-Day Horizontal,'" he told Wilkie.

He wore overalls or cowboy clothes, raised goats and corn for moonshine and published a series of books, including a National Book Award finalist, a memoir of his brother's drug addiction, *Brother to a Dragonfly*. With his wife and three children, Campbell traveled as a social justice advocate and preacher with "a call but no steeple."

By 1965, he had settled his family on a small farm near Mt. Juliet, northeast of Nashville, and from that base he built a national reputation as a writer and speaker and the "personal shepherd to a scattered and eclectic flock of unconventional Christians."

His fame was further etched into popular culture, much to his chagrin, as the caricature for the "Reverend Will B. Dunn" in the Doug Marlette comic strip *Kudzu*.

One of his most treasured books is his hilarious memoir, *Forty Acres and a Mule*. He explained the book's title: "The KAs had abused this goat at Mercer College (Macon, Georgia) where I was teaching. They abandoned it, I guess as a fraternity prank. I adopted it and decided to take it home with me, which was six hours away to Nashville. My wife and kids were waiting for me in the car, and I show up with this goat. My wife was appalled. We're driving six hours, locked up with a goat with the heat on. She said, 'We're trash, poor white trash.'

"Well, at the time we just happened to be driving a Mercedes, one of the few you saw on the road at that time. I told her, 'We're not trash. Trash don't haul no goat in a Mercedes.' I named the goat, Jackson, after the old general. He lived with us for seventeen years."

Will could mix humor and pathos with a sure hand, taking the audience from guffaws to tears in seconds, all the while not seeming to try. He recited the song, "Mississippi, You're on My Mind," the beautiful paean to our state made famous by Jerry Jeff Walker and others. He spoke of meeting the song's author, Jesse Winchester, whom Campbell encountered in Toronto during the Vietnam War. Winchester, also a Mississippi native, was exiled there as a conscientious objector to the war. Campbell had counseled many such young men during his many visits to Canada:

"At one of our meetings with the objectors, Jesse stood up and quietly played that song and brought a hush to the crowd, all of whom were missing some place or somebody. The boy was anguished and missed his home ground."

"It was their conscience to which I was reacting," Will said of those who fled the draft, "not mine. I'd help them get back to their ship or their base, if that was their choice."

In 2002, the publisher David Magee and I drove up to Mount Juliet to talk to Will and spend an afternoon with him. When we knocked on his door, we were greeted by his wife of sixty years, Brenda, who directed us to a small log cabin sitting farther back on their property.

"I shoo him out of here early," she said cheerfully, giving us an immediate snapshot of their relationship. The cabin turned out to be Will's office, comfortably furnished with chairs and sofa, also beset with animal heads and skins, a shelf stuffed with books, a desk, his computer, the back wall decorated with a large Western painting of Indian ephemera. The whole vibe was a man cave for the studious.

"All the modern inconveniences," Will noted, quoting Twain as he waved at his phone and work desk. The highlight of the day was when we went out for lunch at his favorite BBQ place, which turned out to be an all-black establishment. We entered and were seated and appeared to be the only white people for miles. During the course of the meal, David and Will discussed terms of the agreement, which was sparse given our start-up status. Will was gracious and agreeable.

"I'm just happy to see the book have a new life. We need goats now more than ever," he told us.

As we ate, the owner stopped over to shake Will's hand and greet him. Then a couple sitting across from us. Then someone from the kitchen, then the cashier. David and I sat back and watched pure love occur. In all, a dozen people, waitresses and cooks and some of the patrons all came over to the table not just to shake Will's hand but to kiss him. It was one of the most genuine displays of affection I've ever seen. I remember thinking that I was glad Will lived long enough to be rewarded with this moment (and I'm sure many others like it in many of his travels) after all the hate he endured. I looked over at David, and we both smiled knowing David was going to publish Will's book, and we were going to have a part in bringing Will back to Mississippi. You forget how good proud joy feels until it washes over you like happy surf.

It is difficult in our present-day world to imagine how much courage it took for Will D. Campbell to do what he did when he did it. You could get tortured and shot just for whistling back in his time. Campbell stood up to the most enflamed issues of his day, the meanest people and the worst of times and walked tall. He died peacefully and married to the same woman. He cloaked himself in scripture and the ways of the Good Book, but made it seem cool. He wasn't averse to a glass of Jack Daniels on ice. He certainly had no problem with goats, even giving them a lift.

I'm glad Oxford had the good sense to make peace with Brother Will before he made his final passage. May he — and Jackson — rest in peace.

"*A monument only says* At least I got this far
while a footprint says This is where I was when I moved again."
William Faulkner, *The Town* (1957)

39

Home Again

September 16 dawned warm and gray like pipe smoke. Fall was only a week away, but summer has legs in Yoknapatawpha. On this day, the temperature would nudge eighty degrees before sculptor Bill Beckwith and I reached Byhalia on the ride to Memphis to pick up Beckwith's Faulkner statue. We were up early enough to still see coffee steam in the false morning coolness. For Bill Beckwith, slow heat was something he had endured all summer while his sculpture of Faulkner was ninety miles away in Memphis undergoing its finishing touches by the foundry workers.

The deadline of September 25 had pounded toward him like the inevitable Dixie Flyer, but he couldn't jump off the tracks. The statue was literally out of his hands. Since Beckwith's delivery of it on May 15, it had undergone its final waxing and bronzing. Beckwith said the foundry owner, Larry Lugar, told him there was a statue ahead of Faulkner…a full-length likeness of Elvis clutching a guitar and swaying on his tip-toes. The piece was slated for a Memphis city park near Beale Street.

"Not merely endure, but wail," I said.

Beckwith laughed. It had been a long, hot summer. The very existence and location of his heralded piece wasn't entirely, officially finalized until a month before the scheduled unveiling.

"I saw it slipping away several times," he said of the public dust-up, aldermen votes and the myriad legal machinations. He had spent the slow dog days working like one, doing repairs around the house and preparing for his next commission, Lady Justice holding scales, to be placed in front of the courthouse of Lamar County. By late June, while the Mississippi attorney general's office was reviewing a possible injunction to prevent the pouring of concrete to begin construction at Oxford's City Hall, Beckwith waited for the call from the foundry telling him to retrieve his piece.

Arthur Hirsch of *The Baltimore Sun* grasped the story better than most in the national media: "Of all the players in this Southern drama, Faulkner probably would have identified most strongly with Beckwith, the struggling artist trying to work in peace. The commotion, says Beckwith, 'made my life hell for a long time. I never knew if I had the job or not. I couldn't concentrate on the piece for this controversy.'"

Eventually, though, he got down to business in the spring, five months after he signed the contract. The form of Faulkner rose from Beckwith's armature over the next eight weeks, about the same amount of time Faulkner had said it took him to write his fifth novel, *As I Lay Dying.*

"I'm well satisfied with it," Beckwith sighed. "I wanted a kind of intense, inward feeling. I wanted that intensity. His books are like that."

I asked Beckwith, "What was it like, waiting for the foundry to call?"

"Toward the end," he mused, "I had gotten nervous. I called them about every day." In mid-September, a mere ten days before the unveiling, which felt like only a few hours, the foundry finally called Beckwith.

Come get him.

"As you entered the room the thing drew your eyes: you turned sharply as to a sound, expecting movement. But it was marble it could not move… on looking again it was before: motionless and passionately eternal."

William Faulkner, *Mosquitoes* (1927)

40

We arrived at Lugar Foundry, and there was the statue, William Faulkner wearing a hat, seated on a bench, holding his pipe. The piece was dangling in a doorway, hanging from a 3,000-pound hoist. Seeing the life-like image seated there was startling and had a strange, profound effect, as if there were a real person sitting there.

He seemed to have emotions and a spirit.

Maybe it was the quick-mart coffee, but I felt like he was there with us in some kind of otherworldly, freakish, yet soothing kind of way. The figure, with his head tilted back and the legs jauntily crossed, had the presence of a real person. As the foundry workers began alternately wetting then drying the piece with propane blowers, I mentioned the eerie resemblance and the "passionately eternal" human quality to Bill.

"Yeah, the scale is so life-like on this piece — when they're bigger or smaller than life, you get a different sense. When I was working on him at Taylor, I'd have the big doors open, and it was like somebody was walking across the door. I sort of could see it and sort of sense it and just sort of feel it. There was a presence or a visitation or a something, and it happened a lot, like almost every day. There'd be a presence you'd feel. But I was comfortable with the presence — it wasn't a scary thing."

"Has that happened in the past or just on this piece?"

"Just on this piece."

Faulkner at the foundry

"[The artist] can't live forever. He knows that… He can build a bridge and will be remembered for a day or two, but somehow the picture, the poem — that lasts a long time, a very long time, longer than anything."

Faulkner quoted in *Lion in the Garden* (1980)

41

"What's the best part about getting up here and picking this thing up?" I asked, as we watched the workers continue the wetting and drying process.

"I couldn't wait to get up here and see if he was finally in a permanent material. That he had that permanence that I strive for. The piece could be melted, I guess, but that would be a whole chore in itself."

"Will it still be here in 1,000 years?"

"Yeah, should be. Those Greek bronzes and Etruscan bronzes are still around. The immortality of it is kind of exciting... It's also scary, the possibility of critics from now on being able to criticize it."

"Right. You've had one year of critics; now you'll have a thousand."

After a year of all the threats and lawyers and headlines, here Bill Beckwith stood with his creation in its finished stage, its state of permanence. One week away from the end of summer and Faulkner's birthday. As he stood and watched the crew make final preps to load it onto Beckwith's truck, he explained the propane, wax and patina had to be rather painstakingly applied and reapplied in a rinse-and-repeat cycle.

"They had to pull all the wax, which takes a long time. Once they had the wax ready, I brought the bench up here. The wax figure had to be fitted to the bench.

"Then they cut him into eight sections, which makes it more manageable. Then ceramic shell molds were made, which also take a long time.

"Then the process of slurry, stucco, slurry, stucco, back and forth. After that, the piece had to be reinforced with wire and fiberglass. When all that was done, they thrust him into an atmosphere of 1,850 degrees," he said, shaking his head. "They normally need six months to do all that, and this time, they had four."

The foundry crew, owner Larry Lugar and his helpers, Diane Hamberlin and Ann Moore, bustled about like people on a deadline. The trio busted their ass all day on finishing touches prior to Beckwith's arrival. These included sandblasting the piece and spraying it with ferric nitrate. The sculpture was then heated up with propane torches to "open the pores." With the pores open, the patina — or color — was brushed on, and then dried with the torches, painted on again, then dried, back and forth for most of the afternoon. Once the coloring was completely applied and dried, the wax was applied, and the sculpture was completed — at least that stage of it.

"It will change colors over time," Beckwith said. "We'll get a good indication of what's in the Oxford rain water. I imagine it will turn a little darker over the years."

The crew used the 3,000-pound hoist to get the statue onto special ramps Beckwith had built. At five that afternoon, all was finally done, and the crew began pushing Mr. Faulkner up the ramp onto Beckwith's truck. I couldn't help but add my hands to the effort.

It felt like being a pallbearer in reverse.

We were taking him out into the light, giving the great artist a new life. The statue sat upright with its legs crossed and looked so life-like, I tried to buckle Faulkner's seatbelt for him.

Faulkner on Beckwith's truck

"He stood on a stone pedestal, in his frock coat and bareheaded, one leg slightly advanced and one hand resting lightly on the stone pylon beside him. His head was lifted a little in that gesture of haughty pride which repeated itself generation after generation with a fateful fidelity, his back to the world and his craven eyes gazing out across the valley… and the blue changeless hills beyond, and beyond that, the ramparts of infinity itself."

Faulkner, *Sartoris* (1929)

42

For the ride back, Beckwith eschewed a tarpaulin, and we rode with the statue just sitting in the back of the truck. The drive took us from Eads, Tennessee, into the bright sunshine and noise of rush hour in Collierville. Funny how no one, not a single vehicle, honked the horn to ask about the statue. We got a few waves of the hand. Finally, the suburbs played out, and we drove through grassy countryside. I kept looking back at the statue nervously, trying to not make Bill nervous. Had it been anyone else who had strapped the piece down, I'd really worry, but Beckwith gives the air of one who has done this before. I would look back and, in my mind's eye, would imagine one of the straps coming loose and the statue wobbling off the back of the truck, airborne for a second, then thudding onto the pavement, exploding into several pieces and scattering in all directions. A thousand pounds of literature and history, not to mention elbow grease and ulcers, reduced to smithereens.

But it didn't happen. Finally, I was able to just stare ahead, though I noticed Beckwith was using caution and driving under the speed limit. We crossed into Mississippi and reached Byhalia. As the truck twisted through the narrow streets of the town in which Faulkner had died, I had to look back at the statue and feel proud for Faulkner and his triumph. Faulkner was taken to Byhalia numerous times over the years to a sanitarium there where he would dry out and receive rest and treatment after particularly heavy drinking binges. He knew the staff and they him. It was not a happy locale for him, and indeed it is where he drew his last breath with bruised bones in July 1962.

This would be his last pass through town. Faulkner sat above the traffic, but he took it all in; he seemed to scowl at people on their phones, laughing at kids playing soccer.

"I won't finally breathe easy until he's sitting in his spot on the Square," Beckwith said, anxiously glancing back through the rearview mirror. A carload of young kids squealed by, oblivious to the bronze.

"I put that hat on Mr. Faulkner to give him some privacy. That hat defines that little area as his."

I looked back at the figure. "It looks so real I'm wondering why it doesn't blow off."

Beckwith chuckled. "It's a good fit. The whole body language of the piece is not open. It's closed on purpose," he continued. "For privacy, the legs are crossed, and the arms are crossed to lead the eye back to the head. Even in a crowd of tourists, he's alone, lost in his own thoughts."

We grew silent, until we hit the Tallahatchie Bridge and drove into Lafayette County.

"I know this road," Beckwith said, beaming, lighting a victory cigar. "I could push it home from here."

We pulled into Taylor, to Beckwith's shop right next door to the catfish place, which seemed empty and forlorn all closed up. The fading sunset shone off the burnished figure, making it look more like a statue. Today we had made it through the blue hills and back to the

Yocona bottom. Tomorrow, Bill would drive the statue into Oxford, where it would be placed on the right side of the Square. Henceforth — for 1,000 years — drivers will see, to update Faulkner from *The Sound and the Fury* — "…the square facades flow by smoothly, left to right; post and tree, window and doorway," and now statue, "each in its ordered place."

The hushed plaint of wind in stricken trees
Shivers the grass in path and lane
And Grief and Time are tideless golden seas-
Hush, hush! He's home again

Faulkner, *An Armistice Day Poem* (1925)

43

September 25
Unveiling Day

Gray and overcast with intermittent drizzle greeted the day that had finally arrived. For so ugly a day, it was hard to wipe the smile off Bill Beckwith's face. The year-long pressure bubbling around him every day as he sweated over his beloved Faulkner was now over. The critics and gossipers and the ill-informed could flap their lips all they wanted. He put on a tie and a favorite sport coat and stood ready to show the statue to the world, in its eternal position in front of City Hall, and he would cash the check, and everybody could kiss his ass. At least, that would have been my attitude.

Before the unveiling, a press conference was held adjacent to the statue site in what is now Square Books Jr., a children's bookstore, or as they say now, "young adult." Here were gathered the speakers at the event, the Right Reverend A.C. Marble, Jr. of the Episcopal Diocese of Mississippi; U.S. District Judge Neal Biggers; authors Shelby Foote and Willie Morris and the blowhard keynote speaker, former Indiana Congressman John Brademas.

Talking about the Snopes was one of Willie's favorite pastimes, especially in relating them to the present-day Republican party. I stood with about a dozen reporters and patiently waited my turn. The student TV media took up many questions, as did their print counterparts. Luckily, there is a videotape of this press conference, and it's great to see Shelby and Willie, old lions of literature still on their game, still exuding the air of the Southern reader, thinker and writer, over thirty books between them, including Shelby's mammoth, inestimable Civil War trilogy.

Shelby was ten years beyond his TV stardom years, but he still looked great, the very image of distinguished, though his voice had deepened with age. Willie looked relaxed and glowing with a decade of happy married life. Life with JoAnne in Jackson seemed to suit him. Their answers posed on this day make excellent reading, wisdom from the masters.

One of the TV reporters began by asking Shelby what kind of influence Faulkner was on him.

"He was an extremely powerful influence on me for all kinds of reasons. He was a Mississippi writer, and when *Light in August* came out in 1932, it was the first modern novel I had read. It did two things at once: one, it showed me what the novel had progressed to, and he also showed me that you could write about your homeland. I hadn't realized you could write about Mississippi. I thought you had to write about the Land of Oz or Tom Swift and His Electric Rifle or something. The main thing he did for me was show me that writing — if you're good enough at it — can communicate the sensations of things and tell a story. Dickens and some others had already taught me that but not with the same immediacy as Faulkner."

Q: Can you talk about the historical significance of today?

(Here Shelby takes a question he could answer with pabulum but

Sculptor Bill Beckwith with his creation

instead rocks it.)

Shelby Foote: "Faulkner's span of life, covering two-thirds of this century and a little bit of the one before it, is a horrendous set of years. There were probably more people murdered around the world than any other similar seventy-eight years of life, and he portrayed that along with other things. I don't mean he wrote about the concentration camps and everything, but he certainly showed the complexity of modern life. The modern world demonstrated what that complexity could lead to if it turned loose of the values that Faulkner prized highest. It was a murderous stretch of time, and his depiction of that particular corner of the world that he lived in is a sort of mirror of what was going on in the rest of the world. He took a terrible beating for that around here, where he was scorned. 'Count No Count,' various other things simply because he was reflecting a world they couldn't see but he could. Joe Christmas is a fascist, before there were any fascists and there are many such things in Faulkner's work."

Q: At what one point does a prophet become recognized in his own country?

Shelby Foote: "I don't think he ever becomes recognized. Faulkner is beyond the reach of most of us. We can pay obeisance to him, but if by recognize him, you mean appreciate him; I'm not too sure how far we go with that. He's up there with the great writers of all time in my mind. He's a great regional writer, but he's a lot more than that. I hope, in time, that the world will understand that even more than it does now. Faulkner's reputation is sort of like Dante's. Dante wouldn't be read today, except he fascinates the scholars. The literati have kept Dante alive, and so will they with Faulkner. James Joyce used to say, 'I did some work this morning that will keep the professors busy for the next one hundred years.' (Laughter) Faulkner has done some of that, too. Other writers, very good writers, their reputations have faded; that doesn't mean they won't come back. Hemingway is in a sort of trough now because he can't be interpreted the way Faulkner can be interpreted. Other writers, like John O'Hara, whom I admire greatly, have disappeared with scarcely a ripple — not that he won't come back; things swing around. But Faulkner keeps the scholars busy, and they keep people reading him and keep him in print."

Q: I heard you on NPR this morning talking about how Faulkner didn't write real well about the human heart…

Shelby Foote: "That's the thing I'll be talking about later. I consider Faulkner's Nobel speech to be a sort of betrayal of his whole career. He said you must write about the human heart or else you're just writing about the glands. Well, I just want to point out that Faulkner was one of the greatest writers about the glands that ever lived. And when he got to writing about the heart, he tended to drift off into discourses and lectures. Faulkner's later work — to my mind and to many critics' minds — doesn't measure up to *The Sound and the Fury*, *As I Lay Dying*, *Absalom, Absalom*, *Light in August*, much more powerful novels than the later novels in which Ratliff and Gavin Stevens engage in endless conversations about whether we're all going to heaven or not. But I'll also say we have to be cautious in making such judgments. They may be the most admired books of all to a later generation. But to my generation, those later five or six novels can't hold a candle to the first five or six novels. But it's all a matter of taste; what goes around comes around.

Q: Question for Mr. Morris… (My target was now in sight, moving to the podium) **Faulkner felt passionately about the land-**

scape, particularly the landscape of the Delta, where you're from. What do you think he would think of the Delta landscape of today?

Willie Morris: "Well, first of all, I would say that today, this is Faulkner weather. I hope we don't have a torrential downpour and have to move into his courthouse over here. The weather out here reminds me very much of the opening paragraph of probably my favorite Faulkner short story, 'Delta Autumn.' Uncle Ike McCaslin's last hunting trip into that last triangle of the Delta, which I always calculated to be out, kinda south of my Yazoo County — Shelby, you remember? — the 'unhurried Delta rain.' This is Faulkner weather, which means he's really with us today. In terms of the contemporary Delta, of course, Mr. Bill always relished the Delta as hill people always do. The Delta is a riotous place. Shelby has written so eloquently of the Delta because he's from Greenville. I think Faulkner was fascinated with the Delta, and some of his best stuff is set over there. I would think today, if we took off on a little trip with him on his one hundreth birthday to head over to Greenville or Yazoo City he would still be obsessed with the land itself, with the power, the beauty and the fear of the Delta landscape. It really suffused him as Delta people did. I think it would still be the land — the powerful, brooding land of the Delta. If we took him over today over to Greenville to Does Eat Place for a one hundreth birthday party — Shelby do you agree with me? ("Yeah.") I think the land itself would still obsess him."

Q: How did you discover Faulkner?

Willie Morris: "Well, I didn't start reading Faulkner until I was student at University of Texas. When I was in high school, I became obsessed with Thomas Wolfe from North Carolina. For about a year and a half, I lived my life through the pages of Thomas Wolfe. Whose uses of the language… I think he's faded some. I was Eugene Gant in Yazoo County. I started reading Faulkner my freshman year at University of Texas, and it was staggering. Faulkner's work to me — a little ole boy from Yazoo County — was like a blow to the heart. I couldn't deal with it. I started reading his short stories first. I had a professor out there at Texas, Frank Lyle, from Jackson, Mississippi, who was a very close friend of Eudora Welty. In fact, Eudora dedicated her wonderful book *Delta Wedding* to Frank Lyle. He started trying to teach me how to write. I remember the first theme I wrote for Frank Lyle was a 2,000-word autobiographical essay, which I began at a dorm room at the University of Texas, and I described my dog Skip and how he and I roamed the Delta woods, 'shooting squirrels.' And Eudora's friend Frank Lyle gave me a C-minus on my first theme and appended in the margin, 'Who was the better shot, you or the dog?'

"I was enraged. But Frank said you gotta start reading Eudora Welty and William Faulkner because you're from Mississippi. And I did, and I was consumed by both of them but in very, very different ways. (He paused and some seconds passed… no one stepped forward with a question, so I did…)

Q: "Jim Dees, from the *Oxford Eagle*

Willie Morris: Hey, Jim Dees from the *Oxford Eagle*!

Q: Touching on this other question about the landscape, 'Have the Snopeses won?' The South has changed, become homogenized; accents have slipped away; steel and glass buildings, the whole city of Atlanta where old malls go to die…"

Willie Morris: "Well, I think the Snopeses were in their heyday in Mississippi under the era of Ross Barnett, who practically disrupted this university and also whatever civility was in Mississippi in the early

1960s. The Snopses, I wouldn't say the modern-day Republicans are Snopeses; they're much more sophisticated than that in the ways of business. But I do know my old friend and classmate Bill Moyers, who was LBJ's chief of staff in the White House, when he was about to sign the Civil Rights Act of 1964, tuned to Moyers and said, 'After I sign this, this is gonna turn the South over to the Republicans in your lifetime.' I'm not saying that the modern-day Republicans are Snopeses; I think the old Barnett people of that era were much more so. I'm a good friend of Haley Barbour. I disagree with him politically. I do think the heyday of the Snopeses, in terms of power in Mississippi, was back in the '50s and '60s. I may be wrong."

Shelby interjects: "Faulkner said a funny thing about the Snopeses: 'All these people talk about I had genius, and I don't know about all that foolishness, but I know one time I had genius was when I named those people Snopes.'" (Laughter).

Willie Morris: "But also, Shelby, I've been spending a lot of time in Hollywood, which has been a strange experience. Faulkner had to go out there frequently to make a living; he couldn't make a living off his books. He remarked to Howard Hawks or somebody, 'The Snopeses are everywhere; they're multiplying; they're everywhere.' And they didn't know what he was talking about. He also said, 'A leaf drops in a canyon here, and they call it autumn.' And he also told Shelby, who was thinking about going out there to work on a screenplay with Stanley Kubrick, 'It's the only place on earth where you can get stabbed in the back while climbing a ladder.'"

A question about Faulkner's legacy in Oxford was put to Judge Neal Biggers, who demurred.

Neal Biggers: "I'm a fan of Faulkner's, but I am here merely as an introducer. I'm honored to be on a panel of such distinguished writers and scholars, and I would defer that question to Mayor Lamar or Dr. Kartiganer, who is the Faulkner scholar here in Oxford. I will say that I appreciate Willie Morris not saying that modern-day Republicans are like the Snopeses; I appreciate your not going that far, as a political appointee of Ronald Reagan. Mayor Lamar is a recently-elected Republican official."

Willie Morris: "But you are still members of the same party of Thaddeus Stevens and William Tecumseh Sherman."

Neal Biggers: "Whatever that means. (Laughter). I will tell you one story that just occurred yesterday, and that's about all I will say about Faulkner, even though I'm a great fan of his. Dean Faulkner Wells, who was raised by Faulkner, was invited by Bill Beckwith and Mayor Lamar to come to City Hall yesterday at three o'clock to come look at the statue before they moved it out. They were going to move it out at four, so she got there at three. She thought the statue was great. Very impressed with it. She told me last night that while they were looking at it, they were told to move aside, that they were going to move it outside. They brought in convicts to move him. Convicts gathered around the statue and picked him up. And she said Pappy would have loved that. (Laughter) As they went to pick him up, one of the convicts, and I won't quote him verbatim, but he said, *Hmm, this MF heavy.* (Laughter) He didn't say MF. And she said he would have loved that. So that's a little insight into how some people feel about him."

Shelby Foote: "Funny thing about the Snopeses with their rascality and everything else, there never was any mention of belonging to or having anything to do with the Ku Klux Klan. Faulkner left it out. Very strange."

Q: You mentioned Faulkner being out of the reach of most

people. Can you talk about the significance of this day for regular people?

Shelby Foote: "Faulkner is more accessible than he has a reputation for being. When Faulkner's books first came out in paperback released by Signet, New American Library in New York, they were the very best-selling paperbacks anywhere around. Truck drivers read Faulkner with enormous pleasure. They didn't care whether he put in or took out commas; they didn't care whether the sentence was half a page long — he was telling them things. The syntax wasn't a part of what he was telling them. They were getting a feel of what Faulkner was talking about. Faulkner, better than any writer I know, could describe what it was like to be in the woods at dawn, the sequence of things that happen in a way that communicates to you exactly what you would feel if you were there. And he could do that superbly all his life long. It's that, if anything, that will make him live. It's the language; it's his ability to use the language to communicate what's called sensation, that is, the texture of this flower or the feel of this wood. He could do that wonderfully well, often by metaphor or simile, but sometimes just through some magic of language.

(Long pause again, so I jumped in…)

Q: Question for Mr. Beckwith: Would you agree with the convict? (Laughter)

Bill Beckwith: "Lisa Howorth was there, and when she heard that, she said it was the understatement of the century."

Shelby Foote: "What would you say it weighs?"

Bill Beckwith: "A thousand pounds."

• • •

After the press conference, stepping outside into the boisterous cacophony of the crowd and marching band felt like leaving a movie and stepping into daylight. Off and on, drizzling rain clouded the ceremonies, which nonetheless drew 1,000 people. The crowd was treated to a droning hour and a half of local politicians chiming in, most of whom had never read Faulkner. I ran around, tape recorder in hand, trying to cover the event. For me, it felt like the day that would never come, and yet here it was. It was quite moving to share the drive to fetch the piece with Beckwith, a friend since high school, and to now watch him have his day.

It was also a treat to have Willie Morris presiding over the ceremony. Willie had been a great friend to the Hoka during the 1980s. Ronzo and I had gotten to be quite close with him before he decamped for Jackson in 1990. Willie was a night owl, and what a genuine pleasure it was on so many nights to sit up late with him at his small faculty bungalow and have cocktails and hear whatever might be on his mind — usually several things at once, from a campus harangues to football to quoting literature or favorite movies to tales about his famous writer pals who included Truman Capote, George Plimpton and William Styron.

He would tell you to write a novel and really encourage you. Then the pizza delivery guy would come in, and he'd tell him he could write a novel. On this dreary day, Willie looked sporty in a cream-colored blazer and natty tie.

As Willie began his remarks, Chief of Police Bramlett opened an umbrella and held it over Willie as he read. At first I snickered, thinking of 2Live Crew, but as Willie talked and the chief kept the umbrella up, I was proud. Proud for Bramlett, proud for Willie, proud for Oxford.

"This is Faulkner weather. He really is with us today. It is altogether fitting to celebrate his one hundredth birthday on his home soil, here among his own people, in this misty rain. Happy birthday, Mr. Bill."

Shelby Foote recalled meeting Faulkner in 1942 and how privileged he felt to be his acquaintance. "What a great thing to have known such a great man."

The misty rain played havoc with the sound system, and it often cut out completely. Foote took the glitches in stride. He noted, "Faulkner would be pleased with the breakdown of the sound system. He was mostly opposed to most modern mechanisms with the exception of the airplane."

Judge Biggers introduced John Brademas, the keynote speaker. Brademas was a former member of Congress and president of NYU who talked about himself so much I thought we were there for an unveiling of a statue of... John Brademas. I had a copy of his speech and went through it with a yellow highlighter, highlighting when "I" or "me" appeared. Each page was covered in yellow marks. I kept count, and he made references to himself 120 times and to Faulkner eleven times. He was an old friend of John Leslie and thus was offered the "keynote" address.

Amid his interminable bloviating, he was accidentally interesting when he mentioned seeing U.S. Senator Theodore Bilbo in Oxford. Bilbo was a vicious demagogue who advocated violence to keep black citizens — whom he openly called niggers — from the polls. He was governor of Mississippi in the 1920s and U.S. Senator from 1934-1947. Brademas was in Oxford for a year (1946) as a naval officer trainee from Indiana. He recalls Bilbo, in a speech on a flatbed truck parked on the Square, standing before a crowd of mostly poor white farmers in "wool hats, overalls and suspenders" listening as the monstrous Bilbo incited them, shaking his fist: "Let the Yankees come down here with all their money and all their unions, and again, we'll spill their filthy blood on our sacred soil."

Good stuff, but all I could think was that Brademus had absolutely nothing to do with Faulkner. At long last, he finished and finally the moment: Beckwith was asked to say something to the crowd before he unveiled his Faulkner piece. He stepped wearily to the podium.

"It's been a long year. Thank you." There wasn't even time to put an umbrella over him. The statue was covered with a thick sheet, and Beckwith's five-year-old son, Clay, pulled the cord. The canvas came half-way off and stalled. Beckwith stepped up, like a helpful dad, and un-snagged the fabric, and Clay pulled the cord again. The sheet fell completely off, and there was Mr. Faulkner, having a seat and holding his pipe. Thunderous cheers and applause. A section of the crowd was directly next to the statue, stacked on the steps to City Hall, and flashbulbs blasted out in repetition.

True to his unassuming self, Beckwith didn't take on the pose of the victor. No thumbs up or even big smiles. He was exhausted. He probably just wanted to go home. The biggest job of his life had taken its toll, but he delivered. He did his job. He was handed empty air, and he created a monument, a thousand pounds for a 1,000 years.

Later, at two p.m., a series of speeches to commemorate Faulkner were presented on campus at Fulton Chapel, led by the ill but valiant Evans Harrington. Among the speakers was Larry Brown. Larry's inclusion was a wise choice. Though the focus of the day was squarely and appropriately on Faulkner, having Larry speak was not only a tip of the hat to the ongoing literary tradition in Oxford that Faulkner pioneered, it was also an acknowledgement of Lafayette County as

Faulkner's Yoknapatawpha.

To undertake a writing career as a novelist in Lafayette County and use the county as the setting for one's tales of rural intrigue, subterfuge and life in general, in effect plowing the same soil as William Faulkner, is a ballsy move. You'd better be prepared to pull it off with flair, putting your own stamp on it. It's almost a foolhardy mission. Yet, through his ten books (Larry passed away in 2004 at the age of fifty-three) Larry never echoed the Great Man. He took Faulkner's setting and made it his own. Larry did this not only through his talent and perseverance but through the fact that he grew up in the county and knew it first-hand. Richard Howorth, in his remarks that day at Fulton Chapel, quoted noted Faulkner scholar Cleanth Brooks from his review of Larry's novel, *Joe*: "Larry Brown's hometown is the same as William Faulkner's, Oxford, Mississippi. But his novel, *Joe*, is not imitation Faulkner. Brown has his own style and is quite comfortable in it. Nevertheless, the Beat Four district of Yoknapatawpha County peeps through in it."

Larry's love and empathy for his native soil was readily apparent in his remarks: "...when I wasn't in school, I prowled the river bottoms and wooded ridges around Tula, the vast hardwood forests known by their names almost like people: the Big W, London Hill, Round Station, Old Dallas, the Crocker Woods. There were little sand roads that curved through these holdings of timber, and the woods were alive with deer and squirrels, bobcats and raccoons, foxes and hawks and owls and birds of every variety, even the pileated woodpecker, known to old folks as the Indian hen."

Larry had also become our buddy through his visits to the Hoka beginning in the 1980s. It can't be understated what that little funky bohemian enclave meant in terms of the life-long friendships it forged. It had all the appearances of a literary salon — in a tin roof hut — except the conversation wasn't precious or posed. With Larry, I remember many conversations centering on the progress he was making on his house in Yocona. From there, we would touch on many far-ranging topics aided by late night liquids. When his book career took off, his friends rejoiced with him, feeling we had a vested interest by virtue of his taking people into his confidence, detailing the highs and lows of his toil in the Yankee publishing world.

On September 25, 1997, Larry told the Fulton Chapel crowd that he had spent his early childhood years in Memphis as a city boy. When his family finally moved back to Mississippi in 1964, the author reveled in his chance to make up for lost time in pursuits Faulkner surely would have recognized: "I felt like there were many important boy things I had missed: I had never owned a dog. I had never fired a gun. I didn't know how to swim. I had never been able to run wild in Mississippi, and I knew by then that this was my birthright, irrevocably, undeniably mine. So when the chance came, that's what I did. I studied only enough to get from one grade to the next. I spent most of my time totally unencumbered, running around with eight or ten boys my age who lived around Tula, camping out, smoking grapevines or swinging on them, catching fish, riding bicycles for miles over dirt roads, sitting around the store listening to old men tell stories, growing up at long last in the country."

I think Faulkner would have approved.

"Journalism is not a profession or a trade. It is a cheap catch-all for fuckoffs and misfits — a false doorway to the backside of life, a filthy piss-ridden little hole nailed off by the building inspector, but just deep enough for a wino to curl up from the sidewalk and masturbate like a chimp in a zoo-cage."

Hunter S. Thompson,
Fear and Loathing in Las Vegas:
A Savage Journey to the Heart of
the American Dream (1971)

44

Press coverage the next day was fairly perfunctory, but the Jackson *Clarion Ledger*, the state's biggest newspaper, had a very telling front page. The main headline was "Little Rock Nine Embraced," and underneath was a photo of President Clinton greeting the crowd after his speech in Little Rock, Arkansas, on the fortieth anniversary of the forced integration of that high school. The story of the Faulkner statue unveiling was below the fold. Sharing front-page space with Clinton was Ole Miss head football coach, Tommy Tuberville.

Tuberville had issued a statement through *The Daily Mississippian* asking fans not to display Rebel flags at football games starting with that weekend's homecoming game against Vanderbilt.

"We need to educate the new students who really don't know, who bring a flag simply because someone gives it to them. They think it's a novelty item. I think a lot of people are not intentionally trying to make Ole Miss look bad; they're just basically being followers."

The paper noted that Tuberville had taken steps over the summer to rid the stadium of flags, including meeting with student leaders but had decided to take his campaign public. It is difficult to imagine a football coach making proclamations about such things in America today. Perhaps even weirder that such a proclamation was front page news, right alongside the Little Rock Nine and the hundredth birthday of William Faulkner.

Tuberville's statement was heeded to some degree, as a small percentage of students stopped bringing flags. For a while, an "M" flag was tried out to wean fans who were accustomed to flags. For a while, the crowd was half Confederate flags, half M.

Even the student newspaper, the *Daily Mississippian,* in an editorial with the headline, "Move On" by news editor Emily Boling, joined in, perhaps emboldened by the cover the head football coach provided: "For an official at this university to publicly announce his personal feelings about such a controversial issue as this one took courage.

"James Meredith's first day of class was October 1, 1962 — almost exactly thirty-five years ago today. Yesterday, President Clinton spoke in Arkansas to commemorate the fortieth anniversary of the entry of nine black students into Little Rock Central High School. These students also had to be accompanied by federal troops.

"I agree with Tuberville. I think that the presence of the Rebel flag, even though it isn't an official university symbol, hurts the image of the school. The more people argue back and forth about it, the more Ole Miss will suffer. Ole Miss has come a long way since James Meredith walked its grounds in the 1960s. And if you need a reminder of that, just check out the bullet holes in front of the Lyceum. Let's continue to move forward."

Our own *Oxford Eagle* had its own yin-yang coverage. On the front page, there was a beautiful color photo of Beckwith standing next to his piece, with headshots of Willie and Shelby Foote. The statue unveiling story jumped to the back page and there, next to the Faulkner story, was the headline "Meredith Anniversary to be Remembered."

The brief story mentioned a banquet sponsored by a local United Methodist church, where residents would be encouraged to share their memories or what Meredith meant to them. The Associated Press story quoted Elizabeth Leslie, seventy-one, a 1946 Ole Miss graduate and later wife of Oxford mayor, John Leslie.

"When the riot started, you could hear all the noise from our house," she recalled, noting she was five blocks from campus.

"I thought they should have let him enter and not have that big to-do."

The story continued: "Former Mayor John Leslie was working as an Oxford pharmacist during that fall. Elizabeth Leslie said people knocked on his door to see if he had drugs to treat people affected by tear gas on campus. Meredith's admission to Ole Miss brought back memories for others. Members of the Silver Leaf Club in Oxford say they remember fixing dinner for Meredith every Sunday."

In the adjoining statue unveiling story, Beckwith was quoted about the piece he is working on after Faulkner, Lady Justice for the Lamar County courthouse. He was in the process of building her blindfolded, holding aloft the scales of justice.

"I was having trouble getting this one right," he reported. "Then one day, it hit me, and I got over the hump. It all started falling into place, and I knew what I was doing with it.

"Ah, I thought. There is justice."

For Beckwith, that ironic statement could very well have applied to his own travails with the Faulkner statue. With the piece finally unveiled and at long last in its final resting place, Beckwith achieved his own hard-earned justice, which, of course, is the best kind.

45

October
The Rise of Fall

The editor of the *Mississippian*, Jenny Dobson, wrote an editorial calling for banning of the Rebel flag at all sporting events, and the calls and angry letters started up all over again.

Dobson's editorial lit up the campus, and, in a welcome twist, letters of support were the result. A letter from Louise Avent was of particular note. Mrs. Avent was matriarch of a respected Oxford family who ran the town's dairy for decades and also sold land to the city to build veterans' housing after World War II. Gracious and Southern to her core she wrote:

"Many of us who hold the Confederate flag as sacred feel that the way it is being used is a sacrilege. Incidentally, the Ole Miss colors red and blue were not taken from the Confederate flag. The founders of Ole Miss adopted the crimson from Harvard and the blue from Yale — two outstanding schools at the time Ole Miss was established."

Love that last sentence, "outstanding schools at the time Ole Miss was established," as if to say that poor Harvard and Yale have since fallen by the wayside.

Next to Mrs. Avent's letter was one by Alan Alexander, then a first-year law student at the university, now a bankruptcy attorney in town. I quote it at length because the sarcasm is so delicious:

"A few questions regarding the Rebel flag: To everyone who says that athletes who are offended by the flag can go somewhere else, I ask: If you had to choose between the flag and a 2-9 season every year, which would choose? If we went 2-9 every year, would you keep going to the games just to wave your flag and complain about how the coach doesn't do a good job recruiting, because Mississippi's best players keep going out of state?

"To everyone who says they wave the flag to honor their Confederate forefathers, I ask: Don't you get offended when people use their flags to stir their bourbon into their Cokes. Or when they chop up a flag to make a vest or a skirt? Or my personal favorite, when they use their flag as a towel to wipe the bleachers off before they sit down so they don't get their Dockers muddy?

"To all the people who say they wave the flag to support the team, I ask: Why don't you try cheering instead, rather than absentmindedly waving your flag while talking with your friends the whole game about where the keg party's going to be? Last Saturday, I watched Ole Miss take on a hated rival and felt like I was in a mortuary.

"To all the people who now accuse Tuberville of trampling their First Amendment rights and plotting 'open rebellion' against Chancellor Khayat, I ask: Did you even read Tuberville's letter last week? He just asked everyone to act responsibly and think for themselves (as opposed to waving a flag because their fraternity/sorority/parents/dorm mates/etc. expects it), and conspiracy theorists start getting all Machiavellian on us. Granted, a responsible, thinking campus seems almost unimaginable here, but hope springs eternal."

Good stuff.

On October 2, the University of Tennessee student senate adopted a resolution supporting Ole Miss Coach Tommy Tuberville's statement regarding the Rebel flag. It called on Ole Miss fans to not bring the flag to Saturday's game between the two schools in Knoxville. The resolution passed unanimously. A similar resolution was "mentioned" at the Ole Miss student senate, said President Macey Fisher, but "nothing substantial" had happened yet.

• • •

By mid-October, Belle had become dangerously emaciated, and I was watching her closely to determine when to take her in and "put her down," in that awful phrase. I had never done it before but felt confident she'd let me know when it was time. Today, however, she had one of her best days: running, chasing squirrels, playing basketball, including making a steal and running off with the ball. I never did catch her.

I took her and Bingo on a truck ride, always a favorite activity. She smiled but still looked frightful. She was skin and bone, and her breathing was labored, but she was still running, still smiling.

The next day, Saturday, was another in that week's perfect fall weather, cool mornings, followed by highs in the mid-seventies, then cool nights. October is our reward for August. The October light is perfect, clear and vivid. There are occasional echoes of summer, but humidity has broken.

Our good buddy, cookbook author Martha Foose, and her fiancé, Donald Bender, were getting married in Taylor this week in former mayor and Delta photographer Jane Rule Burdine's renovated shop/shed that she called "The Roost." It was located across the street from my house. A team of interior designer friends had transformed the rustic little hut into the Copacabana. There was a big tent set up for the reception. A Memphis jazz band had been engaged. It looked like the circus was in town.

Meanwhile, Belle was unable to get comfortable. Standing, she was a bag of bones heaving heavily. Sitting, she looked awkward. Despite her brave show of running and smiling the day before, I knew what I had to do come Monday.

Today she couldn't even make it out to the basketball court. Instead, she watched me shoot while she sat in the shade of a pecan tree. Every time I looked over at her, her face was contorted. She sat there breathing hard, her head cocked back. Looking for squirrels, maybe? Trying to smell heaven?

After hoops, I put the dogs in their pen. Bingo happily jumped into their dog house while Belle curled up near the pen door. I looked at her and told her it was going to be all right, but she wouldn't look me in the eye. It was almost a sheepish look like she was embarrassed or ashamed of being sick. Dogs live to please, and maybe she felt she couldn't please anymore.

Darkness fell on a perfect Saturday night, comfortable enough for a Hawaiian shirt. I had a beauty picked out for the wedding, a silk number I had found in a New Orleans thrift store that depicted a fisherman in a boat on the front with the fishing line going across the back to reveal a huge marlin jumping up out of the water.

Elizabeth went over ahead of me, and when I finally arrived, saxophonist Jim Spake and The Memphis Jazz Mobile were grooving in the Roost, which looked like a dream, with chiffon streamers adorning the walls. The big tent was full of revelers, and the entire scene was like nothing I had ever seen in Taylor.

We got home around 12:30, and I walked out to let the dogs out of the pen for their late evening bathroom break. Belle never left the pen, never looked at me, never wagged her tail. Bingo did his business, and I locked them both back up. Back inside the house, Elizabeth was snoozing on the couch, still in her party clothes. I mixed a drink, put on some tunes on low volume and sipped my drink. After about ten minutes, I walked back out to the dog pen. I just had a feeling.

I flashed a light into the pen where Belle was curled up, and she was dead in her spot; tongue out, eyes open, a weird smile on her face. Bingo wept as I scooped her up and carried her out and laid her in the back yard near the cornfield. I had always thought when she died, I would bury her near the cornfield in the shade next to the property fence. Well, that time had come and it was two a.m. and I was a few drinks to the good, or bad. Drunk grief isn't the most focused way to approach a difficult task.

I walked into the house, awoke Elizabeth and told her that Belle was gone, and she collapsed into sobs. I went back out and got the shovel from the old outhouse we used as a tool shed. My first stab into the earth felt like digging in concrete. This was going to be an ordeal. I hate to admit it, but standing out there drunk at two in the morning trying to bury my dog, a horrible thought occurred to me. I thought about just loading her up in the truck and driving down to the Yocona River about ten miles away. There, instead of just throwing her in the drink, I would place her softly on a bough in the bulrushes and gently send her off to float serenely out to sea.

I said this to Elizabeth, and she was horrified. Elizabeth pointed out that Belle would soon turn into bloated flotsam and jetsam and that "rednecks would be taking pot shots at her."

OK, back to the dig. I stared at the shovel and the hard ground, and somehow a voice of reason whispered in my head: "Do it tomorrow." Elizabeth wrapped Belle up in a large carpet sample we had stashed under the house that Elizabeth had repeatedly asked me to throw away. We left Belle out in the yard, wrapped up in carpet with lawn chairs all around her as some type of privacy against marauding creatures of the night. We put Bingo back in his pen and staggered back into the house to try to get some sleep. We didn't sleep very well, and I bet Bingo didn't either.

The next morning, I was up with the sun. You don't get much practice for a day like this. The sun was deep in the trees as the coffee cleared its throat. I outlined a good spot near the cornfield. The ground was dewy, thick and cold. I could see my breath as I started shoveling. Soon, sweat and tears were running from my eyes. Elizabeth woke up and grabbed an old ancient hoe and was trying to break up dirt with it.

I remembered that my neighbor, Doug Roberts, just across the fence, had a pick axe. He kept some yard tools in a small hut in the back of his yard, adjoining our yard. He referred to it as the "Hoo Doo Hut," and he and I had many happy hours there. I stepped next door and borrowed the pick axe. Peering at their house, it appeared Doug and his wife, Lyn, weren't up yet. My time in Taylor would not have been as joyful without their friendship. During Elizabeth's many absences off on movie shoots, they had me over for dinner and drinks often. I mowed their yard when Doug was away. I knew he wouldn't mind my borrowing the pick.

Armed with this tool, the hole took shape fairly quickly, though I had to stop every few licks to catch my breath. There were so many feelings going through my head: confusion, utter exhaustion, regret, painful anger.

The early morning cool had faded, and sweat was streaming down my body. I looked over at Bingo, and he was quivering with terror. Another strange thought seized me. I turned to Elizabeth.

"I think Bingo thinks we killed her."

Doug and Lyn eventually awakened and were enjoying their coffee in their back yard, checking their extensive garden, when they heard us digging and walked over. They offered friendship and comfort as we laid Belle into place and covered her grave. We stood there for a moment on a beautiful morning and pondered love and life and the unstinting joy a dog can bring.

After they left, I sat on the back porch trying to reassure Bingo and thought of what the late great Barry Hannah wrote: "God creates the world and says on Saturday afternoon, he must separate the animals from man. So he creates a sudden chasm, like an earthquake, that leaves man on one side and animals on the other, and while the chasm is open, dog jumps over and stands by man. And that's the way it's gonna be; that's the way it's gotta be.

"Felt no mercy lately? Touch a dog's ears."

Amen, brother.

46

On October 14, the university hosted the PBS program, *Firing Line*, hosted by conservative commentator, William F. Buckley, Jr. Buckley hosted quite a line-up for a debate on trade with China, including *Slate* editor Michael Kingsley, Senator Trent Lott, Adrianna Huffington, (pre-*Huffington Post*) former California governor Jerry Brown and former Secretary of State Henry Kissinger. I attended the opening press conference (which Kissinger skipped), but I couldn't help thinking what I would say to him if I had the chance to confront him. I considered him a war criminal and prison fodder, much like his boss, Richard Nixon.

Nixon had ruined politics for my generation with his cheap lies and dumb break-in at the Watergate Hotel, and then, of course, lying about it. Kissinger's crimes were even worse, he had lied about killing people during Vietnam. Instead of prison, he had gone on to be fat, rich and happy, dating movie stars. Any sort of radical-type outburst on my part would get me removed from the proceedings and probably get me fired as well.

Biting your tongue is anathema to a reporter, but this was one of the (few) times my cooler head prevailed. Luckily, one of the "Oxford Nine" felt no such reticence. Ole Miss English professor Peter Wirth penned a thoughtful letter to the *Daily Mississippian*. Though it wasn't scathing enough to get him censured or fired, and seems tame by today's standards, at arch-conservative Ole Miss in the late 1990s, it probably raised hackles in some quarters and eyebrows in others:

"In 1968, Richard Nixon admitted privately about the Vietnam War, 'I've come to the conclusion that there's no way to win the war. But we can't say that, of course.'

"Accordingly, when Nixon was President, he and Kissinger prolonged an unwinnable war for four more years of direct American involvement, at the cost of about $120 billion; 26,000 American lives and untold number of Vietnamese lives. (In the war as a whole, some three million Southeast Asians died, at least a third of them civilians.)

"They did all this in spite of massive popular opposition in the United States and even the American armed forces themselves. Further, Nixon and Kissinger spent three years working, together with the CIA, to undermine the democratically elected Socialist government of Salvador Allende in Chile.

"Their efforts paid off when, in 1973, fascist generals overthrew Allende and killed him and thousands of Chilean men and women who supported him. It is true, as the *Daily Mississippian* says, that Kissinger received the Nobel Peace Prize in 1973. It was awarded jointly to him and Le Duc Tho, the North Vietnamese negotiator at the Paris peace talks.

"Le Duc Tho declined the award because he saw it as an insult to his people. If Kissinger is a man of peace, it is only in the sense in which Tacitus said bitterly of the conquering Romans, 'They make a desert and call it peace.'"

Beautifully said, but I still dream of confronting Kissinger.

• • •

Oxford was fortunate to have the Center for the Study of Southern Culture at Ole Miss. While the name might connote stereotypical "professional Southerners," the center was cool in exploring the South. Led by the dynamic Bill Ferris, Ann Abadie and Charles Reagan Wilson, the Center offered a steady diet of events, readings, music and guest lecturers — all open to the public. This included Sam Phillips, the Memphis record producer who first recorded Elvis Presley. Phillips was a perfect person to visit the university in a year when the school was once again bedeviled by racial issues.

Phillips was an early champion of black culture. Growing up in Florence, Alabama, his family took in a black family friend who was blind, Silas Payne. Making his way to Memphis as a young man in the mid-1940s, Phillips was blown away by all the raw, live music he heard on Beale Street and was convinced the world needed to hear it. Honing his engineering skills with big bands on the Peabody Hotel Skyway, he launched his first studio in 1950. Its mission, as he said, was "for Negro artists in the South who wanted to make a record and just had no place to go."

In his monumental two-volume biography of Elvis, author Peter Guralnick quotes Phillips as saying he was looking for "Negroes with field mud on their boots and patches in their overalls...battered instruments and unfettered techniques."

Phillips earned his bonafides recording the likes of Howlin' Wolf, B.B. King, Ike Turner, Little Milton, Rufus Thomas and Roscoe Gordon. Turner became an unofficial talent scout for Phillips, saying, "I'd check the pool halls to ask the fellows about singers and then check the local churches."

So-called "friends" of Phillips would remark, "Well, Sam, you don't smell so bad today, I guess you ain't been recording no niggers lately." Phillips broke more barriers in the early 1950s when he recorded The Prisonaires, six long-term black prisoners from the state prison in Nashville. The recording required permission from the governor and armed guards to be present at Sun Studios.

Working with such raw talent became Phillips' modus. "I love perfect imperfection," he would say.

Running two businesses at once and the strain of racism socially and in his business induced a nervous breakdown, and Sam was hospitalized and given electro-shock treatments. Upon his release several weeks later, Phillips knew he couldn't keep both jobs, so he gave up his engineering duties at the Peabody and concentrated on his Memphis Recording Service, which would become (after he realized other labels were cheating him) Sun Records.

By the mid-1950s, Phillips was recording a shy teenager named Elvis Presley. Elvis was a white man who sang "black" and thus was exactly what Phillips was looking for to bring black music to a wider audience. Many observers, including record producers Jerry Wexler and Jim Dickinson, credit Elvis with changing the culture in the U.S. regarding race. Phillips would further show his penchant for inclusion in 1954 when he launched radio station WHER, the nation's first all-female radio station.

Anybody who brought the world Elvis and Howlin' Wolf is to be reckoned with — especially on matters of race. In his indispensable book, *It Came From Memphis*, author Robert Gordon crystallized the Phillips legend: "Phillips had come to Memphis from the cotton fields of Alabama and was familiar with the sounds the city slickers gawked at. His rural background gave him the insight to tell Howlin' Wolf to play what he played at home, not the more accessible style he'd adapted for the white folks. Phillips knew the audience could conform to the music. His peers asked him why he spent time with people who smelled like mules. But the recordings he made — Wolf, Ike Turner, B.B. King — found their way to younger white ears, whose failed attempts at imitating them created rock and roll."

Veteran R&B producer Ahmet Ertegun added a succinct point: "You can segregate everything but the radio dial."

It felt like quite the occasion to think I could walk a few blocks from my house and meet the man who, if he didn't invent rock and roll, was its Dr. Frankenstein. The date was October 17, 1997. A music scholar from Liverpool England, David Deacon, was in town working on an article exploring the influence of American soul music on the Beatles. His research brought him to Memphis, and through a circuitous sequence of events (Phillips' former secretary was from Coffeeville and was the daughter-in-law of somebody else — the usual convoluted Mississippi connection), Phillips was invited by Bill Ferris and the center to speak and be awarded an honorary degree.

I had a nice stroll down to the Tupelo Room, an auditorium/quasi-lecture hall on the campus at the center's headquarters, Barnard Observatory. Phillips looked for all the world like a mad scientist of rock and roll, albeit a well-dressed one: a natty, navy blue, double-breasted jacket with pressed khakis. His hair was long in an almost mullet joined together by a full beard. He wore a "TCB" necklace ("Taking Care of Business" jewelry connotes Elvis's inner circle). He was accompanied by his wife, Becky, and his oldest son, Knox.

I sensed that Phillips was truly humbled by the attention.

"This day really means an awful lot to me," he told the crowd. "I'm totally appreciative of the fact that young people come to this university, and they're going to be exposed to the cult of music."

After thanking everyone, Phillips began to talk about his life in an exuberant tone that was half preacher and half snake oil salesman.

"In all my sessions, I wasn't just there to turn knobs. I was there to help an artist and get into his heart and head.

"For two and a half years, I recorded black artists. In gaining their confidence day-to-day, I was able to bring out their real feelings, and we would not accept less. My calling was to communicate with people. That's how I was able to get inner feeling for the music they was making."

Phillips now knows that what he did was historic — and groundbreaking. "If I do have a legacy, it's that we broke down — in the great sort of way — we knocked down a lot of barriers for people who had enough injustice. We created community among races through music that brings people together. I'm not brave. I had to truly love what I was doing."

Phillips then spoke of the great blues singer Howlin' Wolf, born Chester Burnett. "His voice was so attention-getting he could have hummed everything, and I would have loved it. If I didn't get anything on him [recording], it would be my fault not his."

Phillips started in radio in 1942 in Florence, Alabama, with dreams of becoming a criminal defense lawyer. Fate and music took him on a different path.

"I grew up with poor white trash like me. I got interested in church music. A black minister of the gospel can take the Bible and read it to me and say what he believes, and somehow it was more convincing than when I read the same words. Same with music. The people I was with in the fields — people of rhythm — I never heard a complaint from one of them. Gave me inspiration. The power of music, to me, is the power to determine so much in this world."

Again, his humbleness came through: "The greatest privilege I ever had was conferring on the artist, 'You don't have to please the white man behind the glass.' I want to hear what is a part of you, your dreams. I never spent one hour thinking I was going to make a hit. My ambition was to check out the thickets and the forest."

The sounds that Phillips unearthed from the thicket and the forest echoed around the world, all from his unassuming studio on Union Street in Memphis, a fact Phillips was proud to note.

"Sun Records are enjoyed in India, Asia, China. Why? The reason is the honesty. You could hear all the travail and all the happiness.

"Young people didn't have music before rock and roll, especially white kids. In your teenage years, you need something to call your own — rock and roll, rhythm and blues gave that little bit of honest life. They really liked it when it made Mama mad and preachers and politicians — you know they got to get on it!"

Phillips said he never wanted to start a record label: "I had all I could say grace over." But he felt the deal he had signed with distributors gave them rights to the master tapes of music he had discovered and nurtured. So he became his own label, Sun, and developed his own distribution network. Once Elvis, Howlin', Johnny Cash and the other rockers hit the airwaves, parents and preachers became alarmed. The backlash was strong.

"A lot was done to try to kill rhythm and blues and rock and roll," Phillips recalled. "I knew, in time, with more exposure, we'd be accepted by young people."

Phillips honed his engineering skills as soundman for the big bands that played the legendary Peabody Hotel in Memphis after World War II. While his sonic skills improved, he found the color-in-the-lines whiteness of the music stifling.

"At the Peabody Skyway we'd have fifteen to eighteen pieces, all during the war, into the 1950s. They'd play every note as it was on the arrangement; it did not have the liberties you could have. That's where inspiration comes in. That's why blues music is so important. I don't know any gutbucket blues that wouldn't get your ear."

He was asked about the Million Dollar Quartet, a happenstance and historic grouping that casually came together (with helpful phone calls from Phillips) in Sun Studios in December 1956 with Johnny Cash, Jerry Lee Lewis, Carl Perkins and seated at the piano, Elvis. An iconic photo and brief recording remain: "The Million Dollar Quartet was the show of a lifetime. They all just happened to come by. You would have thought all these were brothers. They got into a spiritual. I called the paper, the *Press Scimitar*. The camaraderie was as if they had all been identical twins at the same time. 706 Union Street — something about that day. Johnny cried when he had to leave."

Sitting, listening and jotting notes, I assumed Phillips was probably a little nutty, but who wouldn't be after surviving the dawn of rock and roll? He introduced Elvis to Jerry Lee Lewis. He recorded Howlin' Wolf. At least he was still here with us, in Oxford, no less.

He finished up with a succinct statement on the power of music. "We are blessed that God let us be so restricted in our thinking back in the 1950s before rock and roll. We were messed up, and rock and roll straightened our ass out."

Thank you, Sam Phillips.

Thank you for creating a place for those who had no place. In providing a microphone for what was in the heads and hearts of the "people of rhythm," Phillips brought the races together, one nation under soul.

• • •

Meanwhile, back in Crazyville, the idea to ban sticks as a way to keep Rebel flags out of the Ole Miss football stadium began to receive traction. One student, Brooke Rankins, wasn't impressed. She wrote to the *Mississippian*: "If the intent of banning sticks is to eliminate the waving of the Rebel flag at football games, then the policy-makers had best reevaluate their thinking. This very concept undermines the intelligence of any college student, whether he or she supports the flag or not.

"Does the ever-popular 'chicken on a stick' now become 'chicken in your hand?'"

Say what? I was with her until that last sentence. And just how does one go about "undermining the intelligence of college students" in ways they haven't already done themselves?

Then it happened. From the *Daily Mississippian* on October 21: "In a historic move, Tuesday, the Associated Student Body took a hard stand against bringing the Confederate flag to Ole Miss athletic events. The Senate overwhelming passed the resolution 97-17.

"'I think this is a great message that we're sending to the entire nation,' said Senator Matt Lott."

Unfortunately, the nation could only hear about it because the governing body decided to bar cameras from the proceedings. One senator asked his colleagues if they were voting against the flag because they were "bowing to pressure from the media." One senator, MiMi Montagnet, assured her fellow senators, "I did not do it seeking attention from the press."

In a related development that was surely not a coincidence, UM Chancellor Robert Khayat was, on the very same day as the ASB vote, in Washington, D.C., hand-delivering the school's application for a Phi Beta Kappa chapter.

47

Evans Harrington died on December 2. His hair was gone, and he walked with a cane, but his rare dignity was never diminished. His wife, Betty, and daughter, Donna, debated whether to have "Taps" played, honoring his naval service, but decided against it. There was scant ceremony, just the family clutching each other in a tight cloister — mostly Betty's children rallying around their mother in the newer section of the cemetery. It was a spot he had picked, she said, out of sight of Faulkner.

"Maybe he was tired of fooling with Faulkner," I told her.

The losses seemed to pile up. On January 5, 1998, Duff Dorrough's wife, Debbie, died at age forty-one. I went down for the funeral, a cold, rainy day with big, blobby drops. There was Duff left with two small children. It tore my heart.

Then Carl Perkins, Junior Wells and Junior Kimbrough, Carl Wilson of the Beach Boys (age fifty-one), Sonny Bono and — a real blow — long-time baseball announcer (and Budweiser enthusiast) Harry Caray. They buried Harry Caray and Junior Kimbrough the same week, and it occurred to me that I never got to sing with either of them.

I spent my days at the *Oxford Eagle*, in the months before the millennium, writing obituaries.

48

Settlin' Up

Twenty years after the events in this book, the United States is still grappling with racial issues, and we may have even regressed in our race relations. This despite electing the first black president in our history for two terms beginning in 2008.

National dialogue opened up over the Confederate flag after a church shooting in Charleston, South Carolina, on June 17, 2015, that left nine Bible study members brutally killed by a deranged gunman who identified with Confederate ideals. Walmart, Sears, Amazon and e-Bay, among others, immediately pulled all Confederate-themed merchandise.

Russell Moore, president of the Ethics & Religious Liberty Commission of the Southern Baptist Convention, called for reappraisal of the Confederate flag. On June 14, 2016, the Southern Baptist Convention voted to repudiate the display of the Confederate flag — a huge development in the South.

Nikki Haley, Republican governor of South Carolina, called for removal of the Confederate battle flag from that state's capitol grounds, which indeed happened in a stirring ceremony broadcast live nationwide. Former GOP presidential candidate Mitt Romney, called for the end of Confederate flag displays. Another prominent Republican, Phillip Gunn, the speaker of the Mississippi House of Representatives, called for removal of the stars and bars from his state's flag. Negative comments poured onto his social media.

President Barack Obama, this country's first black president, used the N-word on June 21, 2015, during a podcast interview. On April 30, 2016, HBO comedian Larry Wilmore concluded his remarks at the White House Correspondents' Dinner by turning to the President and saying, "Barry, you did it, my nigga." These are developments my forty-year-old self would not have believed had you told me in 1997.

The website Vice explained Wilmore's use of "nigga" wasn't crude or insulting because it was "code-switching":

"The fact is that code-switching is a pretty common phenomenon, especially among middle-class black folks," journalist Adam Serwer wrote just before Obama's election in 2008. "This isn't a hallmark of anti-intellectualism; rather, it's a way to signify that you're part of a particular culture. The point is that you're supposed to be able to manipulate language to your own ends, not be trapped by it."

Vice concluded: "All debates aside, this much is clear: Somewhere between being born in Hawaii, reared in Indonesia, nurtured by Kenya, educated between California, New York and Boston and then maturing in Chicago and Washington — this Barack, this Hussein, this Obama has learned to speak many languages. He's learned to translate many stories and lead us all to a deeper understanding of the post-racial fairytale and what it means to be black in America."

I have followed the use of "nigger" and "nigga," and as of this writing, they are off-limits to white people, unfit for social utterance, no matter how allegedly funny, edgy or ironic their use. But who knows; like skinny ties, they may come back.

"It doesn't bother me to be writing in the place where he wrote," Mr. Hannah says. "I like the ghosts." In a piece to commemorate Oxford's 150th anniversary, he wrote of Faulkner: "Salute him or go away. You can't walk through a statue."

Barry Hannah, *New York Times* (July 9, 1998)

49

May 5, 2011

I was lying on the couch half-watching a basketball game I didn't care about when God tapped me on the shoulder.

"What's wrong?" my girlfriend, Micah, asked.

"I think I'm having a heart…" the word "attack" got caught, and my voice snapped it off into a whisper.

"Attack —" In an instant, we were dressed and out the door.

We signed in at the desk, and apparently my face conveyed enough pain that I didn't have to sit.

"Go on back," the nurse said. They showed Micah the waiting room and took me back. Just like that, I was placed on a gurney and rolled down a hallway, just like on TV. I was being wheeled very quickly down a hallway, with eight to ten people surrounding the gurney as we rolled, all busy, one strapping an oxygen mask on me, another typing, another removing my socks. Another interviewing me.

"On a scale of one to ten, ten being most severe, how would you rate your pain level?" a nurse with a clipboard asked.

I had the presence of mind to think conservatively and give myself some cushion for down the road — or hall — so I told her, "Eight." By this point, I was hooked up to all manner of gizmos and stickies with wires running into portable blips. My shirt had somehow disappeared. The nurse asked again to rate my pain level, and I kept telling her eight. Finally, she approached me with a needle and said, "This should help a little."

I didn't know it was morphine, but shortly I was out.

When I woke up three hours later, I was in ICU and no worse for wear. I felt no pain; the discomfort was gone, but I was still hooked up to all the gizmos and unaware of what had happened. Finally, a nurse came in.

"How you doing, cowboy? You had a big night."

"I'm fine, what happened?"

"You had a heart attack."

"I was afraid of that."

"Yep. Doctor put in seven stents. You ought to be feeling a lot better now."

She was right about that. The miracle of modern medicine was very much in evidence. Even though I knew I had had a heart attack — I don't think she'd lie about something like that — I still didn't feel like I'd had one, whatever I thought that was supposed to feel like.

Just then, two buddies walked in. Lisa Howorth, the former first lady of Oxford (known affectionately as the Night Mayor, her husband, Richard Howorth, had served two terms as Oxford's mayor.) She was accompanied by Joey Lauren Adams, the movie actress who had adopted Oxford as her second home. I wasn't allowed visitors, but the nurses recognized Joey and, in their awestruck agogness, let them in.

"Dees, how are you? Is this a cry for help? Word on the street is that you got a penile enhancement," Lisa cracked.

"I'm fine. Thanks for coming down here. Ain't this a helluva note?" I couldn't hug them with all the wiry stickies, so we shook hands. They handed me a homemade get well card. "Dees! Get Well Soon Or We Gone Kill You, Love, Lisa and Joey."

What a joy to see these two as soon as I came to. It let me know I was alive. I had made it safely back from Morphine River. I related the night's events to them, and they shook their heads, telling me to lay off biting the Big One.

"Rest easy, boy," Joey said, as the nurses finally shooed them out. Micah came in next and had her laptop with her. I actually emailed family members from ICU to tell them what had happened and that I thought I was ok.

At some point, all visitors were shooed out; the nurses left and there I was sitting alone, all hooked up and beeping, again, just like in the movies. I looked over at the beeper with the jagged green line graphing on the screen, indicating my heartbeat. I took this to be the "flat-line machine," the dreaded green line that, once it flattens as it scrolls across the deadly black background, the alarm goes off, and the nurses rush in, but it's too late. You're already in the Asshole Waiting Room of heaven… you hope…

As I looked at this machine, watching my pulse being reflected back at me, a profound chill came over me…

Holee Shit… now I am one of those people who has had a heart attack. I've joined that club. The Second Chance Club. What would this mean? Can I park in handicapped spots? Will I qualify for a scooter when I go to Walmart? Will the stents set off metal detectors?

What about coffee? Would I have to give up coffee? Or, gasp —

gin? What about omelets? Or my beloved bike rides? Oh Lord, what about my dangling man hammer? Though it's gathered dust of late, it's like a power tool hanging on the wall in the garage. You want it to work when you plug it in.

There was no surgery involved for me, no huge scar down my chest. The stents were applied through a catheter in my leg, a pinpoint incision through which Dr. Purdon ran a ram rod through my arteries and poked them clean like you would a pipe cleaner, a not-unapt analogy.

It's called a heart attack, but mine wasn't so much an attack as I slow build-up of dread, like water seeping up on a porch. I think of heart attacks as, again from TV and movies, the victim clutches his chest and is felled in a swoop of thunderous pain that crumbles him where he stands. Mine was a stomach ache in my chest that rendered me uncomfortable but able to function.

Funny, when you actually die, the benign medical term is "flatline," but if you're a little late with a bullshit news story, that's the much harsher, "deadline."

The many years since the events of this book have been happy ones, for the most part, aside from the natural traumas of life, like having a heart attack. My siblings and I have buried both our parents. I've buried all my dogs. This issue of race has flared up more virulent than ever. The events covered in this book could very easily have happened today, and that saddens me.

The year 1997 had proven to be good training for life in general in all its beautiful ugliness. The same prejudices are in play, if not heightened, more out in the open. Politicians still love a camera and don't feel burdened by facts when they speak into it.

Newspapers are still with us, though thousands have stopped the presses, and those that remain have shrunk the print and the page, laid off the best writers, moved the news online and dumbed it down and misspelled it so it will fit on your phone. The year covered in this book seems to me to be a chronicle of a vanishing, by-gone era, the last gasp of life before we all had the world in our pocket.

The 20th century may turn out to be the last years before humankind developed a hump in its back from looking down all day. One hundred years from now, everyone will be hunch-backed, and conversation will be silent; people will just private message emojis to each other. Even when they are standing next to each other. Newspapers will be in history books. Reporters, if there are any, will be unpaid "content providers."

The year 1997 was part of the vanishing era when people's hometown paper was an important part of their lives. The last of the "this morning's inspiration is that afternoon's finger smudge" generation. The last years when subscribers would read about their local school board meeting from a rubber band-wrapped paper hitting the driveway.

The whole year felt like a dark comedy with all the Faulkner hoohah, the community being confounded yet again by race, the weirdness of 2Live Crew and Mike Gunn and the greatness of Willie Nelson, Myrlie Evers and Shelby Foote.

I am heartened by the fortitude of an artist like Bill Beckwith. He kept his head down and did his work — chipping away at it, literally — while forces outside his door were working to change, postpone, move or even stop his work. He hung strong and did it all with good humor.

As I moved through that year, having to interview people and insert myself into situations for the sake of a story, I realized that turning forty really helped. It is the age when the last of the fucks have been given. You find yourself able to move through existence unshackled by fear or decorum. Once you've buried your parents, it's hard for any other event or slight or hassle or temporary bummer to have lasting effect. Ditto what people think of you. One doesn't feel defiant as much as spent. The emotional capital has been paid out.

Mississippi is an endlessly fascinating place where brilliant art and crushing poverty and ignorance collide. Faulkner knew both sides of the equation and gave his fellow Mississippians a body of work we can point to and say, "Yes, we rank fiftieth in everything except, 'the human heart in conflict with itself.'"

For those of us who love Mississippi while acknowledging its low standing, Faulkner summed it up beautifully in his essay, *Mississippi*: "Loving all of it even while he had to hate some of it, because he knows now that you don't love because: you love despite; not for the virtues, but despite the faults."

I have lived in this state all my life but felt I came closest to it during the year of 1997. My reporter status allowed me to jump squarely into the middle of events that just happened to be matters of history, culture, sports, literature and even life and death. I think I know my state better, but I'm not sure I understand it.

You know, kinda like life.

Epilogue

Hale-Bopp

The Hale-Bopp Comet was that rare "Great Comet" that was visible to the naked eye for most of the year, a rarity with comets. Sci-fi author Sean Mounger put it this way: "From its austere beginnings as a smudge in a telescope in the summer of 1995, it hung around for the better part of a year and a half, becoming most prominent in the skies of the Northern Hemisphere during the spring of 1997. Its last recorded appearance with the naked eye was in December of that year, easily outstripping the previous longest visibility of a Great Comet, which was nine months in 1811-12."

Mounger writes that comets were also thought to presage world catastrophes like world wars or floods. He says in the mid-1990s, the whack-job community suggested Hale-Bopp was more than met the naked eye: "[The comet's appearance] marked an increase in pseudoscience and 'woo' thinking that in the mid-1990s was exploding due to the growing influence of the Internet and 'alternative media' talk shows like Art Bell's *Coast to Coast* radio program. The purveyors of this sort of stuff latched on to Hale-Bopp, and many UFO buffs started talking up the suggestion that there was an extraterrestrial spacecraft following in the tail of the comet. This was rubbish, of course."

Munger recalled the comet's tragic consequences. I seem to remember this story: "Heaven's Gate, a weird UFO cult from Southern California, wove Hale-Bopp into the apocalyptic visions of their leader, Marshall Applewhite. In March 1997, as Hale-Bopp was at its most prominent in the sky, thirty-nine members of the cult committed ritual suicide, believing their souls would ascend to the UFO supposedly trailing the comet. Thus, Hale-Bopp is a celestial object with a body count."

Being "woo-less" in Mississippi, for me, the comet was a beautiful phenomenon that I could see occasionally and thought of as a friend during that turbulent year. A steady flash rocketing across the sky, totally space-made, no men involved, except for the two guys, Hale and Bopp, who discovered it one night by accident in 1995. The comet was a reminder of our smallness on our bright blue orb. Writing, sculpture and art in general would all be burnt to a crispy crisp by a comet. It is interesting to ponder the state of art in the year of Hale-Bopp's return trip, which will be in 4385.

James Meredith

Almost as indestructible as the Great Comet is James Meredith, the civil rights hero who integrated Ole Miss and has lived to tell about it. Despite being shot in 1966 and battling cancer in his later years, Meredith published his memoir, *Mission from God,* in 2012. In it, he wrote: "I am a Zen samurai. I am invincible. Nothing can harm me. I have been put on Earth for a reason, to restore the power and glory to my bloodline and to all Americans.

"I am not a civil rights activist, I am not a protester and I am not a pacifist. I am not a Republican, and I am not a Democrat. My political affiliation is black.

"I am an American citizen and a son of Mississippi. I am a warrior. And I am on a mission from God."

He signed my copy of his book, "To Jim, To our future!"

In 2002, Ole Miss commissioned a statue of James Meredith, and when it was unveiled (after months of the inevitable sniping and complaining), it depicted him walking through a door at a site very near the registrar's office on campus. In 2014, two vandals left a noose around the neck of the Meredith statue, once again sparking international news coverage. The two students, both from Georgia, had placed a noose and an outdated Georgia flag, which contains the Confederate stars and bars, around the neck of the statue. Both were expelled, as was their fraternity, Sigma Phi Epsilon. The two later pled guilty, and one received six months in prison while the other awaits sentencing.

It makes the events of this book from twenty years ago still sickeningly relevant. As of this writing, James Meredith is still alive and feisty at age eighty-two.

Dean Faulkner Wells

Dean Faulkner Wells evoked the very pipe smoke and cedar smell of her uncle in her delightful 2011 memoir, *Every Day by the Sun*, published just months before her death. I knew Dean for thirty years. She was as slight and dark and mischievous as Faulkner was reported to have been and as she said her dad, also named Dean, was. She never knew Dean but was raised by William. Dean's beautiful book and William Faulkner's Nobel Prize-winning universe now belong to the world, but here in Oxford, the two of them will forever belong to us.

Myrlie Evers

Also still alive and feisty is Myrlie Evers, who maintains an office in Jackson, Mississippi, at the Medgar and Myrlie Evers Institute. Of her home state, she told *National Geographic* in 2014, "It represents home, but also the loss of the love of my life."

Evers related to the magazine how she accidentally saw the rifle that killed her husband when she donated his papers to the Mississippi Department of Archives and History in Jackson and attended the opening reception:

"I was proud to see the copy of Medgar's letter to the governor, applying for admission to Ole Miss. And the rejection letter. I started toward a little anteroom, and someone said, 'I don't think you should go in there.' And I stopped in my tracks, because there on a pedestal in Plexiglass was the rifle. It's very difficult for me to explain what I felt. It wasn't panic. It wasn't anger. It wasn't hatred. I don't know what it was. It just stopped me.

"I saw that rifle in three parts. The first part was the trigger, which represented the hatred that was used to pull the trigger. Midway along the rifle, I could see Medgar's body face-down. And it represented this man who loved his people, who loved his state, who loved his country and someone who had given his all, and it was over. As I saw that, I looked at the end of the rifle, and I could literally see the fire coming out of it. It is so interesting how your mind can play these tricks on you. I saw the fire as representing the future, the force of the future. I hope I am right."

In 1997, she spoke to the crowd at Ole Miss about the need to replace "We Shall Overcome" as a civil rights anthem: "We need a new song that moves us into the future. If we don't, we may find ourselves reliving the '50s and '60s."

Reading these words twenty years later in relation to 2015 police shootings of unarmed black citizens and the renewed Confederate flag debate, they seem especially sad and prophetic.

Duff and Charlie

The Tangents were Mississippi's house band and live on in bootleg recordings. Tragedy struck the band in true rock and roll fashion. Charlie died of drug complications; the guitarist, Jerry "Duff" Dorrough, became deathly ill from Hepatitis C; drummer Bob Barbee retired from the road to nurse his wife, who was almost killed after being shredded in a bush hog accident. Bassist Steve Vines became a Nashville music techie, and Jim "Fish" Michie works a government job and plays piano gigs at night. The surviving tapes and CDs of their live performances reveal young, energetic hellhounds who had fully absorbed their heritage of blues records but also rockabilly, Elvis, jazz and the Beatles.

Aside from being friends for thirty years, Duff and I became colleagues for a time. In 2000, I became emcee of the *Words and Music* show, which began its radio life at Blind Jim's tavern as *The Blind Jim's Radio Hour*. The show moved to Off Square Books, a remainder bookstore on the Square, and changed its name to *The Thacker Mountain Radio Hour* (named after a fire tower deep in Lafayette County).

In 2005, Duff came on as front man and lead guitarist for our house band, the Yalobushwhackers. The pianist was Jim Dickinson (and the man who came up with the name Yalobushwhackers), known as a confidant and side man to Bob Dylan, Keith and the Stones (that's Jim on piano on "Wild Horses"), Ry Cooder, Arlo Guthrie, the Replacements, Screaming Jay Hawkins and on and on.

It had to be the coolest small town radio show house band, maybe ever. Duff loved to rehearse, Jim said, "Rehearsal's for pussies," but somehow their shared music, with bassist Slade Lewis and drummer Wallace Lester, had a raw elegance. I stood back and introduced the visiting authors who would read an excerpt from their latest book, then introduce a visiting band flogging their latest release. But, for me, the real show was Duff and Jim. Their deep knowledge of R&B and country music, as well as rock and roll, filled the air like an embarrassment of hipness. They were rowdy scholars and snappy dressers to boot. I loved them both like brothers.

Even with all their hijinks, they treated our guest bands with a certain show biz etiquette, respecting their spotlight and jamming with them when appropriate. We lost Jim in 2009 and Duff in 2012. I'm still the host of the show, but there is definitely a weirdness void. Mark Yacovone has admirably filled the piano bench, and the show is still cranking along at about thirty shows a year. We'll celebrate twenty years on the air in 2017. It's bemusing that a radio broadcast with real musicians and an actual audience can still exist, let alone one with an author reading for twelve uninterrupted minutes from a book made of paper.

Keep radio real!

The Oxford Nine

The Oxford Nine, the literary tree-huggers who were arrested for blocking a construction site, had all charges dropped when it was determined the arrests occurred on university property, and therefore, Oxford police had no jurisdiction.

"And we made it to Disney World that year too," one of the Nine, Ann Phillipi, told me.

The Water Valley watermelon mural

In Water Valley, the mural was completed and depicts black and white citizens enjoying and unloading delicious watermelons from a train. In the intervening years, partly due to inflated rents in Oxford, Water Valley has attracted young families to buy the town's many older homes in which to raise their families. It has turned into a spunky little town with a health food store, art galleries, even its own brewery. The Watermelon Carnival is bigger than ever, and there seems to be no racial tension. It is a town of the future.

Jonny Miles

Within a couple of years of his time at the *Oxford Eagle*, Jonny Miles was writing a drinking column for the *New York Times,* which we found hilarious because he was strictly a Budweiser man during his Oxford days, as his plaque on the City Grocery bar attests. Jonny graduated to an enviable writing career, starting with writing that cocktails column for the *Times*. He also reviewed books for the *Times* Sunday books section, wrote game recipes for *Field and Stream*, celebrity profiles for *Details* and now covers books and drinks for *Garden and Gun*. He has published two brilliant novels and is at work on a third. Now known as Jonathan Miles, he is, simply, the best writer I know.

Mike Gunn

I wondered whatever became of Mike Gunn after he beheaded Robert Khayat at a city near you. A quick Google search came up with this story from 2007 from the website Topix:

"Former State Senator Mike Gunn entered a guilty plea Tuesday morning to the charge of removal and killing of young geese. He agreed to pay a $5,000 fine and will serve a year of probation and must perform eighty hours of community service. He will not serve any jail time.

"Gunn was charged originally with hunting geese out of season by the Mississippi Department of Wildlife, Fisheries and Parks, but that agency turned the case over to the U.S. Fish and Wildlife Service, which handled the prosecution through the U.S. Attorney's Office.

"One of Gunn's neighbors at the reservoir, Carol Boland, says she saw Gunn capture the young geese, put them in a gas grill and then hit them over the head. Seven goslings were killed.

"'I ran afoul of the law and laid a huge egg,' Gunn said as he left the courthouse on Wednesday. 'I have received a gaggle of problems as a result, and I am just glad this wild goose chase is behind us now.'"

The eighty hours of community service was not specified but must be approved by the court.

And one more elucidating tidbit from the Gunn files: "In what was revealed to be a clerical error, Mississippi did not ratify the 13th Amendment (outlawing slavery) until 1995. Leading the charge against ratification was Mississippi State Senator Mike Gunn. He was last in the news for gassing goslings to death in his Bar-B-Q grill, and he is well known in wingnut circles for his quip against gun control: "If guns are outlawed, how can we shoot liberals?"

Back then maybe he was a crackpot. Now, he could run for President.

Ronzo

The Hoka, like so much of funky old Oxford, was eventually razed, and the space now sits empty, a million-dollar piece of real estate, awaiting construction of a boutique hotel with underground parking. Ron Shapiro currently operates a new hangout two blocks away, a Hokaesque coffee shop, albeit, clean and with Wi-Fi. While many may not have taken Ronzo's (Ron's evolved nickname) political career seriously, he always scored a respectable number of votes. Many of his past campaign platforms like arts funding, mass transit and recycling are now Oxford public policy. I've always held that he introduced bagels and, later, wheat grass, to Oxford. Indeed, Faulkner's town has been a more enlightened place for his activism and venues. Best of all, for many of us, Ron, "Ronzo" Shapiro, has become a lifelong friend. He is the walking (dancing?) embodiment of his favorite Tom Robbins quote: "It's never too late to have a happy childhood."

Robert Khayat

Robert Khayat survived the death threats he received as Ole Miss chancellor. He has also lived to see his efforts vindicated: there are no Rebel flags at Ole Miss football games and few on campus. The old man mascot is gone. Ole Miss received the Phi Beta Kappa chapter and enrollment, and campus construction exploded. Khayat looked evil in the eye and didn't blink. Even under personal duress, he set his alma mater on a solid course, left it better than he found it.

He has since become a personal friend, but before we became acquainted, I remember him from the old Hoka days. Whenever he saw Ronzo and me and our scraggly, flannel-shirted group, he would always speak. Even coming out of Handy Andy (a delicious downhome BBQ and police hangout) with his snooty colleagues.

He has been on *The Thacker Mountain Radio Hour* with country singer Marty Stuart and sung Hank Williams songs. Robert Khayat is an American patriot, a hero and a fine storyteller, plus he can kick field goals. When we took a road trip to Delta State University recently to perform *Thacker Mountain Radio*, he was our author and read from his memoir, *The Education of a Lifetime*. Rather than drive to the gig in the comfort of his own car, he rode in the van with our crew, telling us, "I'm used to being with the team."

I am proud to love him.

Willie Morris and Shelby Foote

Both of these greats have left us, Willie in 1999 and Shelby in 2005. Go have a peek at the volumes they left behind, millions of words. Their contribution to American letters, and particularly Southern literature, is towering. I was fortunate to spend time with both of them and actually became good friends with Willie. Both were shining examples of how to conduct yourself on the page and off. As great as they were as writers, both were also Southern gentlemen, incredibly well read and just plain good company. They were both deeply Mississippian.

Bill Beckwith

Bill Beckwith went on to create numerous sculptures, including statues of B.B. King for his hometown of Indianola and one of Elvis Presley for his hometown of Tupelo. Beckwith still resides in Taylor with his wife and son, still keeps his hands in clay, still is every inch the artist his mentors and teachers back in Greenville knew he would be.

To use Mr. Faulkner's phrase, "he endured and prevailed."

Oxford

Our town survived the statue controversy, the Ole Miss image review, the five-laning of West Jackson Avenue...even the skanky antics of 2Live Crew. The statue of Faulkner sits serenely in front of City

Hall amid Chester McLarty's monkey grass and flowers, just as he envisioned it. Ole Miss has flourished after abandoning its Old South trappings. Minority enrollment is up, as is enrollment in general, as well as the school's endowment. This despite the announcement that it will retain the name "Ole Miss" and the nickname, "Rebels" for its sports teams.

West Jackson was widened to five lanes, and now, twenty years later, the road is surrounded by trees and foliage. Even members of the "Oxford Nine," who I run into periodically out and about in town, concede the area is landscaped very well, and the one hundred or so trees that were cut aren't missed aesthetically.

Still, all the passions, irate letters, dramatic board meetings and expressions of emotion were necessary. The outpouring of opinion showed that this town cared about itself. The fiery debates proved that the people of Oxford were passionate about their town and were willing to fight for it.

Twenty years later, Oxford is a progressive city that has fulfilled Faulkner's literary promise with some thirty nationally published authors. The town and its environs are still beautiful, still green and lush, still have that "light in August." Faulkner captured his hometown like a painter; "arrested motion" as he put it, holding his world up to the light for all to see.

Even now, after all these years, I still feel the mojo of this locale and feel blessed to be here. And thankful that Faulkner is still here, too. When you visit his house off South Lamar, you can smell the cedars and feel the ghosts. His whiskey is there and his boots. A few paces out his door, you can gaze outward to what he saw, "the blue changeless hills beyond, and beyond that, the ramparts of infinity itself."

Bingo

After Belle passed, Bingo would live on to be a seventeen-year-old. We acquired another female Shepherd, Juno, who lived to be twelve and who stayed quiet and shy all her life. Bingo, the dog we ridiculed as a bit dim, outlived them all. He would get me through two moves, four jobs and three girlfriends. He and I walked three miles most every morning for fifteen years. I calculated we logged about 12,000 miles together, many of those miles with me talking, pouring out my secrets to him. He was really good at keeping them.

Living in the country with dogs is the antidote to a world of hurt and sorrow. When I think back to 1997, I see myself on the back porch in Taylor, pecking on a laptop with the dogs sprawled around me. Their peace and abiding nature got me through that year. I have to admit, I haven't had a dog since those three. I guess my heart is gun shy. They would be hard to live up to.

On his last day, the day I took Bingo for his final vet visit, he was deaf, half blind and couldn't stand up to get himself a drink of water.

But he never stopped smiling.

Bingo and Juno, Taylor, Mississippi,
Spring 1998

Acknowledgements

The late, great Barry Hannah spoke of what it takes to "make" a book. Not write one, but make one. I always thought it was strange verb choice, but I now understand what he meant. It takes a village – and a patient one at that.

Big thanks to Neil White and his very cool crew at Nautilus Publishing and to Chancellor Robert Khayat for kicking me like one of his game-winning field goals.

Love, thanks and respect to Kathryn McGaw York and my *Thacker Mountain Radio* family, and to Square Books, still the mothership after all these years.

Thanks and love to Ronzo Shapiro (arrangements), Randy Yates (poolside counsel), and Semmes Luckett (key to Gonzo). City Grocery, Ajax Diner, Proud Larry's, Star Package and Oxford Bicycle Company.

Love and thanks to Lynn and Debbie Hewlett and the sanctuary that is Taylor Grocery.

Thanks to Dan and Tim Phillips and the Phillips family for hiring me at the *Oxford Eagle* and for being the best bosses — and friends.

Inspiration: Mark Richard, Roy Blount Jr., George Singleton, Tom Franklin and Beth Ann Fennelly, Ace Atkins, Rheta Grimsley Johnson, Jack Pendarvis, Harrison Scott Key, Lisa Howorth, Curtis Wilkie, James Meredith, Myrlie Evers, Jesse Robinson and Bobby Rush.

Love and respect to Ron and Becky Feder.

My pals Jonny Miles, Steve Mullen, Bruce Newman. My bro, Bill Beckwith. Jane Rule Burdine. Elizabeth Dollarhide. Nicky Hewlett, Lyn and Doug Roberts and the town of Taylor.

Jim "Fish" Michie, Diane, Rosemary and Cathy Jacobs and the Tangents. Moon Morgan and the tailgate team at Swayze. Mark Smith for the Grove. Chan Patel for the swims. Butch Scott for lunches.

And finally, thanks and love to my family and to the people of Oxford and to Micah who was always game for "story time" and happily listened while I read her this whole book.

Photo Credits

Cover photography: Bruce Newman, Danny Clinch and *New York Times.*

Interior photography:
Bruce Newman, *The Oxford Eagle*: Pages 25, 28, 43, 74, 89, 118, 123, 139, 175, 229, 281
Tom Rankin: Page 159
Danny Clinch: Page 237
Elizabeth Dollarhide: Pages 269, 271
Jim Dees: Pages 182, 339